W9-AYW-004

Jossey-Bass Teacher

Jossey-Bass Teacher provides K–12 teachers with essential knowledge and tools to create a positive and lifelong impact on student learning. Trusted and experienced educational mentors offer practical classroom-tested and theory-based teaching resources for improving teaching practice in a broad range of grade levels and subject areas. From one educator to another, we want to be your first source to make every day your best day in teaching. *Jossey-Bass Teacher* resources serve two types of informational needs—essential knowledge and essential tools.

Essential knowledge resources provide the foundation, strategies, and methods from which teachers may design curriculum and instruction to challenge and excite their students. Connecting theory to practice, essential knowledge books rely on a solid research base and time-tested methods, offering the best ideas and guidance from many of the most experienced and well-respected experts in the field.

Essential tools save teachers time and effort by offering proven, ready-to-use materials for in-class use. Our publications include activities, assessments, exercises, instruments, games, ready reference, and more. They enhance an entire course of study, a weekly lesson, or a daily plan. These essential tools provide insightful, practical, and comprehensive materials on topics that matter most to K–12 teachers.

HANDS-ON

GENERAL SCIENCE ACTIVITIES

WITH REAL-LIFE APPLICATIONS

Ready-to-Use Labs, Projects, & Activities for Grades 5–12

SECOND EDITION

PAM WALKER • ELAINE WOOD

JOSSEY-BASS
A Wiley Company
San Francisco

Copyright © 2008 by John Wiley & Sons, Inc. All rights reserved.

Published by Jossey-Bass
A Wiley Imprint
989 Market Street, San Francisco, CA 94103-1741—www.josseybass.com

No part of this publication may be reproduced, stored in a retrieval system, or transmitted in any form or by any means, electronic, mechanical, photocopying, recording, scanning, or otherwise, except as permitted under Section 107 or 108 of the 1976 United States Copyright Act, without either the prior written permission of the publisher, or authorization through payment of the appropriate per-copy fee to the Copyright Clearance Center, Inc., 222 Rosewood Drive, Danvers, MA 01923, 978-750-8400, fax 978-646-8600, or on the Web at www.copyright.com. Requests to the publisher for permission should be addressed to the Permissions Department, John Wiley & Sons, Inc., 111 River Street, Hoboken, NJ 07030, 201-748-6011, fax 201-748-6008, or online at www.wiley.com/go/permissions.

Permission is given for individual classroom teachers to reproduce the pages and illustrations for classroom use. Reproduction of these materials for an entire school system is strictly forbidden.

Readers should be aware that Internet Web sites offered as citations and/or sources for further information may have changed or disappeared between the time this was written and when it is read.

Limit of Liability/Disclaimer of Warranty: While the publisher and author have used their best efforts in preparing this book, they make no representations or warranties with respect to the accuracy or completeness of the contents of this book and specifically disclaim any implied warranties of merchantability or fitness for a particular purpose. No warranty may be created or extended by sales representatives or written sales materials. The advice and strategies contained herein may not be suitable for your situation. You should consult with a professional where appropriate. Neither the publisher nor author shall be liable for any loss of profit or any other commercial damages, including but not limited to special, incidental, consequential, or other damages.

Jossey-Bass books and products are available through most bookstores. To contact Jossey-Bass directly call our Customer Care Department within the U.S. at 800-956-7739, outside the U.S. at 317-572-3986, or fax 317-572-4002.

Jossey-Bass also publishes its books in a variety of electronic formats. Some content that appears in print may not be available in electronic books.

Library of Congress Cataloging-in-Publication Data
Walker, Pam, 1958–
  Hands-on general science activities with real-life applications : ready-to-use labs,
projects, and activities for grades 5-12 / Pam Walker and Elaine Wood. — 2nd ed.
      p. cm. — (Jossey-Bass teacher)
  Includes bibliographical references and index.
  ISBN-13: 978-0-7879-9763-2 (alk. paper)
  1. Science—Study and teaching (Elementary) 2. Science—Study and teaching
(Secondary) I. Wood, Elaine, 1950– II. Title.
  LB1585.W25 2008
  507.1—dc22
                                                                2007047721

Printed in the United States of America

FIRST EDITION

HB Printing   10 9 8 7 6 5 4 3 2 1
PB Printing   10 9 8 7 6 5 4 3

About This Resource

All teachers deal with the issue of how to elicit student interest. Teachers in the field of science have an advantage over others: science is clearly relevant to everyday life. Even so, not every student finds science engaging, so teachers are constantly striving to improve their courses. *Hands-On General Science Activities with Real-Life Applications* is an excellent tool for science teachers in grades 5 through 12. This book provides teachers with lessons, activities, and projects that are related to daily life, connected to prior student experience, and fun to perform. These labs and activities can serve as core teaching material or as supplemental material that supports, reviews, re-enforces, and extends textbook lessons.

Both students and teachers like the material in this resource. Students enjoy the material because it is relevant and interesting. Consequently, they are not left wondering "Why do I need to know this?" Teachers find the resource valuable because the labs and activities are inexpensive and require little specialized equipment or training. Even out-of-field science teachers can use the book with ease. Most of the supplies for activities can be purchased in grocery and general merchandise stores, and none are hazardous. In addition, the lessons require very little advance preparation by the teacher. Labs and activity worksheets are reproducible for class use, and the labs lend themselves well to either individual or cooperative group work.

In this second edition of *Hands-On General Science Activities with Real-Life Applications*, the resource has been updated to include techniques and approaches that are current in science education. Several performance assessment activities are included to provide alternative methods of assessing student work. Each performance assessment activity is accompanied by either a checklist or a grading rubric to make the grading process fair and pain free. We recommend that you provide students with copies of the appropriate checklists or rubrics before the activity so they know up front how to prepare for a good grade.

In addition, this edition includes several inquiry labs. Although traditional labs, with their detailed procedures and explicit directions, are still important and highly recommended, the use of some inquiry labs is encouraged. These types of activities give students opportunities to act like scientists, selecting their own methods and materials for solving scientific problems. Inquiry labs also teach students to handle and report scientific data. Through inquiry, students use higher level thinking skills and participate in true science.

The five units in this book feature earth science, physics, astronomy, chemistry, and biology—all of the core areas of middle and high school science. There are twenty-two complete lessons in the book. Each lesson includes background information to provide context, a vocabulary activity to review critical terms, and one or more labs and activities to explore the content in detail.

The goal of *Hands-On General Science Activities with Real-Life Applications* is to improve science education. Whether the resource is used every day or only occasionally, it is an excellent collection of material for every science classroom.

Pam Walker
Elaine Wood

About the Authors

Pam Walker, a teacher at Alexander High School in Douglasville, Georgia, has been in the science classroom since 1981. She has taught physical science, biology, applied biology and chemistry, chemistry, human anatomy and physiology, physics, health, and physical education in grades 9 through 12. Pam earned a B.S. in biology from Georgia College and a M.Ed. and Ed.S. in science from Georgia Southern University. Pam was selected as the 2007 Georgia Teacher of the Year, a position that enabled her to visit teachers and administrators across the state of Georgia and throughout the entire United States. In this position, Pam served on committees that scrutinized all aspects of science education and worked to develop implementation plans for improvement.

Elaine Wood earned an A.B. in biology and secondary education in 1971, an M.S. in biology in 1988, and an Ed.S. in science education in 1993, all from West Georgia College. She interned at Georgia State University, conducting research in genetic engineering. Elaine has taught physical science, biology, chemistry, applied biology and chemistry, and human anatomy and physiology. Currently she is teaching at Chapel Hill High School in Douglasville, Georgia.

Pam and Elaine are coauthors of dozens of science teacher resource books, including *Crime Scene Investigations: Real-Life Science Activities for Elementary Grades; Crime Scene Investigations: Real-Life Science Labs for Grades 6–12;* and *Science Sleuths: 60 Forensic Activities to Develop Critical Thinking and Inquiry Skills.* Both educators participate in local, state, and national conferences on science education, and work from the premise that all students can learn when provided with the right support.

Acknowledgments

We appreciate the constant support and best wishes of our families, who always understand when we need to work and encourage us to keep at it.

Kate Bradford of Jossey Bass has been instrumental in planning and completing the second edition of *Hands On General Science Activities with Real-Life Applications*. She has overseen the entire project and organized the resources needed for us to tackle this task. Kate leads a double life; she is an expert in her field who cares about the quality of work as well as a concerned and sympathetic collaborator who is truly concerned about the individuals involved in this work. We owe her many thanks.

The editing of this manuscript was handled by Michele Jones. Her enthusiasm and talent made this second edition a painless process for us. Michele has keen eyes, amazing intuition, and asks all the right questions. Thank you Michele!

The king of organization is Justin Frahm, who managed the finished manuscript, keeping all of us—writers, editors, and artists—in line and on task. Justin is a superb chief, and the final tone and polish of the book is due to his expertise. It has been a joy and privilege to work with Justin and we appreciate all he has done.

Table of Contents

SECTION 1: EARTH SCIENCE—*1*

SECTION 2: PHYSICS—*65*

SECTION 4: CHEMISTRY—*193*

SECTION 1

Earth Science

LESSON 1: PLATE TECTONICS

1-1 AS THE EARTH MOVES
Content on Plate Tectonics

Copyright © 2008 by John Wiley & Sons, Inc.

❧❧❧

Moving Plates

You may not realize it, but you are a passenger on a moving mass of earth. The surface of the earth is divided into pieces called plates, which are in constant motion, and you are traveling along with one of them. You cannot feel the motion of the plate because it is very slow, about the same as the rate of growth of your fingernail.

The study of the formation and the movement of Earth's plates is called plate tectonics. The latest scientific data indicate that about one dozen plates make up the surface of the earth. Some plates are moving apart (diverging), and others are colliding. Why are these plates moving? What is providing the power to push them along? To understand these concepts, you must know a little about the composition of the earth.

Probing Deep into the Earth's Interior

The earth is divided into three major layers: the crust, the mantle, and the core (see Figure A). The crust is the solid portion that we stand on. Beneath the crust is the molten, flowing mantle. The core, made of solid and molten iron, is the innermost part of the earth. The crust and the upper portion of the mantle collectively make up the lithosphere, which is broken into gigantic plates. The lithospheric plates float on top of the asthenosphere, a region of the mantle that flows by means of convection currents. Convection currents are created by heating that causes material to expand and rise, and by cooling that makes material contract and sink (see Figure B).

Convection currents bring new material to the surface of the earth, driving aside older matter and pushing some of the plates apart. The South American and African plates are currently being pushed apart by molten lava brought to the surface in the middle of the Atlantic Ocean. Plates come together and collide in locations where cooler currents of the asthenosphere are sinking. For example, the Nazca plate in the Pacific Ocean is colliding with the South American plate. As a result, one of the plates is sliding beneath the other on the western coast of South America.

3

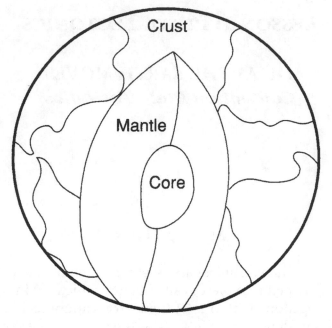

FIGURE A

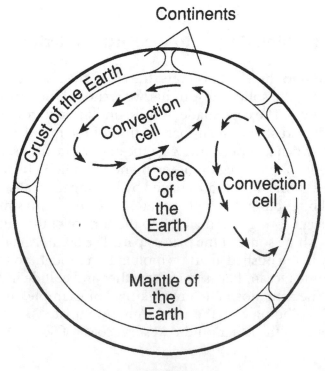

FIGURE B

Copyright © 2008 by John Wiley & Sons, Inc.

Copyright © 2008 by John Wiley & Sons, Inc.

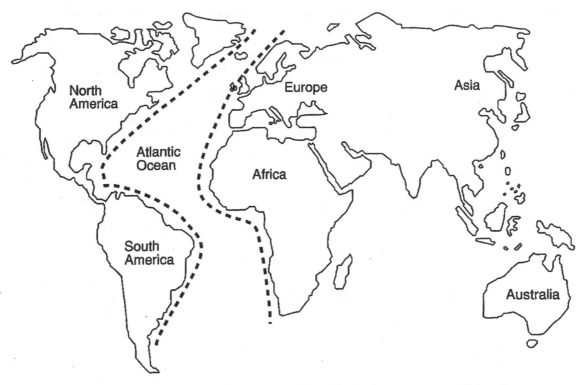

The East and West Coast lines of the Atlantic Ocean seem to fit together

FIGURE C

Supporting Evidence for Plate Tectonics

The theory of floating plates was initially proposed by Alfred Wegner in 1915. Although the theory seemed a little farfetched at the time, it has gained widespread acceptance. Evidence to support the theory is strong. For example, the shapes of South America's eastern coast and Africa's western coast seem to fit together like a jigsaw puzzle (see Figure C). This suggests that at one time they were both a part of a single, large land mass that broke apart and formed the two continents we know today. Other evidence includes the discovery of the reptilian fossil Mesosaurus in both Brazil and South Africa. Mesosaurus has not been found anywhere else in the world. The union of the two continents at one time would explain the unusual distribution of this fossil.

Over time, the theory of drifting continents was expanded into the theory of plate tectonics. This theory explains several geological processes, including the occurrence of volcanoes and earthquakes. Earthquakes and volcanoes do not just take place randomly throughout the earth. They are limited to the areas or belts where two or more plates share a boundary. As the boundaries move relative to one another, stresses build up and fractures occur, causing earthquakes. The high heat flow in these areas can trigger volcanoes. The largest belt of volcanic and earthquake activity is located in the Pacific Ocean, and about 90 percent of all earthquakes occur in this zone (see Figure D).

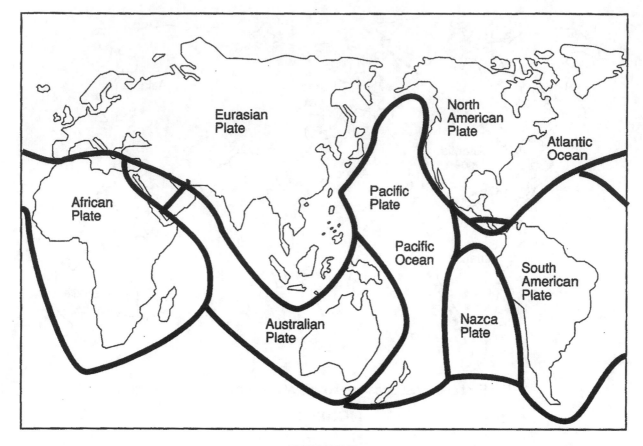

FIGURE D

Copyright © 2008 by John Wiley & Sons, Inc.

In ocean areas where the plates are moving apart, lava wells up from within the earth and forms new rocks, forcing older rocks away from the boundary. This process, called sea floor spreading, carries the continents and creates spreading centers, or mid-oceanic ridges.

Cracking, Rumbling, and Erupting

When lithospheric plates slide past each other, faults, which are breaks or cracks in the earth, can occur. Earthquakes occur along these fault lines. The San Andreas is a famous fault in southwest California. Its average rate of movement is about 5 centimeters (cm) per year.

Mountains can be built when plates converge or collide. The collision may cause the lithosphere at the boundary to be pushed upward into a mountain range. The Himalayan mountains were built when the Indian-Australian plate pushed into the Eurasian plate.

If one plate plunges beneath another when plates collide, a deep subduction zone forms. The lower plate is crushed and melted, forming new magma. On the overriding plate, volcanic islands are created. Most of the world's active volcanoes occur at subduction boundaries.

Although the theory of plate tectonics is not endorsed by every geologist, it is the most widely accepted explanation for many geological processes. The theory clarifies the similarity in borders of continents, the presence of fossil remains on seemingly unrelated areas of Earth, the reversal of the planet's magnetic poles of the earth, and the occurrence of such phenomena as earthquakes and volcanoes.

Copyright © 2008 by John Wiley & Sons, Inc.

ACROSTIC—VOCABULARY ACTIVITY ON
AS THE EARTH MOVES

Directions

After reading *As the Earth Moves,* answer the following questions. Enter your answers vertically in the blanks. The numbers are written across the top of the puzzle. When you complete the acrostic, your answers will form a two-word message horizontally in the boxes in the puzzle.

Clues

1. Breaks or cracks in the lithospheric plates that may result in earthquakes are _____.

2. Earth's surface is made up of several moveable _____.

3. A(n) _____ can form when one plate is subducted beneath another, permitting hot molten rock to move upward toward the surface of the earth.

4. At spreading centers in the ocean, hot _____ wells up from within the earth to form new rocks and push older material aside.

5. The _____ is the partially melted region of the mantle that flows and carries the plates along with it.

6. The crust and the rigid, upper portion of the mantle make up the _____.

7. Sometimes plates collide, pushing up the lithosphere to form _____.

8. Hot lava comes to Earth's surface at the mid-oceanic _____, pushing plates apart.

9. The appearance of the same _____ in Africa and South America supports the plate tectonic theory.

10. The _____ is a semisolid layer of the earth between the core and crust.

11. The _____ is the topmost layer of the earth.

12. The _____ Ocean has the majority of volcanic activity.

13. Plate _____ is the study of the formation and movement of the plates of the earth.

14. The theory of continental _____ preceded the idea of plate tectonics.

15. Due to convection currents, cooler regions of the mantle _____, pulling some of the plates together.

Copyright © 2008 by John Wiley & Sons, Inc.

Vocabulary Acrostic

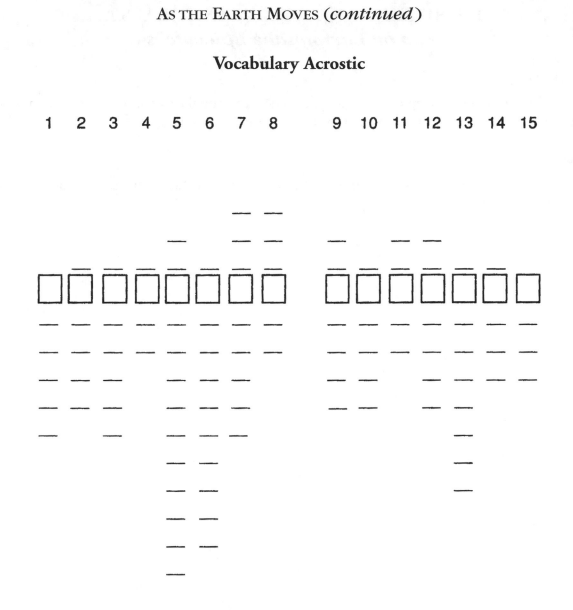

Copyright © 2008 by John Wiley & Sons, Inc.

1-2 ROCKIN' AND ROLLIN' IN THE U.S.A.
Lab on Earthquake Epicenters

Objectives

Students will calculate the epicenter of a hypothetical earthquake by using data on the primary and secondary waves collected at three seismographic locations.

Teacher Notes

A lesson on wave motion preceding this activity might facilitate a more thorough student understanding of this material.

Copyright © 2008 by John Wiley & Sons, Inc.

Copyright © 2008 by John Wiley & Sons, Inc.

Name _____ Date _____ (1-2)

Rockin' and Rollin' in the U.S.A.
Lab on Earthquake Epicenters

Introduction

When objects are subjected to extreme pressure or stress, they build up potential energy. This potential energy can be released in a variety of ways. The crust of the earth, for instance, can release its potential energy in the form of vibrations that we call earthquakes. Earthquakes result from sudden movements along fault lines or from volcanic activity.

Vibrations in the earth's crust travel in the form of wave energy. During an earthquake, these waves spread out in all directions. Some of the waves cause rocks to vibrate from side to side; other waves cause a backward-and-forward vibration. The various kinds of waves travel through rock material at different speeds. Primary waves, or P waves, travel at 6.1 kilometers per second (km/sec), and secondary waves, or S waves, travel at 4.1 km/sec. P waves cause backward-and-forward vibrations and can travel 100 km in 16.4 seconds. S waves create side-to-side vibrations and require 24.4 seconds to travel 100 km.

Seismographs are instruments that measure the arrival time of both P and S waves at various locations around the world. This arrival time can help geologists find the exact location of an earthquake. The focus, or point of origin, of an earthquake is the place where the stress energy changed to wave energy. The point on the earth's surface directly above the focus is the epicenter. Seismologists, scientists who study earthquakes, can pinpoint the exact location of the epicenter of an earthquake by calculating the difference in arrival times of the two types of waves.

Seismographic stations are located in various places around the world to collect wave data. Seismologists can use the arrival time of waves at three or more stations to calculate the exact epicenter of an earthquake. The greater the difference in the arrival time of the P and S waves to a station, the farther that station is from the epicenter of the earthquake.

Seismologists also determine the energy given off by an earthquake by using a special rating scale called the Richter scale, which ranges from 1 to 10. Each increment on the Richter scale represents a tenfold increase in energy, so a level 5 earthquake is 100 times more powerful than a level 3 earthquake.

You and your lab partner are training to be seismologists for the U.S. government. As part of your training, you will analyze data on earthquake waves from various seismographic stations to determine the epicenter of a hypothetical earthquake.

Prelab Questions

1. What does a seismologist study?

2. Explain how a seismologist determines the exact location of an earthquake.

3. How long would it take a P wave to travel 500 km? An S wave?

4. What does the difference in arrival times of the P and S waves at a seismographic station indicate about the distance of the epicenter from that station?

5. How are the epicenter and focus of an earthquake different?

6. What is potential energy?

7. Besides arrival time of shock waves, what other kinds of earthquake information do seismologists measure?

Materials

Figure A, hypothetical records of earthquake waves

Figure B, a map of the eastern United States

Compass and ruler

Calculator (optional)

Procedure

1. Examine the data in Figure A, the records of earthquake waves from three recording stations in the United States. Figure A shows the arrival time of the P and S waves at each station. The peak of the P and S waves corresponds to the number of seconds on the line beneath the reading. You will notice that the S wave always arrives later than the P wave. These differences in arrival time will help you determine how far the earthquake is from each of the stations that recorded the data. Calculate the difference in time for the P and S waves at each of the three stations and record these calculations on the data table.

2. Use these calculations to compute the distance of the earthquake from each of the three recording stations. To do so, use this formula:

distance = difference in time between P and S waves × 100 km ÷ 8 seconds

This formula is applicable because 8 seconds is the difference in the amount of time required for a P wave to travel 100 km and an S wave to do the same. Consider the following example: If a P wave arrived in Pittsburgh at 4:10:00 P.M. and the S wave arrived at 4:10:35 P.M., you can calculate the distance of the earthquake from Pittsburgh by using the formula above. Your answer would be

distance = 35 seconds × 100 km ÷ 8 seconds = 437.5 km

This calculation tells you that the earthquake is located 437.5 km from the Pittsburgh station. However, you need the readings from two other cities to triangulate the precise location of the epicenter. Use differences in P and S wave times in the data table and the formula provided above to calculate the distance of each of the three stations from the earthquake epicenter. Record your findings in the data table under the heading Distance.

Copyright © 2008 by John Wiley & Sons, Inc.

FIGURE A: HYPOTHETICAL RECORDS OF EARTHQUAKES
FROM THREE STATIONS IN THE UNITED STATES

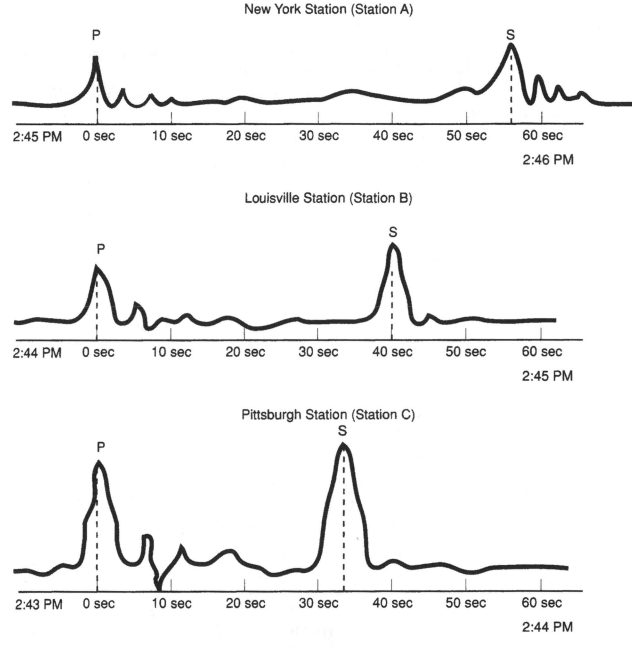

FIGURE A

Copyright © 2008 by John Wiley & Sons, Inc.

3. Locate a compass, a ruler, and the map of the eastern United States (see Figure B). Notice the scale in kilometers at the bottom of the map. Each 100 km is represented by about 1 cm on the map. Use the information in the data table to pinpoint the epicenter of your earthquake. To do so,

   a. Place the compass point on zero of the kilometer scale.

   b. Maintaining this position on the scale, place the compass pencil on the distance of the earthquake from New York (according to the data table).

   c. Remove your adjusted compass, and place the point of the compass on the dot representing New York City on the map.

   d. Draw a circle around New York with the compass.

   e. Repeat steps a through d for Pittsburgh and for Louisville.

FIGURE B

4. If you have done your computations and drawings correctly, you will notice that the three circles intersect in one area. This marks the exact epicenter of the earthquake.

5. Answer the postlab questions.

Copyright © 2008 by John Wiley & Sons, Inc.

ROCKIN' AND ROLLIN' IN THE U.S.A. (*continued*)

DATA TABLE

City	Difference in P and S Wave Arrival Times (seconds)	Distance (km)
New York City		
Louisville		
Pittsburgh		

Postlab Questions

1. Which of the three cities was the closest to the earthquake? Which was the farthest away?

2. In what state was the focus of the earthquake located?

3. If a seismographic station in Savannah, Georgia, detected the earthquake you measured, would it receive its reading before or after 2:45 P.M.? Explain.

4. With the map in Figure B, establish the distance of the earthquake from New Orleans. Now put this information into your formula and calculate the difference in arrival time between the P and S waves in New Orleans.

Copyright © 2008 by John Wiley & Sons, Inc.

1-3 QUAKES AND PLATES
Lab on Plate Tectonics and Earthquakes

Objectives

Students will plot the positions of 50 earthquakes and compare their locations to the edges of tectonic plates.

Teacher Notes

For each lab group, prepare the following:

1. Transparency of Figure A, a world map showing tectonic plates

2. Paper copy of Figure B, a world map showing latitude and longitude

You can extend this activity by asking students to indicate the severity of each earthquake based on the number of fatalities. One way to do this would be to use a red dot for an earthquake that caused less than 100 fatalities, a blue dot for a quake that caused 101 to 500 fatalities, a yellow dot for a quake that caused 501 to 1000, and a green dot for a quake that caused more than 1000 fatalities. Students could also plot the locations of volcanoes and indicate these geological events with stars or boxes.

Before the activity, review the term *magnitude* with students. You may also need to remind students how to locate points on a map using latitude and longitude.

If you want to omit the student research portion of this activity, go to one of the following Web sites and print a list of earthquakes. You can print a list of most recent earthquakes or a list of most severe earthquakes.

USGS, Latest Earthquakes in the World—Past 7 Days

http://earthquake.usgs.gov/eqcenter/recenteqsww/Quakes/quakes_all.php

Answers.com, List of Earthquakes

www.answers.com/topic/list-of-earthquakes

USGS Earthquakes Hazards Program, Earthquakes Worldwide in the Last 30 Days

www.iris.edu/seismon/last30days.phtml

USGS, Most Destructive Earthquakes on Record in the World

http://earthquake.usgs.gov/regional/world/most_destructive.php

Copyright © 2008 by John Wiley & Sons, Inc.

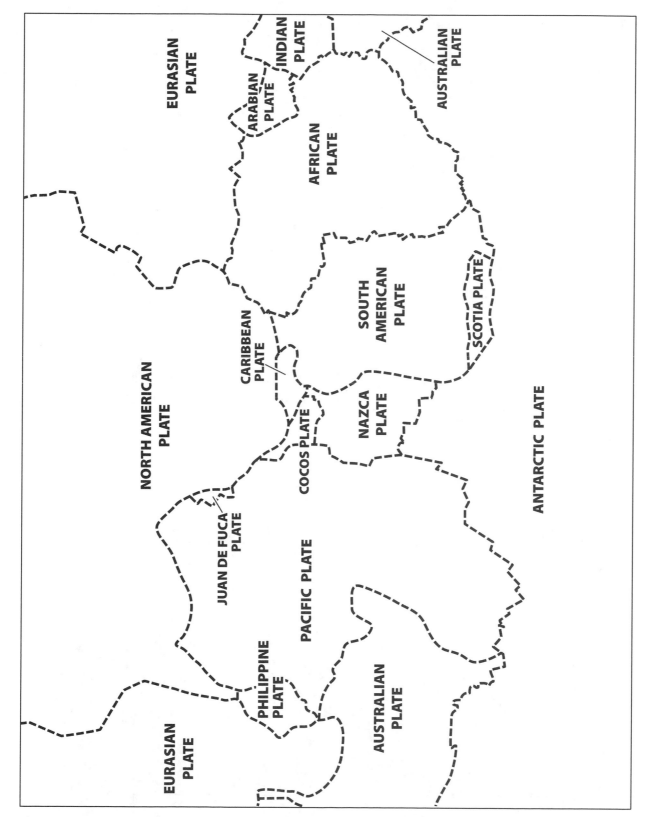

Copyright © 2008 by John Wiley & Sons, Inc.

FIGURE A

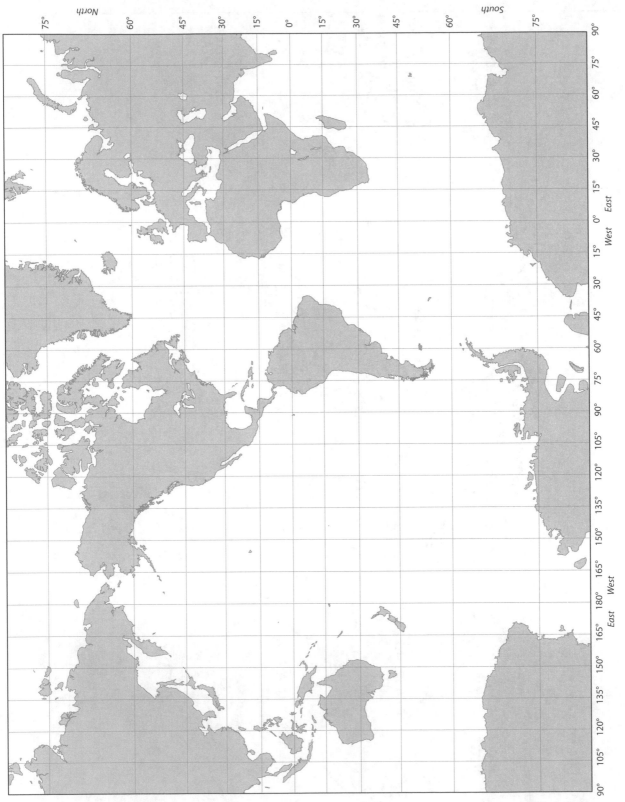

FIGURE B

Copyright © 2008 by John Wiley & Sons, Inc.

Copyright © 2008 by John Wiley & Sons, Inc.

QUAKES AND PLATES
Lab on Plate Tectonics and Earthquakes

Introduction

Most scientists agree that Earth's crust is broken into 14 large tectonic plates. These gigantic plates float on top of a hot layer of the mantle, which has fluid-like properties. The plates travel slowly, powered by convection currents within the layer beneath them. Plate movement has created the continents and formed ocean basins.

As they move, plates interact along their edges. Some plates scrape each other as they slide in opposite directions. In other cases, plates slowly collide, causing one to be pushed down under the other. Areas where plates collide are called convergent zones.

The advancement of Earth's plates is not smooth and continuous. Plates are slowed, and sometimes even stopped, by the force of friction. When the force of the collision overcomes this friction, the plates lurch forward in jerky motions. These movements release energy as seismic waves, earthquake waves that travel through Earth's crust.

In this experiment, you will determine and plot the locations of 50 earthquakes around the world. You will analyze the relationship between the locations of earthquakes and the edges of tectonic plates.

Materials

    Red pencil

    Figure A

    Figure B

Prelab Questions

1. What is a tectonic plate?

2. Why do tectonic plates move?

3. Why do tectonic plates produce seismic waves?

Procedure

1. Use the Internet or resource books on earthquakes to determine the dates, magnitudes, and locations (latitude and longitude) of 50 earthquakes.

2. Create a data table similar in design to the one shown on page 20. Your data table should have 50 rows, one for each earthquake.

3. For each of the earthquakes listed on your data table, draw a red dot on Figure B at the proper latitude and longitude.

19

DATA TABLE

Date	Magnitude	Latitude (N-S)	Longitude (E-W)	Occurred Near Plate Boundary

Copyright © 2008 by John Wiley & Sons, Inc.

4. When all dots have been marked on Figure B, lay Figure A, the transparency of plate boundaries, over Figure B. Compare the positions of the earthquakes with the edges of the tectonic plates. Put a check mark on the data table beside each earthquake that occurred within 5 degrees (latitude or longitude) of a plate boundary.

5. Answer the postlab questions.

Postlab Questions

1. Are earthquakes randomly scattered around the earth, or are they more common in some areas than others?

2. What percentage of the earthquakes that you plotted in this activity occurred near the edges of tectonic plates?

3. Offer an explanation for the location of earthquakes in relation to the edges of tectonic plates.

4. Would you expect the central portion of Africa to be an area that experiences a lot of earthquakes? Explain your answer.

5. From what you've learned in this experiment, do you think that understanding the movements of plates can help predict earthquakes? Explain your answer.

LESSON 2: ROCKS AND SOIL

2-1 THE SCOOP ON SOIL
Content on Rocks and Soil

Copyright © 2008 by John Wiley & Sons, Inc.

Why Rocks Crack

As time passes, the appearance of Earth's surface changes. New rocks are made through volcanic activity, and existing rocks are worn down and transported to new locations. Many factors contribute to the breakdown of rocks. The process of breaking down rocks is called weathering. Weathering can be chemical or physical.

Physical and Chemical Weathering

Physical weathering alters the size of a rock, but not its composition. Temperature is one factor that causes physical weathering. Rocks expand in the summer and contract in the winter. Alternating episodes of expansion and contraction weaken rocks and cause them to crack and break into pieces. Roots from shrubs and trees can also cause physical weathering as they grow in the cracks in rocks, breaking them apart.

Chemical weathering modifies the composition of a rock. In this type of weathering, new material is formed. Oxidation and carbonization are two forms of chemical weathering. In oxidation, oxygen combines with other materials to form new substances. Some rocks take on black, brown, or orange coloration because of oxidation. Iron oxide, or rust, develops in rocks when the iron in them is exposed to the atmosphere. In carbonization, carbon dioxide in the atmosphere unites with water vapor to form carbonic acid. When carbonic acid falls on limestone rocks, it dissolves the rocks and carves out caves.

Where Does Soil Come From?

A combination of physical and chemical weathering eventually breaks rocks down into fine grains of soil. As it accumulates, soil forms horizons, or layers. The uppermost layer (Horizon A) is composed of the nutrient-rich topsoil that nurtures plants. Decaying plants and animals form humus, which enriches the topsoil. Beneath the topsoil is the subsoil, or Horizon B. This layer has some nutrients, but not as many as the topsoil. Horizon B has an orange color due to its high content of clay particles. Water and most plant roots have great difficulty penetrating the subsoil. Horizon C is the layer below the subsoil and just above the bedrock. It is composed of broken pieces of rock. Rock that has not been completely broken down by weathering is called immature soil.

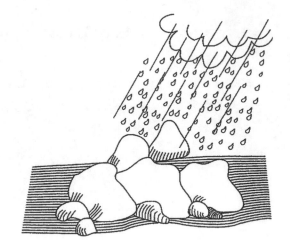

As weathering occurs, pieces of rock break off and fall to the ground. Some of these pieces remain in their original locations, and other pieces are carried away by natural agents, such as wind or water. The transportation of these broken pieces is called erosion. The four most common agents of erosion are running water, glaciers, gravity, and wind.

Erosion by Water

Running water is the dominant agent of erosion in most areas. Rivers and streams transport tons of eroded material. All the material carried by moving water is called the stream load. The weight and composition of a stream load influences when and where the particles will be deposited. The heaviest particles of the load bounce along the bottom of the stream. They cause abrasion, grinding down surfaces by contact. Lighter particles are easily suspended in fast-moving water, but will drop if the stream slows. Running water can even be so powerful that it creates new landscapes, such as valleys between two mountains.

Erosion by Glaciers

Glaciers are mounds of sliding snow and ice. Glaciers move slowly and cover much less area than running water. As they creep forward, glaciers erode the soil beneath them in several ways. Through a process called plucking, areas of glacial ice melt, seep into the bedrock, then refreeze. Refreezing causes rocks to be dislodged and picked up by the glacial mass. In abrasion, plucked rocks act like sandpaper, grinding other rocks into fine dust.

Erosion by Wind

Because of the great velocity wind can generate, it can pick up and move sediments easily. Wind-blown sediments rub against rocks and other surfaces. If you have ever been caught in a wind gust on a sandy ball field or playground, you know that

Copyright © 2008 by John Wiley & Sons, Inc.

Copyright © 2008 by John Wiley & Sons, Inc.

whirling sand particles sting as they strike your body. Imagine the damage a huge dust storm might do to plants, animals, and buildings. In the 1930s, a dust storm occurred in the Great Plains because long dry spells in that area had killed the vegetation and left the topsoil exposed to the air. Violent storm winds picked up loose, dry topsoil and bombarded nearby crops and buildings. The abrasive action of these storms caused massive devastation.

Although clay and silt in soil can cause damage, the most destructive particles are grains of sand. Sand grains are much larger and more abrasive than clay or silt. They can damage structures and pound giant boulders and small rocks into shapes called ventifacts. Sand particles can also erode materials to form facets, or smooth surfaces.

The wind eventually loses energy and slows, dropping the sand. In extremely sandy locations, wind creates mounded sand dunes. These dunes can move over time; as they migrate, they cover and destroy objects in their path.

Erosion by Gravity

Gravity is the underlying force behind all types of erosion. Gravity causes water to run downhill and glaciers to flow. It also produces winds by pulling heavier cold air down beneath lighter warm air. Such phenomena as landslides, rock slides, and snow slides are all caused by gravity.

Preventing Soil Erosion

What effect does erosion have on the surface of the earth? The loss of valuable topsoil reduces soil fertility and lowers crop production. Such loss can cause severe environmental and economic damage. The depletion of topsoil can be controlled by a variety of soil conservation methods.

Farmers routinely practice soil conservation techniques. They use vegetation to cover topsoil and prevent erosion. The plants' roots extend down into the soil and hold it in place. When farmers do not have crops planted, they allow wild vegetation to grow in their fields as a protective measure.

Soil conservation is important to our future and our food supply. Some methods employed by farmers to conserve topsoil include the following:

1. *Planting windbreaks.* Belts of trees are planted along the edge of a field to slow wind erosion.

2. *Contour plowing.* Crops are planted in rows parallel to the contour of the land to prevent the rapid flow of water downhill.

3. *Terracing.* The slope of a hill is flattened by building small terraces or ridges that resist erosion.

4. *Strip cropping.* Different kinds of crops are planted next to one another, rather than having bare ground between rows. An example is corn and alfalfa planted side by side with no uncovered soil in between.

5. *No till.* An area is plowed, planted, and fertilized all at once so that the ground is not disturbed again until harvest.

Even though erosion changes the earth, humans can help control some undesirable alterations. Erosion of farmland can be prevented. Soil conservation is important to our generation as well as to future generations. Our food supply depends on it.

Copyright © 2008 by John Wiley & Sons, Inc.

Copyright © 2008 by John Wiley & Sons, Inc.

Name _____ Date _____ (2-1)

WORD TRACE—VOCABULARY ACTIVITY ON
THE SCOOP ON SOIL

Directions

After reading *The Scoop on Soil*, complete the following sentences. Locate each of your answers in the word trace puzzle. Trace over the word in an unbroken line.

Clues

1. _____ is the process of breaking down rocks that make up Earth's crust.

2. Plant _____ can cause physical weathering by widening the cracks in rocks.

3. The material that is found beneath Horizon C soil is called _____.

4. The decayed plant material found in the topsoil is _____.

5. Horizon A is also called _____. It is rich in nutrients and minerals, which plants need to grow.

6. A(n) _____ is an agent of erosion composed of packed snow on a layer of moving ice.

7. _____ is the grinding down of a surface due to friction caused by contact.

8. _____ is the underlying force behind all erosion.

9. Shapes created by sand abrasion are called _____.

10. A belt of trees planted outside a field to block the wind is called a _____.

11. Most wind abrasion is caused by large soil particles called _____.

12. _____ are created when sand is dropped as the wind loses energy.

13. A(n) _____ _____ is material transported by a stream from one location to another.

14. _____ is planted on top of soil to prevent erosion.

15. Soil _____ includes practices that prevent erosion.

16. _____ plowing is the planting of crops in rows parallel to the contour of the land to prevent the flow of water down hillsides.

17. _____ is the flattening of a slope on a hill to prevent erosion.

18. When all three horizons are found in the soil, the soil is said to be _____.

19. _____ is the process in which oxygen combines with another material.

20. _____ is a form of chemical weathering that results when carbonic acid reacts with limestone to make caves.

25

21. _____ is another name for iron oxide.

22. _____ _____ is the orange-colored compound formed on iron-bearing rocks during chemical weathering.

WORD TRACE PUZZLE

Example

```
b   i   o   m   t   z
k   m   l   z   b   t
u   t   o   r   e   b
k   m   g   y   b   v
j   w   p   c   v   t
```

The study of life is called biology.

```
K  J  D  F  B  W  B  I  R  O  N  O  X  I  D  D  U  D
S  A  O  V  M  E  E  D  R  O  A  B  R  T  E  L  N  C
C  N  X  E  T  A  M  N  B  C  G  L  A  E  B  T  E  R
O  D  I  G  K  T  A  T  U  K  L  R  S  R  K  V  S  T
N  P  D  E  Z  H  E  R  R  H  A  E  I  R  M  J  D  V
T  R  A  T  A  T  T  I  E  U  C  I  O  A  B  N  L  W
O  U  T  I  O  I  O  N  R  M  U  S  N  C  I  N  G  Y
U  S  T  D  N  O  P  G  R  O  O  T  S  V  E  N  T  Z
R  S  C  I  O  N  S  O  I  L  W  I  N  D  B  R  I  B
N  T  O  T  N  G  M  I  G  R  A  T  N  G  V  E  F  T
D  R  N  A  Q  R  A  V  I  T  Y  I  O  R  F  A  A  X
V  E  S  V  D  P  C  O  R  N  Z  O  I  A  K  K  C  M
K  A  E  R  L  J  A  K  M  U  M  N  T  N  B  R  T  L
J  M  L  O  A  D  R  B  O  N  I  Z  A  I  T  E  S  D
```

Copyright © 2008 by John Wiley & Sons, Inc.

2-2 BREAKING UP IS EASY TO DO
Lab on Weathering of Rocks

Objectives

Students will observe the mechanism behind the physical and chemical weathering of rocks into soil.

Teacher Notes

The rocks in the materials list are common rocks, but you may substitute other types of rocks that might be more convenient for your location. In this experiment, use samples of rocks that are small enough to fit in containers A through H. You can use a variety of items for containers—plastic tubs, beakers, cups, or glasses. This lab is written to be conducted for 48 hours, but the results will be adequate if you want to do only a 24-hour reading. You also can wait several days and still get good results if you cannot observe the results the day immediately following the start of the activity.

Copyright © 2008 by John Wiley & Sons, Inc.

BREAKING UP IS EASY TO DO
Lab on Weathering of Rocks

Introduction

The rocks composing Earth's crust are subjected to a variety of environmental factors that break them down into smaller particles. Through weathering, rocks undergo physical and chemical changes. Physical weathering changes the size of the rock, but not its composition. Chemical weathering alters the composition of a rock, forming a new substance.

Agents of physical weathering include wind, water, ice, plants, and animals. The roots of plants can penetrate cracks in rocks, causing crumbling. In a similar way, water can seep into the crevices in rocks. If the water freezes, it expands, making the cracks even larger, in a process called ice wedging.

Chemical weathering brings about a chemical change in the materials that make up a rock. As a result, new materials are formed. In the type of chemical weathering known as carbonization, carbon dioxide from the air dissolves in water and forms carbonic acid. The strength of carbonic acid is equivalent to the strength of acid in carbonated beverages. Over long periods of time, this acid reacts with the minerals in the rock. Carbonic acid is very effective at dissolving limestone, a type of rock made of calcium carbonate from the remains of dead animals. Limestone caves result from the process of carbonization over periods of thousands of years.

What determines the speed and intensity of the weathering process? Three important factors are the type of rock, the hardness of the materials in the rock, and the climate. Rocks composed of materials that dissolve easily in water or acid weather much more quickly than insoluble rocks. For example, sandstone weathers faster than many other rocks because it is made of sand grains that are cemented together with natural materials. Weathering naturally occurs faster in areas that get a lot of precipitation, as well as places with hot, humid climates. As weathering takes place, large pieces of rock are changed into smaller pieces. Some of the pieces remain in their original location, but others are carried away by natural agents, such as wind and water. Soil is the final product of rock weathering.

Prelab Questions

1. Explain the differences between physical and chemical weathering.

2. Explain ice wedging.

3. Explain carbonization.

4. Why is sandstone more prone to ice wedging than granite?

5. Why is limestone more prone to carbonization than granite?

6. What three factors determine the rate of weathering a rock undergoes?

Copyright © 2008 by John Wiley & Sons, Inc.

Materials

Limestone (two rocks)	Vinegar
Marble (two rocks)	Eight small containers
Granite (two rocks)	Platform balance or electronic scale
Sandstone (two rocks)	Water
Grease pencil or pen and labels	Towel

Procedure

1. Label the eight containers A, B, C, D, E, F, G, and H with a grease pencil.

2. Use the balance or scale to find the mass of each rock. Record this mass on the data table in the Initial Mass column. Place each rock in the designated container.

   Limestone rock—container A

   Marble rock—container B

   Granite rock—container C

   Sandstone rock—container D

   Limestone rock—container E

   Marble rock—container F

   Granite rock—container G

   Sandstone rock—container H

3. Add water to containers A, B, C, and D. Place enough water in these containers to cover the rocks completely.

4. Add vinegar to containers E, F, G, and H. Place enough vinegar in these containers to cover the rocks completely.

5. Set these eight containers aside for 24 hours.

6. Remove the rocks from their containers one at a time and towel-dry them. Weigh each rock on the platform balance or electronic scale, and record the mass on the data table under the heading Mass After 24 Hours. Do this for rocks A through H. Return each rock to its proper container when you finish measurements.

7. Set the containers aside for another 24 hours then repeat step 6. Record the mass in the data table under Mass After 48 Hours.

8. Clean up the containers and answer the postlab questions.

Copyright © 2008 by John Wiley & Sons, Inc.

DATA TABLE

Rocks Placed in Water			
Container	Initial Mass	Mass After 24 Hours	Mass After 48 Hours
A Limestone			
B Marble			
C Granite			
D Sandstone			
Rocks Placed in Vinegar			
A Limestone			
B Marble			
C Granite			
D Sandstone			

Copyright © 2008 by John Wiley & Sons, Inc.

Postlab Questions

1. Which rock would be the best candidate to undergo ice wedging? Explain.

2. Which rock would be most likely to undergo carbonization? Explain.

3. Which rock seemed unchanged by either water or vinegar?

4. Do you think smog and humidity can affect the surface of rock statues? Explain.

5. Explain what the water in this lab represents in a real-life situation.

2-3 SHAKING SUGAR
Lab on Physical Weathering

Objective

Students will simulate the actions of physical weathering, observe the consequences of these actions, and predict future changes.

Teacher Notes

Each lab group will need a jar with a lid that has the capacity to hold 10 sugar cubes. Make a copy of the Lab on Physical Weathering: Student Answer Sheet for each student or student group.

Copyright © 2008 by John Wiley & Sons, Inc.

SHAKING SUGAR
Lab on Physical Weathering

Introduction

Weathering includes all the destructive forces that change the size, shape, and position of Earth's rocks. Weathering may be physical or chemical in nature. In physical weathering, rock is mechanically abraded into smaller pieces by wind, glaciers, and freezing water. Chemical weathering is the breakdown of rock through chemical processes, primarily with water and gases in the atmosphere.

During erosion, rock particles are physically picked up and moved. Erosion helps break solid rock into the small particles that make up soil. In this experiment, you will simulate the effects of physical weathering and erosion on rocks.

Prelab Questions

1. What is weathering?

2. What are some of the factors that cause weathering?

3. Where does soil come from?

Materials

Container with lid	Weighing boat
Sheet of sandpaper	Graph paper
Ten sugar cubes	Triple beam balance or electronic scale

Procedure

1. Trim a sheet of sandpaper to fit inside the container. Line the container with the sandpaper.

2. Find the mass of the weighing boat and write it on the answer sheet.

3. Place all 10 sugar cubes in the container. Place the lid on the container.

4. Shake the container vigorously 50 times.

5. Open the container and set aside the pieces or chunks of sugar cubes. Pour the sugar grains that have accumulated in the container into the weighing boat.

6. Find the mass of the sugar grains and the weighing boat. Calculate the mass of the sugar grains by subtracting the mass of the weighing boat from the total mass of the sugar grains and weighing boat. Record the mass of the sugar grains on the row of the data table corresponding to 50 shakes.

Copyright © 2008 by John Wiley & Sons, Inc.

7. Return the sugar grains and the sugar cubes to the container. Place the lid on the container.

8. Repeat steps 3 through 6 for another 50 shakes. Record the mass of the sugar grains on the row of the data table corresponding to 100 shakes.

9. Repeat the procedure for 150 shakes, 200 shakes, 250 shakes, and 300 shakes.

10. Create a graph that shows how the mass of sugar grains changed with each additional 50 shakes. Plot the number of shakes on the x-axis and mass of sugar grains on the y-axis.

11. Answer the postlab questions.

Postlab Questions

1. What is the relationship between the mass of sugar grains in the container and the number of shakes?

2. In this experiment, what is represented by shaking the jar?

3. In this experiment, what do the sugar cubes represent?

4. How did the sugar cubes look at the end of the experiment?

5. Based on the results of this experiment, explain how you think the sugar cubes would look if you continued this experiment for another 300 shakes.

6. In your own words, define *physical weathering*.

Copyright © 2008 by John Wiley & Sons, Inc.

LAB ON PHYSICAL WEATHERING
Student Answer Sheet

Prelab Questions

1. _____

   _____

2. _____

   _____

3. _____

   _____

Mass of weighing boat _____

DATA TABLE

Number of Shakes	Mass of Sugar Grains
50	
100	
150	
200	
250	
300	

Postlab Questions

1. _____

   _____

2. _____

   _____

Copyright © 2008 by John Wiley & Sons, Inc.

3. _____

_____

4. _____

_____

5. _____

_____

6. _____

_____

Copyright © 2008 by John Wiley & Sons, Inc.

LESSON 3: WEATHER

3-1 THE WEATHER REPORT
Content on Weather

Weather Indicators

Before you plan any outdoor activity, you probably check the weather forecast. Meteorologists, scientists who predict the weather, make reliable forecasts by studying weather patterns. To understand the weather, meteorologists must be familiar with how the atmosphere heats and cools, how clouds form and produce rain, and what makes the wind blow. They use an assortment of instruments to help them understand weather patterns and anticipate future weather events.

Tools of the Trade

Meteorologists rely on barometers to measure air pressure, or the weight of the air. Rising air pressure is usually a sign that the weather is going to improve. A fall in air pressure may indicate the approach of bad weather.

Thermometers are instruments that measure atmospheric temperature. Fluctuations in air temperature directly influence many other weather conditions. For example, the capacity of the air to hold water varies with its temperature. Warm air can hold more water than cool air. Specific humidity is the name given to the amount of water vapor actually present in the air.

A more useful measurement dealing with this concept is relative humidity. During a weather forecast, a meteorologist reports the relative humidity, the percentage of water vapor in the air compared to the maximum amount of water vapor the air can hold at that temperature. Two instruments that measure relative humidity are the hygrometer and the psychrometer. The point at which the atmosphere is saturated and can accept no more water vapor is known as 100 percent humidity. In warm weather, 100 percent humidity prevents sweat from evaporating from your skin, causing a sticky, uncomfortable feeling.

The direction and speed of the wind are two more factors that influence weather patterns. Wind information is gathered from a variety of locations, including

36

Copyright © 2008 by John Wiley & Sons, Inc.

Copyright © 2008 by John Wiley & Sons, Inc.

weather ships, weather stations, and satellites in space. Wind patterns are influenced by regional differences in the air pressure. Air always moves from an area where pressure is high to an area where pressure is low. This air movement is what we commonly call wind. Wind vanes are simple mechanisms that show the direction from which the wind blows. The direction of the wind can be a key in weather predictions. In the northeastern part of the United States, a wind from the northeast can mean a blizzard in winter, whereas in the summer it may bring rain.

Anemometers are used to determine wind strength or speed, another good weather predictor. In 1806, the English admiral Sir Francis Beaufort worked out a scale from 0 to 12 to indicate the strength of the wind. Zero on the Beaufort scale indicates wind with speeds below 2.5 miles per hour. Hurricanes are at the other extreme of his scale. These storms, whose winds exceed 95 miles per hour, carry a rank of 12 on the Beaufort scale.

Interrupting for a Weather Bulletin

Has your favorite television show ever been interrupted by a severe weather warning from the local meteorologist? Sometimes thunderstorm watches and warnings are issued to alert viewers of dangerous weather. A thunderstorm watch indicates that conditions are favorable for a thunderstorm to develop, whereas a warning means that a storm has been sighted in the area. A thunderstorm is a small-area storm formed by strong upward movements of warm, moist air. The two major types of thunderstorms exist: air mass thunderstorms and frontal thunderstorms. Air mass thunderstorms begin when warm, moist air masses are strongly heated. They usually occur in the spring and summer and last less than an hour. Frontal thunderstorms form in warm, moist air on or ahead of cold fronts. These thunderstorms often occur in lines along the frontal surface. Slow-moving cold fronts, which produce heavy rain and flooding, are commonly called squall lines. Frontal storms are stronger and of longer duration than air mass thunderstorms.

Both types of thunderstorms are accompanied by lightning and thunder, and they usually produce rain. Very strong thunderstorms may cause high winds, hail, and even tornadoes. The lightning from thunderstorms comes from discharges of electricity between thunderclouds and the ground or from one cloud to another. The high temperatures in a lightning bolt heat up the air, causing thunder, a sudden, explosive expansion of the air. Because sound travels much more slowly than light,  you will see lightning before hearing thunder. Lightning can be seen immediately because light travels at 186,000 miles per second. The sound of thunder takes about

5 seconds to travel one mile. To determine how far away in miles lightning strikes are, count the seconds between a flash and a boom and divide by five.

Violent Storm—Take Cover

Tornadoes, violent wind storms that form funnel-shaped cloud patterns, may accompany violent thunderstorms. They are more frequent in the United States than in any other place in the world. Most tornadoes occur in the Mississippi River valley and the Great Plains, which receive warm air from the Gulf of Mexico. The funnel of a tornado is composed of a mixture of clouds and dust. Air pressure is low near the center of a tornado, which causes the condensation level to dip downward and form a funnel. The funnel-shaped column extends downward from the cloud base toward the ground. The strength of tornadoes varies greatly, but the strongest winds can reach 311 miles per hour. A tornado will generally follow an irregular path that is less than 15 km long and will usually survive no longer than an hour before running out of energy. These storms are often accompanied by heavy rain, lightning, and hail.

Hurricanes are violent storms that occur most often on the Gulf and Atlantic coasts, with average wind speeds of 75 miles per hour. A hurricane has a calm central area of sinking air called the eye, which is usually 20 to 40 miles in diameter. The air in the eye of the hurricane sinks without producing rain or wind. However, winds just outside the eye are extremely violent and can reach speeds of 155 miles per hour or higher.

You may wonder where the custom of naming hurricanes originated. World War II pilots began the tradition by naming hurricanes after their girlfriends and wives. They even went as far as naming one after President Truman's wife, Bess. In 1950, the Weather Bureau began issuing an alphabetical list of women's names for the hurricanes they expected each year. In the late 1970s, the Weather Bureau began naming hurricanes after both men and women after objections from the female population.

Copyright © 2008 by John Wiley & Sons, Inc.

WEATHER CROSSWORD—VOCABULARY ACTIVITY ON *THE WEATHER REPORT*

Copyright © 2008 by John Wiley & Sons, Inc.

Across

4. When air pressure _____, it is usually a sign that better weather is approaching.

6. The study of the weather and atmosphere is called _____.

8. The name given to the amount of water actually present in the air is _____ (two words).

10. A(n) _____ is an instrument used to detect humidity.

12. The funnel of a tornado is a mixture of clouds and _____.

13. The movement of air creates _____.

15. A(n) _____ thunderstorm lasts less than an hour and starts when warm, moist air masses are strongly heated (two words).

16. A thunderstorm or tornado _____ means that conditions are right for these storms to develop.

17. Because _____ travels at 186,000 miles per second, we can see lightning before hearing thunder.

18. One feature of a(n) _____ is wind that spirals toward the center of the storm.

Down

1. A(n) _____ is used to detect wind speed.

2. The _____ is the central area of sinking air in a hurricane.

3. A(n) _____ is used to measure air pressure.

4. A percentage that compares the actual amount of water vapor in the air to the amount that the air can hold is _____ (two words).

5. A(n) _____ thunderstorm lasts several hours and forms ahead of cold fronts.

7. The eye of a hurricane has little wind and no _____.

8. The air is _____ when the relative humidity is 100%.

9. The _____ scale ranges from 0 to 12 to indicate the strength of wind.

11. Lightning heats the air and causes a rapid _____ of air molecules, producing thunder.

14. When air pressure is _____, it may be a sign that the weather is going to turn bad.

Word List

AIR MASS	HURRICANE	RISES
ANEMOMETER	HYGROMETER	SATURATED
BEAUFORT	LIGHT	SPECIFIC HUMIDITY
DUST	LOW	WATCH
EXPANSION	METEOROLOGY	WIND
EYE	RAIN	
FRONTAL	RELATIVE HUMIDITY	

Copyright © 2008 by John Wiley & Sons, Inc.

3-2 HYGROMETER ENGINEERING
Lab on Measuring Relative Humidity

Objectives

Students will construct and use a hygrometer to measure relative humidity.

Teacher Notes

None

Copyright © 2008 by John Wiley & Sons, Inc.

HYGROMETER LAB
Lab on Measuring Relative Humidity

Introduction

The weather forecast tells you that the temperature is 65°F, so you decide its perfect weather to run a few laps around the track. But after just two laps, you feel hot and sticky—not what you expected on such a pleasant day. What's the problem?

When you checked the forecast, you did not wait around long enough to hear the relative humidity. Unfortunately, you chose to run on a day when the relative humidity was high. A high relative humidity reading indicates that the air is holding a lot of water vapor. As a result, sweat cannot evaporate from your body to help keep you cool. Your run would have been much more pleasant if the humidity were low.

Meteorologists, scientists who study the weather, use hygrometers to measure relative humidity. One of the simplest types of these instruments is the hair hygrometer, which is based on the principle that human hair stretches when it is humid. To construct a hair hygrometer, a human hair is attached to a fixed point on one end. The other end of the hair is connected to a pointer. When the hair is damp, it stretches, and the pointer moves up. When the hair dries, it contracts, and the pointer moves down.

Another type of hygrometer is a psychrometer. It works on the principle that evaporation causes cooling. A simple version of this instrument can be constructed by using wet- and dry-bulb thermometers and comparing the differences in temperature between these two thermometers. In the following activity, you will construct a psychrometer to detect relative humidity.

Prelab Questions

1. What is relative humidity?

2. What does it mean when the relative humidity of the air is 75%?

3. Would it be more comfortable to jog in weather that is 60°F at 98% relative humidity or 70°F at 20% relative humidity? Explain.

4. What does it mean when someone describes the atmosphere as "saturated"?

5. Explain why you get hotter and stickier in humid weather than in dry weather.

Materials

Two standard thermometers (Fahrenheit)	Table of relative humidity
Cotton or cotton fabric about 3 to 4 inches long	Tall container
Narrow-mouth bottle (for example, a soda bottle)	Rubber bands
Water	Modeling clay

Copyright © 2008 by John Wiley & Sons, Inc.

Procedure

1. Wrap the bulb end of one thermometer with cotton fabric that has been soaked in water. Use a rubber band to secure the cotton fabric to the thermometer.

2. Add enough water to one bottle to fill it about one-fourth full. Lower the cotton-wrapped end of the thermometer into the bottle of water. Submerge only the part of the thermometer covered with fabric.

3. Use modeling clay to secure the thermometer in that position in the bottle, preventing it from slipping deeper into the water.

4. Position the bottle with the thermometer (the wet-bulb thermometer) in a convenient location in the room.

5. Lower the second thermometer into the other bottle. (This bottle does not contain water.) Attach the thermometer in the bottle with clay. This is a dry-bulb thermometer.

6. Place the wet- and dry-bulb thermometers side by side (see Figure A), and observe their temperature readings each day over the next several days. Record the temperatures in the data table. In the blanks at the bottom of the table, make notes about the way you feel during those days. Also indicate whether you think the humidity is high or low.

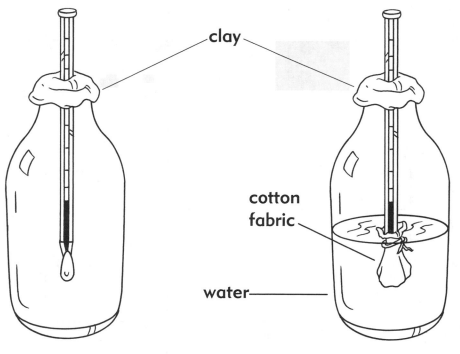

clay

cotton
fabric

water

FIGURE A

Copyright © 2008 by John Wiley & Sons, Inc.

7. Calculate the difference in the two temperature readings and record this calculation in the data table.

8. Find the relative humidity for each day. To do so, locate the dry-bulb temperature in the first column and the difference in the wet- and dry-bulb temperatures on the top row of the chart in Figure B. The point where these readings intersect gives you the relative humidity. Record the relative humidity for each date on the last line of the table.

Example: If the dry-bulb temperature was 72°F, you would locate 72 under the dry-bulb column. If the wet bulb was 68°F, subtract 68 from 72 to get 4. Find 4 along the top of the chart for difference between wet and dry. Then find the intersection of the two readings to find 82% as your answer. If there is no difference in the readings, the relative humidity is 100%.

9. Answer the postlab questions.

DATA TABLE

Day of the Week	Dry-Bulb Temperature	Wet-Bulb Temperature	Difference in Wet- and Dry-Bulb Reading	Relative Humidity

Copyright © 2008 by John Wiley & Sons, Inc.

Notes on how you feel each day:

_____

_____

_____

_____

_____

_____

FIGURE B. RELATIVE HUMIDITY CHART

Copyright © 2008 by John Wiley & Sons, Inc.

Dry Bulb Reading	Difference Between Dry and Wet Bulb											
°F	1	2	3	4	5	6	7	8	9	10	11	12
66	95	90	85	80	75	71	66	61	57	53	48	44
68	95	90	85	80	76	71	67	62	58	54	50	46
70	95	90	86	81	77	72	68	64	59	55	51	48
72	95	91	86	82	77	73	69	65	61	57	53	49
74	95	91	86	82	78	74	69	65	61	58	54	50
76	96	91	87	82	78	74	70	66	62	59	55	51
78	96	91	87	83	79	75	71	67	63	60	56	53
80	96	91	87	83	79	75	72	68	64	61	57	54
82	96	92	88	84	80	76	72	69	65	61	58	55
84	96	92	88	84	80	76	73	69	66	62	59	56
86	96	92	88	84	81	77	73	70	66	63	60	57
88	96	92	88	85	81	77	74	70	67	64	61	57
90	96	92	89	85	81	78	74	71	68	65	61	58

Postlab Questions

1. Which is usually higher, the temperature on the dry or wet bulb? Why do you think this is so?

2. As humidity increases, does the difference between the temperature readings on the two thermometers increase or decrease? Explain.

3. Why is the relative humidity 100% when the readings are the same?

4. As the temperature of the dry bulb decreases and the difference in temperatures increases, does the humidity increase or decrease? How would you describe the air under these conditions?

5. Add all your humidity readings and divide by the number of days you recorded them to find the average humidity for the week.

6. Describe any days on which you could tell that the humidity was high or low, and explain why.

Copyright © 2008 by John Wiley & Sons, Inc.

3-3 WEATHER TRACKING
Performance Assessment on Tracking, Interpreting, and Predicting Weather

Objectives

Students will observe and record local weather conditions over a period of two weeks, analyze their data, and use the data to make predictions on future weather.

Teacher Notes

An ideal situation would be an outdoor location where you can set up the weather instruments and leave them for the experimental period. If this is not possible, students can carry the instruments to the same outdoor location every day. If you do not have access to the outdoors, students can collect this information on the Internet or from local weather forecasts.

Show students each of the instruments they will use in this lab and teach them how to use the instruments.

This experiment is a performance assessment that evaluates students' abilities to use a variety of standard weather instruments, collect and analyze their own data, and use their own data to make predictions. If your students can spend more than two weeks on the project, they will be able to make better predictions.

Following is a suggested grading rubric. If you plan to grade student work with this rubric, give each lab group a copy before they begin the activity so that they will know how you will assess their work.

Copyright © 2008 by John Wiley & Sons, Inc.

SUGGESTED GRADING RUBRIC

	Excellent Quality (4 points)	Good Work (3 points)	Satisfactory (2 points)	Poor Quality (1 point)
Prelab questions	All 4 prelab questions answered correctly	3 of 4 prelab questions answered correctly	2 of 4 prelab questions answered correctly	1 of 4 prelab questions answered correctly
Chart	Chart has all 60 entries for the experimental period	Chart has 40 to 59 entries for the experimental period	Chart has 11 to 39 entries for the experimental period	Chart has less than 10 entries for the experimental period
Graphs	All 6 graphs labeled correctly and color-coded correctly	All 6 graphs attempted, but some mislabeling on 1 or 2 graphs	3 to 5 graphs completed and correct, OR all 6 attempted, but color-coding or labeling incorrect	Only 1 or 2 graphs attempted
Postlab questions	All 6 postlab questions answered correctly	4 or 5 postlab questions answered correctly	3 postlab questions answered correctly	1 or 2 postlab questions answered correctly

Comments: _____

_____

Points possible: 16

Points earned: _____

Copyright © 2008 by John Wiley & Sons, Inc.

Copyright © 2008 by John Wiley & Sons, Inc.

WEATHER TRACKING

Performance Assessment on Tracking, Interpreting, and Predicting Weather

Introduction

A person who studies the weather is a meteorologist. By collecting data on the weather, meteorologists learn about weather patterns. They use this knowledge to make predictions about weather in the future.

Meteorologists take readings from a variety of weather instruments. Barometers are devices that indicate air pressure, thermometers show air temperature, and psychrometers indicate relative humidity. Instruments that determine wind speed are anemometers; wind vanes show wind direction. A rain gauge can tell you how much rain has fallen in the last 24 hours.

If you observe weather conditions and collect weather data in your local area for a period of time, could you make predictions about future weather? In this experiment, you will find out.

Prelab Questions

1. What is the job of a meteorologist?

2. What tool does a meteorologist use to measure air pressure?

3. What tools does a meteorologist use to gather information about wind?

4. Why do you think that weather forecasting is important?

Materials

Thermometer	Barometer
Psychrometer	Rain gauge
Anemometer	Graph paper
Wind vane	Colored pencils

Procedure

1. Find a location where you can measure weather conditions once a day for the next two weeks. If possible, set up an outdoor weather station that can remain in place for the duration of the experiment.

2. In your science notebook, create a data table like the one shown below. Draw 10 rows on your data table so that you can record conditions five days a week for two weeks.

DATA TABLE

		Weather Instrument Readings				
Date	Thermometer	Psychrometer	Anemometer	Wind Vane	Barometer	Rain Gauge

Copyright © 2008 by John Wiley & Sons, Inc.

3. At the same time each day, visit the weather station. At the weather station, determine air temperature, relative humidity, air pressure, wind speed, wind direction, and the amount of rain that has fallen in the last 24 hours. Record these observations on the data table.

4. At the end of the two-week period, create a line graph that shows the air temperature each day of the experimental period. Use a red pencil to plot temperature. Place time (the dates) on the x-axis and temperature on the y-axis.

5. Create similar graphs that show the other weather variables (relative humidity, air pressure, wind speed, wind direction, and rainfall). Use a different-colored pencil for each weather variable.

6. Compare the graphs. Can you see any patterns or trends? For example, does relative humidity increase as temperature increases? What about air pressure or wind speed?

7. Answer the postlab questions.

Postlab Questions

1. According to your graphs, how did relative humidity change as temperature changed?

2. According to your graphs, how did barometric pressure change as temperature changed?

3. According to your graphs, is there a relationship between air pressure and wind?

4. On the basis of the weather data you collected and the graphs you analyzed, can you make some general predictions about the kind of weather your area may experience in the next few days? Explain.

5. Meteorologists keep extensive records on weather conditions. Why do you think they do so?

LESSON 4: WATER

4-1 THE WATER PLANET
Content on Water

Water Everywhere

Water is essential for life on Earth. This simple, life-sustaining molecule is abundant, covering three-quarters of the planet's surface. However, not all water on Earth is fit for human consumption; 97 percent is salty. The remaining 3 percent is fresh water, but 2 percent is tied up in glaciers around the polar caps. That leaves only 1 percent of the planet's total water supply for human use.

The Water Cycle

New water is never created, so the total volume of water on Earth has remained constant for millions of years. Today's water was here when the dinosaurs roamed the planet. Water molecules spend thousands of years traveling through a circuit called the water cycle (the hydrologic cycle), which includes terrestrial, oceanic, and atmospheric reserves.

FIGURE A. THE WATER CYCLE

51

Copyright © 2008 by John Wiley & Sons, Inc.

In the water cycle, water can be found in all three states of matter—solid, liquid, and gas. Figure A illustrates the water cycle. Energy from the sun provides the power that causes water to evaporate from the land and seas. Water also enters the atmosphere by transpiration, an evaporative process in which plants lose water. Water frozen in glaciers can evaporate to a gaseous form in the process of sublimation.

Water vapor in the atmosphere condenses into droplets of liquid and forms clouds. Water falls from these clouds in various forms of precipitation and replenishes supplies in the ground, rivers, and oceans. Rain, snow, sleet, and hail are forms of precipitation.

Once it falls to the earth's surface, water can follow one of several possible routes. Some percolates through the soil to become groundwater. Most of the groundwater in the United States is in underground reservoirs. Groundwater within 1000 feet of Earth's surface can be recovered economically. The total volume of available groundwater is about nine times the volume of water in the Great Lakes. About 50 percent of the U.S. population gets its water from groundwater.

Groundwater Depletion

Groundwater supplies can be exhausted if the rate of withdrawal exceeds the natural rate of replenishment. One large underground reservoir, the Ogallala aquifer, is located under the Great Plains of the United States. People began pumping water from the Ogallala in the 1930s to irrigate the land, converting this naturally dry region into the lush "breadbasket of America." Today, water is being removed from this aquifer 50 times faster than it can be replenished by rain. As a result, the water table, the topmost level of underground water, is dropping drastically. The loss of water in the reservoir is forcing farmers to change their agricultural methods to raise crops that require little or no water.

Water that does not infiltrate the ground becomes runoff, which travels in streams and rivers to the sea. Water flows from high elevations to lower ones due to the force of gravity. The land area that delivers the water, along with its load of sediment and dissolved materials, to a stream or river makes up the watershed or drainage basin. The kinds and amounts of substances dissolved in water depend on the climate, the rock and soil composition, and human activities in the basin. Pollutants in the drainage basin can include gasoline and oil from road surfaces, fertilizers from fields, animal manure from feedlots, and pesticides from farms.

Water that falls as precipitation can also join existing water bodies, such as rivers, lakes, and oceans. If water molecules fall into freshwater systems, they are available to plants and animals. Living things use water to carry out normal metabolic activities. These molecules are eventually excreted from the animals and evaporated from the plants to reenter the atmospheric water supply.

Copyright © 2008 by John Wiley & Sons, Inc.

WATER PUZZLE—VOCABULARY ACTIVITY ON
THE WATER PLANET

Directions

After reading *The Water Planet,* complete the sentences in the following clues and fill in the corresponding spaces in the raindrop. The letters in the numbered circles will spell out a water word at the bottom of the puzzle.

Clues

1. The _____ provides energy that drives the water cycle.

2. A river's _____ is composed of sediment plus materials from the watershed area.

3. Running water can cause soil to _____.

4. Water vapor condenses to form _____ in the atmosphere.

5. A large, underground reservoir is a(n) _____.

6. Rain helps refill or _____ an aquifer.

7. The land area that delivers water and its load to a stream is the _____.

8. Runoff may include oil, gas, fertilizer, and other _____.

9. _____ occurs when ice changes to a vapor.

10. The water cycle is also called the _____ cycle.

11. Water can _____ into the atmosphere from lakes and rivers.

12. _____ means to change from a gas to a liquid.

13. A(n) _____ is a large body of ice.

14. Water can exist as a solid, _____, or gas.

15. Water changes from a gas to a liquid and back to a gas in the water _____.

Copyright © 2008 by John Wiley & Sons, Inc.

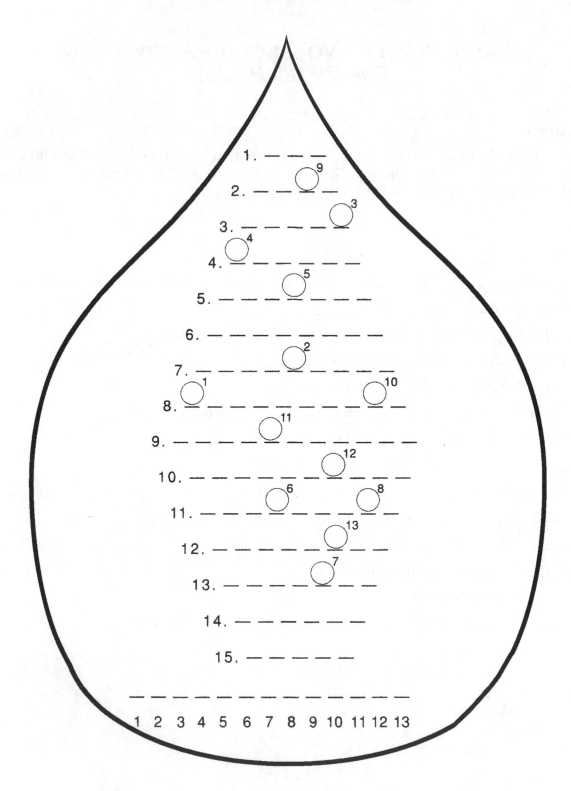

Copyright © 2008 by John Wiley & Sons, Inc.

4-2 BEARLY RAINING
Lab on Drainage Basins

Objectives

Students will read a topographic map, determine the volume of rain that falls on an area, and explore ways a drainage basin affects water quality.

Teacher Notes

A hypothetical school campus is used in this example. However, you can determine the volume of water that falls on your campus by measuring the area with a trundle wheel or tape measure. An estimate of the size of school grounds is also acceptable for an activity such as this. The amount of annual rainfall in your area can be obtained from almanacs, newspapers, and TV weather stations. You can also use a rain gauge to determine the volume of rain that falls during one rainfall event.

Copyright © 2008 by John Wiley & Sons, Inc.

Bearly Raining
Lab on Drainage Basins

Introduction

Figure A is a topographic map that shows the Little Dipper High School (LDHS) campus and surrounding area. A topographic (topo) map shows elevations, which can be determined by reading the numbers written on one of the topo lines. Each line represents a 50-foot change in elevation. Creeks and rivers are on the lowest elevations, and roadbeds are generally built on ridges.

The school campus is marked with four Xs. The campus width is 320 yards, and its length is 599 yards. The annual rainfall for this locale is 59 inches per year. LDHS is part of two drainage basins, the Bear Creek drainage basin and the Little Bear Creek drainage basin.

A drainage basin includes all the land area from which runoff flows to a waterway. Water always flows downhill, and because LDHS is on the top of a hill, the rain that falls on campus flows toward both creeks. The quality of this runoff from the school campus is affected by the activities of people in the drainage basin.

Materials

Topographic map

Colored pencils

Procedure

1. Determine the annual volume of rain (in cubic feet [ft3]) that falls on this campus by multiplying the length of the campus (ft) by the width of the campus (ft) by the annual average depth of rain (ft).

   Volume (ft3) = length (ft) × width (ft) × depth of rain each year (ft)

   Record this calculation in the data table.

2. Divide the annual rainfall on campus by 12 to determine the average monthly volume of rain. Record your answer in the data table.

3. Determine how much the yearly rain volume weighs in pounds. One cubic foot of water weighs 62.5 pounds. Record the answer in the data table.

4. Convert this weight to kilograms. There are 0.454 kilograms in one pound. Record your answer in the data table.

5. Determine the monthly rain volume weight in pounds. Multiply the monthly rain volume (ft3) by 62.5 pounds. Record your answer in the data table.

6. Convert the monthly weight of rain to kilograms. There are 0.454 kilograms in one pound. Record your answer in the data table.

Copyright © 2008 by John Wiley & Sons, Inc.

Copyright © 2008 by John Wiley & Sons, Inc.

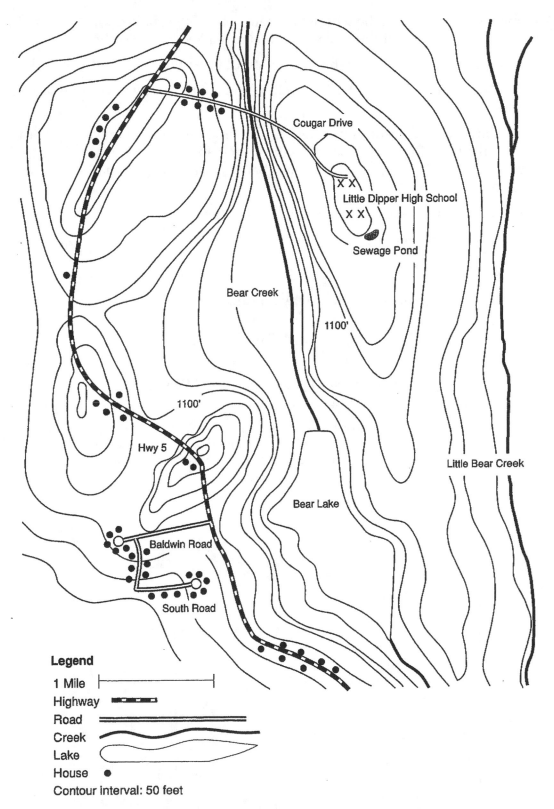

Legend

1 Mile	
Highway	
Road	
Creek	
Lake	
House	●

Contour interval: 50 feet

FIGURE A. BEAR CREEK DRAINAGE BASIN

7. Determine the elevation of the school by reading one of the marked topo lines and counting the number of 50-foot lines between the one marked and the school.

8. Use the topo map to determine the destination of water that falls on the school campus.

9. Shade the Bear Creek drainage basin in yellow and the Little Bear Creek drainage basin in pale blue.

10. Draw in some possible features that might affect the quality of the water in the Bear Creek basin and the Little Bear Creek basin on the topo map. These features could include, but are not limited to, homes, roads, pastures, barns, businesses, and parks. See the key for appropriate symbols.

11. Use dots to indicate areas that might support wildlife.

12. Answer the postlab questions.

Postlab Questions

1. Complete the data table with data from your calculations.

DATA TABLE

Rain on Little Dipper High School Campus					
Annual Rain Volume	Monthly Rain Volume	Weight of Annual Rain in Pounds	Weight of Annual Rain in Kilograms	Weight of Monthly Rain in Pounds	Weight of Monthly Rain in Kilograms

Copyright © 2008 by John Wiley & Sons, Inc.

2. What is the elevation of Little Dipper High School?

3. What structures did you add to the drainage basin of Bear Creek? How might your additions affect the quality of water in the creek?

4. How might wildlife in the area be affected by changes in the runoff to these two creeks?

5. If all the vegetation between LDHS and Bear Creek were removed, how would the runoff and the creek be affected? Explain your answer.

Copyright © 2008 by John Wiley & Sons, Inc.

4-3 AQUIFER PROJECT
Inquiry Lab on Groundwater

Objectives

Students will develop a model of an aquifer.

Teacher Notes

Make a variety of materials available to students. Several items are listed in the Materials section, but you can alter the list according to the items you have available. If you want students to demonstrate ground wells or pumps, be sure to include drinking straws, syringes, or hand pumps (from spray bottles) in the materials.

You could expand the experiment by asking students to add a "pollutant" (such as oil or colored water) to the model. They could track the movement of the pollutant, then develop methods of removing the pollutant.

A suggested grading rubric follows. You can use the rubric as it is or tailor it to your needs. Give the students a copy of the rubric before they begin the lab so that they will know how you will assess their work.

Copyright © 2008 by John Wiley & Sons, Inc.

SUGGESTED GRADING RUBRIC

Criteria	Scale			
	4	3	2	1
Prelab questions: number of questions answered correctly	4 of 4	3 of 4	2 of 4	1 of 4
Design for aquifer model meets these criteria: • Transparent • Uses approved materials • Drawing of design clear and neat • Design includes list of materials	4 of 4 items present	3 of 4 items present	2 of 4 items present	1 of 4 items present
Model constructed as designed	Model follows design perfectly	Only very minor design flaws	Several design flaws	Many design flaws
Demonstrated and described flow of water with arrows on design drawing	Demonstrated and explained fully; added arrows appropriately	Demonstration and explanation incomplete; arrows correct	Either demonstration and explanation or arrows incorrect	Could not demonstrate or explain water movement; arrows incorrect
Postlab questions: number of questions answered correctly	4 of 4	3 of 4	2 of 4	1 of 4

Comments: _____

_____

Points possible: 20

Points earned: _____

Copyright © 2008 by John Wiley & Sons, Inc.

AQUIFER PROJECT
Inquiry Lab on Groundwater

Introduction

When it rains, water flows into streams or rivers. However, much of the precipitation soaks into the soil, traveling slowly down through the layers until it reaches an aquifer. Aquifers are made up of porous materials, such as small rocks, sand, gravel, and sandstone. Porous materials are permeable to water because they contain a lot of space in which water can collect. The area of an aquifer that contains accumulated water is the saturated zone, and the top of this area is the water table (see Figure A). The depth of the water table can vary from a few feet to thousands of feet below the surface. The water table may rise or fall, depending on the amount of rain and the rate at which water is removed. Extracting water from aquifers for use in homes, agriculture, and industry lowers the water table.

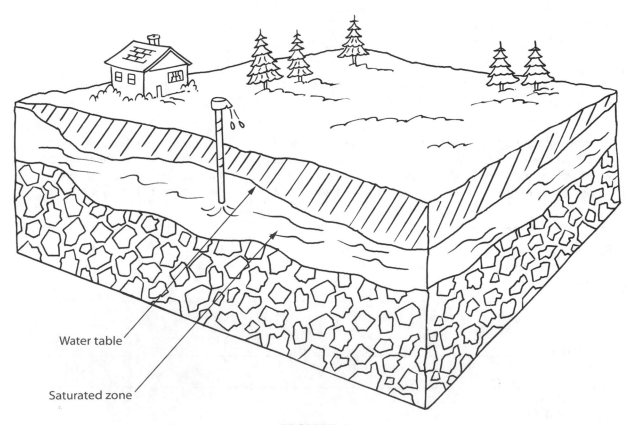

Water table

Saturated zone

FIGURE A

Copyright © 2008 by John Wiley & Sons, Inc.

Groundwater participates in the water cycle. Water in the soil constantly drains to lower elevations. Eventually, this water is discharged into a lake or river. In some places, water rises to the surface through natural springs. Once groundwater makes its way to the surface, water molecules evaporate and return to the air. When it rains, water falls on the recharge zone, the area above an aquifer, and percolates back down to the groundwater.

Prelab Questions

1. What is an aquifer?

2. How does water enter an aquifer?

3. How does water leave an aquifer?

Materials

Clear soda bottle	Hand pump
Plastic food container	Straws
Large, clear plastic cups	Plastic tubing
Gravel (about 2 cups)	Syringe (without needle)
Sand (about 2 cups)	Scissors
Clay (about 2 cups)	Rubber bands
Water	Coffee filters (any size or shape)

Procedure

1. Work with a group of two or three other students.

2. The job of your group is to design and build a model of an aquifer. As a group,

   a. Develop a design for your model of an aquifer. The model aquifer should be transparent so you can see what is happening inside. Keep in mind the materials that are available to you. You can use any of the materials available, but you do not have to use all of them.

   b. Draw your design for the model aquifer.

   c. Make a list of materials that you will need to build your model.

   d. Show your design and materials list to your teacher.

   e. If you get teacher approval, collect the materials and construct the model aquifer.

3. Once your aquifer is complete, slowly add water to it. As you add the water, closely observe the system and notice how water moves through it. Add arrows to the drawing of your design to show the path of water moving in the model.

4. Add a well to your model aquifer. Construct the well from any of the materials that are available. Demonstrate how you can remove water from the aquifer.

5. Answer the postlab questions.

Copyright © 2008 by John Wiley & Sons, Inc.

Postlab Questions

1. On the basis of your model, what do you think happens to a natural aquifer when it rains? What do you think happens during periods of drought?

2. What do you think might happen to the land over an aquifer if all the water in the aquifer were removed? Explain your reasoning.

3. The soil in some regions is primarily clay on top of bedrock. Would you expect to find aquifers in these regions? Explain your answer.

4. Suggest some ways that a pollutant might enter an aquifer.

Copyright © 2008 by John Wiley & Sons, Inc.

SECTION 2

Physics

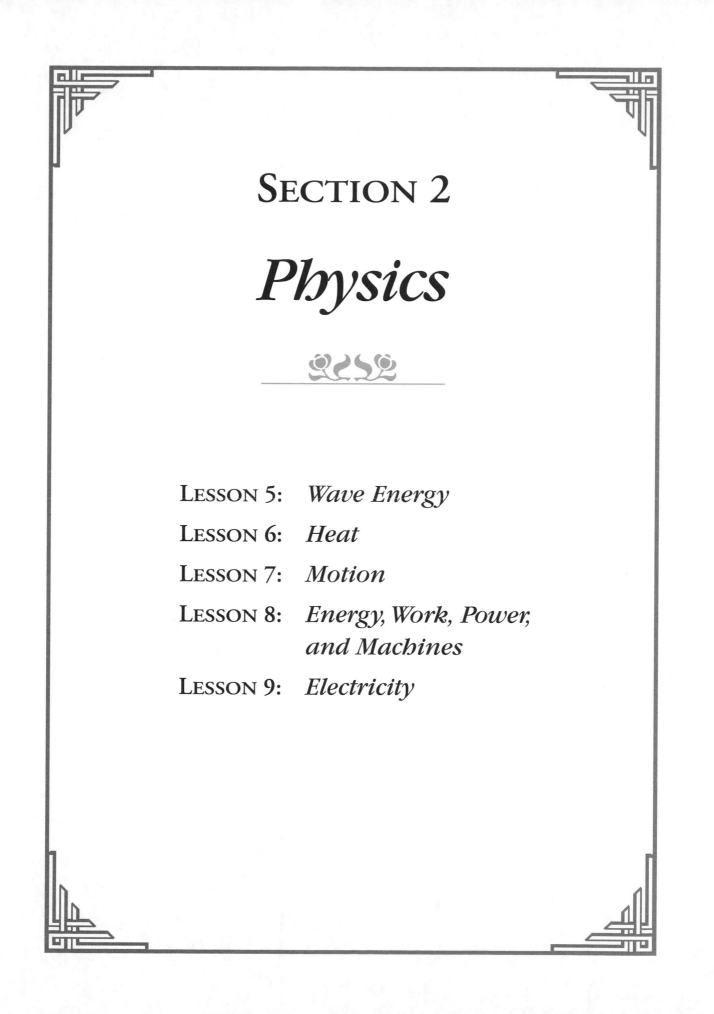

Copyright © 2008 by John Wiley & Sons, Inc.

LESSON 5: WAVE ENERGY

5-1 WAVE ON
Content on Wave Energy

❧❧❧

What Wave?

Have you ever done "the wave" at a baseball game? This undulating motion produced by spectators standing in sequence, one after another, reminds us of the motion of waves in nature. Many waves are invisible, but we see some of them every day.

If you drop a marble into a pool of water, you create a wave. The marble has kinetic energy because it is moving, and it transfers some of this energy to the water particles, causing them to move. The particles of water transfer the energy to adjacent particles, and the wave moves outward from the center.

A Disturbance

A wave is a disturbance that moves energy through matter and space. The matter through which a wave moves is referred to as the medium. For example, air is a medium for sound waves. As a wave travels through a medium, the medium does not move along with the wave. Only the energy is transmitted. To see this, tie a string to a doorknob and move it up and down to form a wave (see Figure A). The string, or medium, is not moving toward the doorknob, but the energy of the wave moves from your hand to the doorknob.

Transverse and Longitudinal Waves

There are two types of waves: transverse and longitudinal. An ocean wave is a transverse wave because the medium, the ocean, moves at right angles to the wave. Just like the string you tied to a doorknob, the ocean moves up and down, but the wave moves toward the shore. The crest of a transverse wave is the high point, and the trough is the lowest downward point (see Figure B).

In a longitudinal wave, the medium moves back and forth in the same direction as the wave travels. Ask a friend to hold one end of a Slinky. By pushing your end of the Slinky in and out, you can create a longitudinal wave. Particles of the medium are compressed or pushed together in areas called compressions. As a compression moves forward, it leaves behind a rarefaction, a space containing fewer particles. Sound waves travel as longitudinal waves.

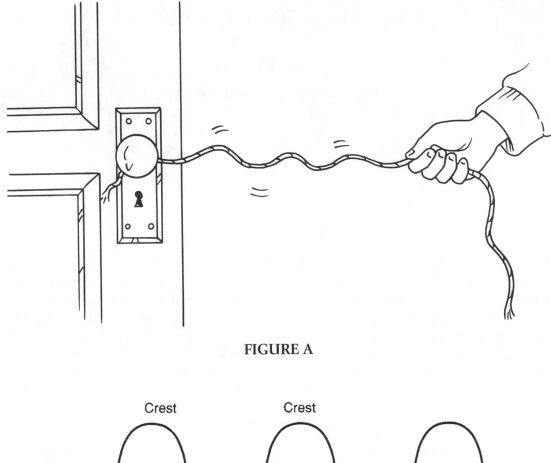

FIGURE A

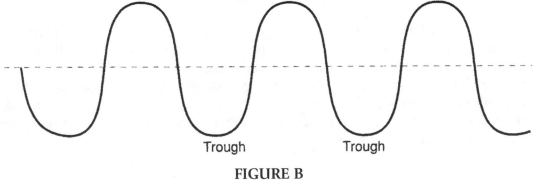

FIGURE B

Copyright © 2008 by John Wiley & Sons, Inc.

Wave Characteristics

There are many types of waves, including sound waves, light waves, and radio and television waves. All waves share the characteristics of amplitude, wavelength, and frequency.

Amplitude refers to the maximum distance molecules of the medium are displaced from their original position. If you push the Slinky very gently, the waves you create have small amplitude. However, if you shove the Slinky forward with a lot of force, you can create waves with large amplitudes.

Wavelength is the distance between two successive identical wave parts, such as two crests. Many wavelengths are measured in meters or centimeters, but wavelengths of light are measured in millionths of a meter, or micrometers.

Copyright © 2008 by John Wiley & Sons, Inc.

The number of waves that pass a point in a certain amount of time is the wave's *frequency*. For example, if 1000 waves pass a point in one second, they have a frequency of 1000 cycles (or waves) per second. Wave frequency is measured in units called hertz (Hz). A frequency of 1 Hz is equal to one wave per second. Higher frequencies are measured in kilohertz (kHz), and extremely high frequencies are measured in megahertz (MHz). AM radio waves are broadcast in kilohertz, but FM waves are broadcast in megahertz. If a station is 140 MHz on the FM radio, it is broadcasting waves with a frequency of 140,000,000 Hz. These waves are produced by electrons vibrating at the same frequency in the radio station's transmitting antenna.

Sound

Sounds are generated by vibrating objects that cause the surrounding medium, usually the air, to vibrate. Sound waves have two important components: intensity and pitch. Intensity, the amount of energy in a sound wave, determines the loudness of a sound, and is measured in units called decibels. The decibel scale begins at zero, the point at which we can just hear. The sound of a rocket engine is deafening at 200 decibels. All sounds with intensities near 120 decibels can cause pain to humans. Sounds above 85 decibels can damage hearing. Loud music, especially played through earphones, damages many people's hearing.

Sound waves also have the property of pitch, which is determined by the frequency of the vibrations in the molecules of the medium. High-frequency sound waves have high pitches. A high note by a female singer may be about 1000 Hz, and a male bass may sing at 70 Hz. Humans can hear sounds between 20 Hz and 20,000 Hz. Dogs can hear pitches of up to 25,000 Hz, and porpoises can hear them up to 150,000 Hz.

The Doppler Effect

Have you ever listened to the sound of an approaching siren? The pitch of the siren gets higher as the siren gets close to you due to the Doppler effect. When there is motion between the observer and the source of sound, the frequency of sound waves changes. As the sound approaches the observer, the waves are compressed, and they reach the observer sooner than they would have if the source of the sound were stationary. Therefore, sound waves seem to have a higher pitch when they reach the observer because their frequency has increased. As the source of the sound moves away from the observer, the sound waves are farther apart, and the pitch drops.

RIDE THE WAVE—VOCABULARY ACTIVITY ON *WAVE ON*

Directions

After reading *Wave On,* select a word from the wave below that fits in the following sentences. Some words are used twice.

wave   amplitude   dogs
medium   rarefaction   hertz   intensity
transverse   compression   frequency   sound
longitudinal   trough   Doppler   decibels
crest   ultrasonic

Clues

1. The _____ of a sound wave determines the sound's pitch.

2. Ocean waves are _____ waves because the water and the waves move at right angles to each other.

3. In a longitudinal wave, the space where there are few particles of medium is called a(n) _____.

4. _____ are better at hearing very high pitched sounds than humans.

5. A(n) _____ is a disturbance that moves energy through space and matter.

6. Sound is a(n) _____ wave because the medium moves back and forth in the same direction that the wave travels.

7. The _____ of a transverse wave is the highest point, or point of maximum displacement, of the wave.

8. The sound of an approaching train whistle increases in pitch because of the _____ effect.

9. Sounds that people cannot hear are called _____ sounds.

10. Air is one _____ through which sound can travel.

11. The frequency of sound waves is measured in units called _____.

12. In a sound wave, the space where air particles are pushed together is a(n) _____.

13. A(n) _____ wave is produced by a vibrating object that causes the air molecules to vibrate.

14. The intensity or loudness of a sound is measured in units called _____.

15. Wave _____ refers to the maximum distances medium molecules are displaced.

Copyright © 2008 by John Wiley & Sons, Inc.

16. The lowest displacement of a wave is called the wave's _____.

17. A rocket engine produces a wave of high _____, which registers 200 on the decibel scale.

18. Porpoises can hear _____ sounds in the 150,000 Hz range.

19. FM radio stations broadcast at frequencies in the mega-_____ range.

20. Sounds above 85 _____ can damage our ears.

Copyright © 2008 by John Wiley & Sons, Inc.

5-2 TELEPHONE WAVES
Lab on Sending Waves Along Strings

Objectives

Students will carry out their own experiments to find out the best combination of materials to construct a set of talking cans.

Teacher Notes

Make a variety of materials available. You can include all the materials listed in this lab, or modify the list according to your supplies.

Copyright © 2008 by John Wiley & Sons, Inc.

TELEPHONE WAVES
Lab on Sending Waves Along Strings

Introduction

Have you ever made a set of "talking cans" like those in Figure A and used them to send a message to a friend? Two empty cans that are attached to each other with a long string make a pretty good communication device. They work because a speaker sends out sound waves. Talking into the can directs those sound waves toward the bottom of the can, causing the bottom of the can to vibrate at the same frequency as the speaker's voice. Talking produces more than 1000 sound waves per second. As the bottom of the can vibrates, it pulls the string along with it. The string transmits its vibrations to the bottom of the second can, which then vibrates. A listener can hear those vibrations. In this experiment, you will make several sets of talking cans to determine the best combination of materials for transmitting sound waves.

FIGURE A

Copyright © 2008 by John Wiley & Sons, Inc.

Materials

Two clean metal cans with labels and one end removed

Thin wire (several feet)	Two small paper cups
Ruler or tape measure	Two large paper cups
Scissors	Two small plastic cups
Wire cutters	Two large plastic cups
Thin nail	Plastic wrap
Hammer	Twine or kite string (several feet)
Needle	Fishing line (several feet)
Rubber bands	Thread (several feet)

Prelab Questions

1. In your own words, define the term *vibrate*.

2. What is sound?

3. You are talking to your friend sitting next to you. How do the sound waves produced by your voice travel to your friend's ears?

Procedure

1. Work with a partner to make a set of talking cans similar to the ones in Figure A. To do so,

   a. Use the thin nail and hammer to punch a tiny hole in the end of each can. Take care when working with the hammer and nail.

   b. Measure and cut a 3-foot length of kite string.

   c. Thread one end of the string into one of the cans, from the outside to the inside. Be careful not to cut your hands on the metal around the holes in the cans. Inside the can, either tie a knot in the string or tape it so that the string cannot pull out.

   d. Repeat the same procedure with the other can and opposite end of the string.

2. Experiment with the talking cans. As one partner speaks into one can, the other can listen at the other can.

   a. Try varying the tension on the string between the cans to find the optimum tension for transmitting sound waves.

   b. See if the cans can carry a message around a corner.

   c. Replace the 3-foot kite string between the cans with a 6-foot kite string. Compare the transmitting quality of the two strings.

Copyright © 2008 by John Wiley & Sons, Inc.

3. Redesign the talking cans to see if you can improve on the original plan. Try using paper or plastic cups, or try different types of string. For each new design, compare it to the original set of talking cans that you made in procedure step 1.

4. Answer the postlab questions.

Postlab Questions

1. How are sound waves transmitted along the talking can apparatus?

2. When you experimented with the talking cans, what did you find out about talking around corners?

3. When you experimented with the talking cans, what did you learn when you replaced the 3-foot string with a 6-foot string?

4. When you redesigned the talking cans, what changes did you make? Did your changes improve the transmission of sound?

5. Your friend wants to make a set of talking cans. Based on your experimental results, what would be the best design for her to follow?

Copyright © 2008 by John Wiley & Sons, Inc.

5-3 ASSESSING THE VIBRATIONS OF MUSIC
Performance Assessment on Sound Waves

Objectives

Students will create a musical instrument composed of strings that vibrate at different frequencies. Students will also relate the pitch of a vibrating string to the number of times the string vibrates.

Teacher Notes

Because this is an inquiry lesson, students should not receive explicit directions for construction of their musical instruments. Encourage students to be creative in their designs. If you have additional materials other than those suggested in the materials list, please make them available to your students when they are in the planning stage. Foot-long pieces of 2-by-4-inch lumber are suggested as the base of the musical instrument. However, different sizes of wood are just as useful. Anything that can support four strings can be used in this lab.

A suggested grading rubric follows. You can use the rubric as it is or tailor it for your needs. Give the students a copy of the rubric before they begin the lab so that they will know how you will assess their work.

Copyright © 2008 by John Wiley & Sons, Inc.

SUGGESTED GRADING RUBRIC

Excellent Quality 4 points	Good Work 3 points	Satisfactory 2 points	Poor Quality 1 point
Answered all 4 prelab questions correctly	Answered 3 of 4 prelab questions correctly	Answered 2 of 4 prelab questions correctly	Answered 1 prelab question correctly
Design for the instrument is written and explained well	Design for the instrument is written but incomplete	Design for the instrument is written but not fully explained	Design for the instrument contains minimal information
Instrument has at least 4 strings that produce sounds	Instrument has 2 strings that produce sounds	Instrument has 3 strings that produce sounds	Instrument has 1 string that produces sounds
Each string produces a different pitch	3 of the strings produce different pitches	2 of the strings produce different pitches	All of the strings have the same pitch
Instrument was used to play a simple melody	Instrument could be played, but the melody was not clear	Instrument could be played, but a melody was not produced	Instrument could not be played
Instrument is constructed well enough to be played by several students	Instrument is fragile, but could be played by 2 other students	Instrument is fragile, but could be played by 1 other student	Instrument was not constructed well enough for other students to play
Answered all 4 postlab questions correctly	Answered 3 of 4 postlab questions correctly	Answered 2 of 4 postlab questions correctly	Answered 1 postlab question correctly

Comments: _____

_____

Points possible: 28

Points earned: _____

Copyright © 2008 by John Wiley & Sons, Inc.

ASSESSING THE VIBRATIONS OF MUSIC
Performance Assessment on Sound Waves

Introduction

How can you make musical sounds? To make a sound, something must vibrate. A sound is considered music if it has a pleasing quality, an identifiable pitch, and a rhythm.

People have been making musical instruments for centuries. Woodwind instruments, such as flutes and clarinets, produce sounds by vibrating a column of air within the instrument. Drums and other percussion instruments vibrate when they are struck. Stringed instruments pulsate when they are rubbed or plucked. Guitars (like the one in Figure A), violins, and pianos produce sounds when their strings are vibrated. The pitch of a stringed instrument can be changed by changing the length, tightness, or thickness of the string.

A short string vibrates at a higher frequency than a long one and thus produces a higher pitch. Musicians change the pitch of a string by placing their fingers along it, thus altering its length. A finger placed near the center of an instrument shortens the string much more, producing a very high pitch.

A tighter string will have a higher frequency of vibration. Pianos, guitars, and violins are tuned by tightening or loosening the strings. When a string is tightened, it produces a higher pitch.

Thick strings vibrate more slowly, and thus at a lower frequency, than thin strings. The strings on a bass guitar are much thicker than those on a lead guitar. Likewise, the strings on the bass keys of a piano are thicker than those on the treble keys.

In this lab, you will create a musical instrument that has at least four strings. You will use this instrument to play a tune of your own creation.

FIGURE A

Copyright © 2008 by John Wiley & Sons, Inc.

Prelab Questions

1. What is a sound?

2. What is music?

3. How can a musician change the pitch of a string on an instrument?

4. How does the thickness of a string affect its sound?

Materials

Four or more pieces of monofilament fishing string or thin wire	Tape
Small pieces of wood, Styrofoam, cork, or other material	Scissors
Foot-long piece of wood (2 inches by 4 inches)	Tacks

Copyright © 2008 by John Wiley & Sons, Inc.

Procedure

1. Design a simple stringed musical instrument that can be made from the materials available. You can use any of the materials available, but you do not have to use all of them. As you are planning the instrument, keep these points in mind:

   a. The instrument should have four stings that produce four different pitches.

   b. The first string should have the lowest pitch, the second a higher, the third a still higher, and the fourth the highest pitch.

   c. The instrument must be constructed well enough for you and your classmates to use it to play a tune.

2. Write the steps you will follow to assemble the instrument. Show these steps to your teacher.

3. If you get teacher approval, collect the materials you need and assemble your instrument.

4. Use your instrument to play a simple melody.

5. Swap instruments with two or three classmates. Try playing your tune on their instruments.

6. Answer the postlab questions.

Postlab Questions

1. What are some problems you encountered in construction of your instrument? How did you solve these problems?

2. Ukuleles are small, guitarlike instruments that have four strings. The first string has the lowest pitch and the last string the highest pitch.

   a. Which string is probably the tightest?

   b. Which string is probably the thickest?

3. A guitar is made of six strings that are strung over a bridge. To play this instrument, a guitarist holds down the strings at different points. Why does holding down the strings change the pitch of the sound produced by those strings?

4. A piano is a stringed instrument. When a pianist strikes a key, a hammer strikes a string. Some of the strings are very thick; others are thin. Would you expect bass (low-frequency) sounds to be produced by thick or thin strings? Explain your reasoning.

LESSON 6: HEAT

6-1 DOING THE ATOMIC SHAKE
Content on Heat Energy

The Heat Is On

Anything that has mass and occupies space is matter. All forms of matter are made up of atoms and molecules that are constantly moving and jiggling about. All this shaking and moving is due to the kinetic energy that these molecules possess. The kinetic energy in molecules can be detected by the amount of heat given off by a particular form of matter. As the temperature of matter increases, the kinetic energy increases.

You can easily detect the increase in kinetic energy in matter. If you hit a baseball with an aluminum bat and then touch the point of impact on the bat, it will feel warm. The impact causes molecules within the metal bat to move and shake faster. Rub your palms together quickly and you will notice that they begin to get warm. This warmth is the result of speeding up the molecules in your hands. As molecules speed up, they give off heat.

The Temperature Is Rising

If you want to know exactly how much heat matter is giving off, you need to determine its temperature, a measurement that tells how warm or cold a body is with respect to some standard. A thermometer is an instrument that measures temperature. Thermometers contain either mercury or colored alcohol, substances that expand and rise up the tube of the thermometer when the temperature increases. Thermometers can be marked in the Fahrenheit scale, the Celsius scale, or the Kelvin scale.

Fahrenheit is the English temperature scale. On the Fahrenheit scale, 32 degrees signifies the freezing point of water, and 212 degrees its boiling point. The Celsius scale is the metric scale most often used to measure temperature. On the Celsius scale, the freezing point of water is 0 degrees and the boiling point is 100 degrees. Kelvin is another metric temperature scale. On this scale, temperature is measured in units called kelvins (K). This is a particularly useful scale because zero degrees Kelvin (0°K) is the lowest possible temperature that anything can reach; furthermore, 0°K is known as absolute zero, the temperature at which all molecular motion stops.

Copyright © 2008 by John Wiley & Sons, Inc.

Copyright © 2008 by John Wiley & Sons, Inc.

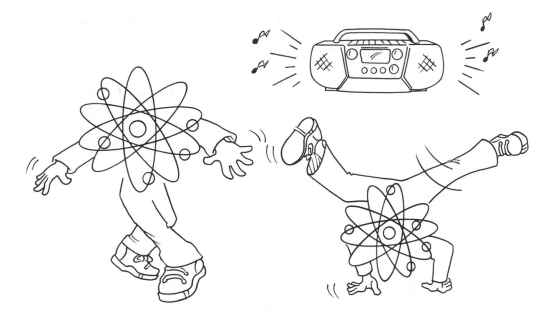

Temperature measures the motion of molecules or atoms in a substance. Heat is the energy that is transferred from one object to another because of a temperature difference between the objects. An increase in temperature indicates the addition of heat. Likewise, a decrease in temperature represents the removal of heat.

A calorie is one of the units used to measure heat. One calorie is defined as the amount of heat required to raise the temperature of one gram of liquid water one degree Celsius. The amount of heat needed for a given temperature change depends on the mass and the specific heat of the substance being heated. Specific heat refers to the ability of a substance to absorb heat energy. In fact, the specific heat of a substance is the number of calories needed to raise the temperature of one gram of that substance one degree Celsius. Water has a specific heat of 1.0 calorie per gram. Mercury has a specific heat of 0.03, and wood has a specific heat of 0.42. This tells you that it takes a lot more heat to raise the temperature of one gram of water than it does to raise the temperature of an equal amount of mercury or wood.

Bulging Cans and Sagging Lines

Have you ever left an aluminum can of soda unopened in your car on a sunny day? Chances are that the soda expanded, causing the can to bulge. As the temperature of a substance increases, its molecules move faster and farther apart. The result of this movement is expansion. The opposite of expansion is contraction. Cold weather slows the molecular motion of substances,

and the molecules move closer together. These concepts of expansion and contraction must be considered when buildings are designed and constructed. The extent of expansion of a particular substance depends on the amount of heat it absorbs. For example, why are telephone and power lines allowed to sag when they are strung between poles in the summer? The answer lies in expansion and contraction. In the summer heat, the lines are longer, and in the cold of winter, they are shorter. If the lines are strung too tightly, they might snap in the winter because they contract when it is cold.

Almost all liquids expand when they are heated and contract when they cool. However, you may know of an exception. Place some water in your ice trays and pop them in the freezer. What happens? The water freezes and expands. This behavior is not seen with other liquids. The odd crystalline structure of ice explains the expansion of freezing water.

Up, Up, and Away

Gases also expand and contract. Have you ever thought about why warm air rises? When air is warmed, it expands and becomes less dense than the surrounding air. As a result, it is buoyed up like a balloon. The buoyancy is upward because the air pressure below a region of warmed air is greater than the pressure above. Thus the warmed air rises because the buoyant force is greater than the weight of the gas. If this is true, why is the temperature not warm at high altitudes? Why are mountaintops usually cool and covered with snow? The warm air moves from a region of greater atmospheric pressure on the ground to a region of less pressure above it. Because it is moving to a region of less pressure, the gas expands. Expansion causes cooling, so the temperature drops.

Copyright © 2008 by John Wiley & Sons, Inc.

ATOMIC CROSSWORD—VOCABULARY ACTIVITY ON
DOING THE ATOMIC SHAKE

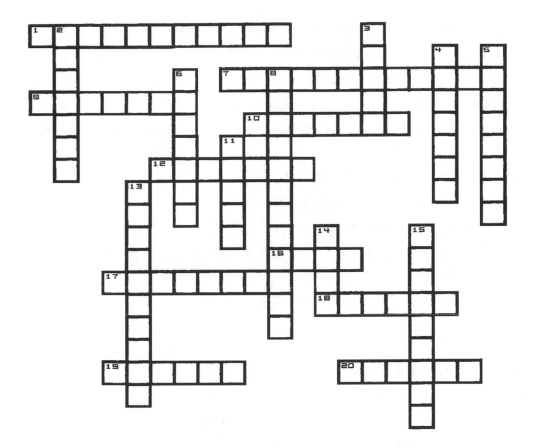

Copyright © 2008 by John Wiley & Sons, Inc.

Across

1. The measurement that tells how warm or cold a body is with respect to some standard.

7. The lowest possible temperature anything can reach; 0°K. (2 words)

9. The amount of heat required to raise the temperature of one gram of liquid water one degree Celsius.

10. A liquid metal used in thermometers that responds to temperature changes by contracting or expanding.

12. This type of energy can be detected by the amount of heat given off by matter.

16. This is the energy transferred from one object to another because of temperature change.

17. This is lower beneath a region of warmed air than above it.

18. Power lines will often sag due to expansion during this season.

19. A metric scale used to measure temperature; absolute zero is found on this scale.

20. When a gas expands, its temperature becomes _____ .

Down

2. When the temperature of a substance increases, the substance may _____ .

3. The specific heat of this substance is 1.0.

4. The units used in the Kelvin scale.

5. When substances cool, they _____, or decrease in size.

6. The metric temperature scale most often used to measure temperature; on this scale, 100° is the boiling point of water.

8. The ability of a substance to absorb heat energy.

11. Warm air is less _____ than cold air, so it rises above it.

13. When gases are _____, they get warmer.

14. The amount of heat needed for a given temperature change depends on the _____ of the matter being heated.

15. These move and shake due to kinetic energy in matter.

Word List

ABSOLUTE ZERO	EXPAND	MOLECULES
CALORIE	KELVIN	PRESSURE
CELSIUS	KELVINS	SPECIFIC HEAT
COMPRESSED	KINETIC	SUMMER
CONTRACT	HEAT	TEMPERATURE
COOLER	MASS	WATER
DENSE	MERCURY	

Copyright © 2008 by John Wiley & Sons, Inc.

6-2 UP, UP, AND AWAY
Performance Assessment on Heat Energy

Objectives

Students will discover how hot air causes objects to rise by building a hot air balloon.

Teacher Notes

Inflate students' balloons by holding them over a piece of 6-by-8-inch stovepipe that is sitting over one of the burners of a camp stove. If a camp stove is not available, a portable Bunsen burner or a commercial heat gun will work. Do not let the students operate any of this equipment.

For best results, fill the balloons on a day when the air is very calm.

A suggested grading rubric follows. You can use the rubric as it is or tailor it for your needs. If you opt to use this rubric, give the students a copy before they begin the lab so that they will know how you will assess their work.

Copyright © 2008 by John Wiley & Sons, Inc.

SUGGESTED GRADING RUBRIC

Excellent Quality 4 points	Good Work 3 points	Satisfactory 2 points	Poor Quality 1 point
Answered all 4 prelab questions correctly	Answered 3 of 4 prelab questions correctly	Answered 2 of 4 prelab questions correctly	Answered 1 prelab question correctly
Design for the hot air balloon is written and thoroughly explained	Design for the hot air balloon is written, but explanation is not thorough	Design for the hot air balloon is written, but explanation is incomplete	Design for the hot air balloon contains minimal information
Hot air balloon floats easily	Hot air balloon floats, but does not achieve altitude	Hot air balloon barely floats	Hot air balloon holds the hot air, but does not float
Answered all 4 postlab questions correctly	Answered 3 of 4 postlab questions correctly	Answered 2 of 4 postlab questions correctly	Answered 1 postlab question correctly

Comments: _____

_____

Points possible: 16

Points earned: _____

Copyright © 2008 by John Wiley & Sons, Inc.

UP, UP, AND AWAY
Performance Assessment on Heat Energy

Copyright © 2008 by John Wiley & Sons, Inc.

Background Information

If you were to hold a piece of tissue paper above a hot radiator, you would see the tissue begin to float upward. Air warmed by the radiator rises, carrying the tissue paper along with it. Warm air rises because it is lighter than cool air. As the rising air gains altitude, cool air moves under it to take its place. This is one reason that the top floor of a two-story home is hotter than the bottom floor in the summer.

The movement of cool air underneath warm, rising air creates air currents. Birds take advantage of these currents and float for long distances with little effort. Gliders can also travel on air currents once they are high enough in the sky.

When air is warmed, it expands. As air warms, its molecules become more active and push away from each other. If you don't believe this, blow up a balloon and hold it over the top of a radiator. The balloon will eventually burst due to expansion of air inside it.

Just as their name suggests, hot air balloons are filled with air, which has been heated by a gas burner. The heated air is lighter and less dense than the air around the balloon. As a result, the balloon is buoyed upward.

Prelab Questions

1. Explain why hot air rises.

2. Describe how hot and cold air can cause currents in a home or outdoors.

3. Explain why a bottle of hair spray might explode if left in a hot car all day.

4. Imagine an experiment in which you fit one balloon over the mouth of a bottle filled with hot water and another balloon over the mouth of a bottle of cold water. Which balloon would you expect to expand? Explain your answer.

Materials

One sheet of tissue wrapping paper for each group of two or three

Thread or lightweight string

Scissors

Index card

Glue

Tape

Procedure

1. Work with a group of two or three other students.

2. Your group will design and build a hot air balloon using the materials available. Your goal is to create a balloon that can rise the highest in the air when the teacher fills it with hot air. As a group,

   a. Develop a design for your hot air balloon. The balloon should be lightweight (less than 16 ounces), and it will need a length of string or cord to act as a tether. In addition, your balloon must have an opening through which it can take on hot air. Hot air will be supplied by your teacher from a camp stove and delivered through a 6-inch stove pipe.

   b. Draw your design for a hot air balloon.

   c. Make a list of materials that you will need to build the hot air balloon.

   d. Show your design and materials list to your teacher.

   e. If you get teacher approval, collect the materials and construct the hot air balloon. If you do not get teacher approval, review and change your design.

3. Once your balloon is complete, show it to your teacher. When all the balloons have been completed, the teacher will hold them, one at a time, over the stove pipe and fill them with hot air. The balloon that gains the most height wins the class competition.

Postlab Questions

1. Describe the balloon that floated the highest.

2. Explain why you think the balloon you described in question 1 won the competition.

3. How would you build your balloon next time if this experiment were repeated?

4. Summarize in one sentence what you learned from this lab.

Copyright © 2008 by John Wiley & Sons, Inc.

LESSON 7: MOTION

7-1 LET'S GET MOVIN'
Content on the Energy of Motion

It Depends on How You Look at It

Look at your desk. Is it moving? Do you see any motion? Whether you answer yes or no to these questions, you are right. The motion of an object depends on the frame of reference you use to evaluate it. The desk is at rest if you judge it relative to the floor or to yourself, but it is in motion compared to the sun. Because it is located on Earth, the desk is revolving around the sun continuously. No object on Earth is ever at rest relative to the sun.

For the purpose of our discussions on motion, we will use the earth rather than the sun as our frame of reference. When objects on the earth are placed in motion, they travel certain distances in a given time. The distance an object travels in a given time frame is called speed. Speed is determined by the following formula:

$$speed = distance \div time$$
$$S = d/t$$

Is It Speed, or Is It Velocity?

There are two types of speed we need to consider in our discussion—instantaneous and average. Instantaneous speed is an easy concept to grasp if you think of a speedometer on a car. The speedometer registers the speed at the particular instant that you look at the dial. There will be some fluctuations in the car's speed over time, even if it has cruise control. Red lights, stop signs, and slower motorists will cause the instantaneous speed to vary.

Average speed is the concept that we discuss more often when traveling. Average speed is the total distance an object travels over the entire time span it took to

Copyright © 2008 by John Wiley & Sons, Inc.

89

achieve that distance. If you went on a road trip and wanted to calculate your average speed, you could do this by watching your odometer (the distance dial on the dashboard) and your watch. Let's say you went 80 miles in 90 minutes. What was your average speed? You would divide 80 miles by 90 minutes to determine your speed in miles per minute, so your average speed was 0.89 miles per minute. You could calculate your answer in miles per hour by dividing 80 miles by 1.5 hours, making your average speed 53.33 miles per hour.

Most people think of speed and velocity as the same concept, and to everyone but the physicist, this may be true. In physics, however, velocity is speed in a given direction, and it is determined by dividing displacement by time. Displacement is the length and direction of an object's path from its starting point straight to its ending point. This means that the speed and velocity of an object may differ depending on the route the object takes to get to its destination.

It might be easier to understand speed and velocity if you picture a walk with your dog from your house to your grandmother's house. You would probably stay on the sidewalk and walk directly from your house to your grandmother's by the shortest route. If your dog is not on a leash, he would probably veer off the sidewalk, sniff some trees, and chase a few squirrels on the trip. This would increase the distance the dog travels, but not his displacement. Therefore, the dog's speed would be different from your speed, but the velocity for both of you would be the same if you both arrive at the house at the same time.

When computing velocity, you state not only the size, or magnitude, of the velocity but also the direction traveled. Velocity is a vector quantity, meaning that it has both magnitude and direction. Speed is a scalar quantity because it has only magnitude.

Let's return to our walk with the dog to review these concepts. It is 4 miles to your grandmother's house by the shortest route you can travel. She lives due west of your home. You and your dog, Doc, cover this distance in 60 minutes. You took the straight path of 4 miles, but Doc logged in 6 miles as he veered off the path for some dog adventures. Your speed was 4 miles per hour. Your velocity was 4 miles per hour west. Doc's velocity was 4 miles per hour west, but his speed was 6 miles per hour (distance traveled divided by time).

There's No Cruise Control on Roller Coasters

Another vector quantity is acceleration, the rate of change in velocity. Because acceleration is a vector quantity, it can involve a change in speed, a change of direction, or both. Have you ever experienced or felt acceleration? You can answer yes to that question if you have braved the amusement park's roller coaster ride. Changes in speed can be detected easily as the roller coaster slows down and speeds up. The formula for finding the magnitude of acceleration is as follows: acceleration (a) equals change in velocity divided by time, or

$$\text{acceleration} = \text{final velocity} - \text{initial velocity} \div \text{time}$$
$$a = V_f - V_i \div t$$

Acceleration can be represented by either negative or positive numbers. When objects speed up, there is positive acceleration. When objects slow down, acceleration is negative (known as deceleration).

Copyright © 2008 by John Wiley & Sons, Inc.

Copyright © 2008 by John Wiley & Sons, Inc.

Free Fall

The last concept we want to examine is free fall. All objects that fall toward the earth due to the pull of gravity fall with the same acceleration, regardless of their mass. This is acceleration due to gravity, *g*, which is approximately 10 meters per second squared. If you were to climb to the top of the highest building in your town and drop a tennis ball and a bowling ball off the building at the same time, they would both hit the ground simultaneously. These two balls maintain equal accelerations due to the pull of gravity and the effects of inertia.

Inertia and Newton

No discussion of motion is complete without the mention of Newton's three laws of motion. Newton's first law of motion is called the law of inertia. It states that an object at rest will remain at rest and that an object in motion will remain in motion unless some outside force acts on it. *Inertia* ("a resistance to change") often is the measure of the mass of a substance. To understand the first law of motion, imagine a boulder on the edge of a cliff. It remains perched on the edge unless something or someone nudges it forward. This force could be a person pushing it or a vibration of the earth. Or imagine that your car hits the car in front of you, and you lunge forward until your seat belt stops your forward motion. Inertia keeps your body in motion, even when the car is stopped by a collision.

It's a Matter of Mass

The second law of motion says that the acceleration produced by the net force on a body is directly proportional to the magnitude of the net force, in the same direction as the net force, and inversely proportional to the mass of the body. Or, to shorten this explanation, think of this formula:

$$\text{acceleration} = \text{force} \div \text{mass}$$

$$a = F \div m$$

You can turn this formula around and say that $F = m \times a$, or $m = F \div a$. To understand this concept, think of a golf ball on a tee. The more force you use to strike the golf ball, the greater the acceleration of the ball. Now think of a lead ball on the tee. You might increase the force you use to hit the ball, but not reach the acceleration you did before because of the greater mass of the object being moved. In other words, acceleration is directly proportional to force (if you increase one, you increase the other). Mass is inversely proportional to acceleration (if you increase the mass, you will decrease the acceleration if the force is not increased). The second law of motion might help explain why race cars are built of lightweight materials, such as fiberglass, to increase acceleration.

It is important to remember that forces applied to an object may be resisted by friction. Friction is a force that always acts in a direction to oppose motion. Greater masses may experience more friction when being moved than lighter masses. The surface on which the object is resting will dictate the amount of friction involved. Air resistance is also a type of friction. For objects that fall downward through the atmosphere, air resistance does not present a problem unless the mass of the object is so light that air currents can slow its progress (as in the case of feathers and pieces of paper).

Actions and Reactions

You have probably heard the third law of motion. It states that whenever one body exerts a force on a second body, the second body exerts an equal and opposite force on the first. In simpler terms, for every action there is an equal and opposite reaction. Forces always occur in pairs. As you walk across the floor, you push down on the floor, and the floor pushes back up on you. As a rocket fires out gases that push on the air molecules, the air molecules push back, propelling the rocket upward. The force that initiated the reaction is called the action force. The force that responded to the initial action is called the reaction force. You might have experienced this law of motion in a frightening way the first time you jumped from a rowboat onto a pier. As you jumped forward off the front of the boat, the boat floated backward in response to your forward push. We hope you took this into account as you leaped forward, or you might have gotten a little wet.

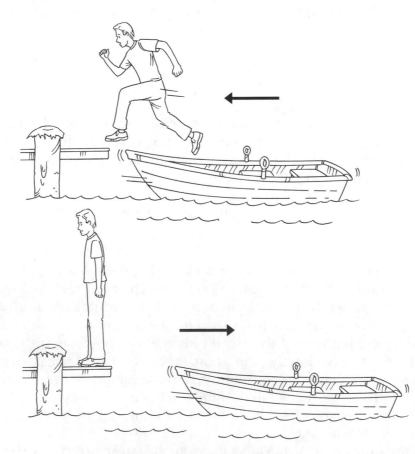

THE THIRD LAW OF MOTION

Copyright © 2008 by John Wiley & Sons, Inc.

Copyright © 2008 by John Wiley & Sons, Inc.

Name _____ Date _____ (7-1)

WORD FIND—VOCABULARY ACTIVITY ON
Let's Get Movin'

Directions

After reading *Let's Get Movin'*, read the following statements and determine the best word to complete each one. Circle the word on the word find puzzle. If you cannot find a word horizontally, vertically, or diagonally in the word find, you probably have an incorrect answer for the statement.

Clues

1. Distance divided by time is known as _____.

2. The _____ on a car registers the distance you have traveled.

3. Your _____ speed is determined by dividing the total distance traveled by the total time it took to travel that distance.

4. Another term for resistance to change or a measure of mass is _____.

5. The second law of motion is stated as _____ equals mass times acceleration.

6. According to the second law of motion, the mass of an object is _____ proportional to the acceleration of that object.

7. When deciding if an object is in motion, it is important to determine your _____ by which to judge that motion.

8. Velocity is defined as _____ divided by time.

9. When a quantity requires both the magnitude and the direction, it is classified as a(n) _____ quantity.

10. A change in velocity divided by the time required to achieve the change is _____.

11. The speed of an object at that moment in time only is called the _____ speed.

12. The acceleration of an object due to _____ is 10 m/sec^2.

13. In the third law of motion, the _____ force is a response to the initial force.

14. Negative acceleration is called _____.

15. The force that opposes motion when an object moves over a surface is _____.

16. A _____ quantity expresses magnitude but does not express direction.

17. The first law of motion explains that force is required to initiate motion for objects at _____.

18. Which law of motion explains why football players who are running backs weigh less than line backers, due to the need for acceleration?

93

19. What object is used for the frame of reference if you were to say that a dead mosquito is in motion even though it is lying on the ground?

20. Inertia is really a measure of the _____ of an object. Objects with greater inertia are often harder to move.

```
E  I  A  D  S  S  A  M  O  G  R  A  V  I  T  Y
C  N  V  T  M  K  V  J  D  S  R  D  B  D  R  U
N  V  E  P  O  K  M  P  O  A  E  E  K  E  Z  S
E  E  R  L  B  C  S  Q  M  I  A  E  M  C  M  U
R  R  A  F  I  R  S  T  E  T  C  P  Z  E  K  O
E  S  G  R  S  T  L  J  T  R  T  S  R  L  C  E
F  E  E  M  E  B  B  V  E  E  I  R  V  E  B  N
E  L  J  D  L  S  R  S  R  N  O  O  U  R  O  A
R  Y  B  N  J  V  T  K  B  I  N  T  S  A  L  T
F  T  V  L  B  N  K  S  M  P  U  C  T  T  P  N
O  S  M  C  R  O  F  U  D  R  V  E  L  I  D  A
E  P  E  C  R  O  F  N  K  S  K  V  B  O  F  T
M  D  I  S  P  L  A  C  E  M  E  N  T  N  J  S
A  S  E  C  O  N  D  R  D  K  J  M  L  T  S  N
R  N  O  I  T  A  R  E  L  E  C  C  A  B  R  I
F  F  R  I  C  T  I  O  N  J  R  A  L  A  C  S
```

Copyright © 2008 by John Wiley & Sons, Inc.

7-2 SOLVING YOUR PROBLEMS IN MOTION
Activity on the Energy of Motion

Objectives

Students will solve physics problems on speed, velocity, and acceleration using the appropriate formulas.

Teacher Notes

Students must read *Let's Get Movin'* to complete this activity. A calculator may be helpful. You might want to solve some sample problems on the board before giving this assignment.

Copyright © 2008 by John Wiley & Sons, Inc.

SOLVING YOUR PROBLEMS IN MOTION
Activity on the Energy of Motion

Directions

Use the information and formulas discussed in the content of *Let's Get Movin'* to solve the following motion problems. Please show your work for each problem as well as the final answer. If you need more room for your computations, you may use the back of the worksheet.

I. Read the scenario below and consult the map to answer the following questions about this paragraph:

Joe works with a team of emergency medical technicians (EMTs) in Atlanta. He is often called on to use his superior driving skills when rushing to the scene of an accident and delivering a patient back to Hardy Hospital. On May 14, Joe received a call that a car collision had occurred on Radburn Road in Douglasville. Joe knew he must cover the 25-mile distance in as little time as possible. He jumped into his car at 10:00 P.M. and arrived at the scene of the accident at 10:15 P.M. He worked from 10:15 to 11:00 P.M. getting the patient ready to transport. At 11:00 P.M., Joe got into his EMT vehicle and headed back toward Atlanta with his patient. When he departed the scene of the accident, he went from 0 to 60 miles per hour in 2.5 seconds. He had almost made it back to the hospital when a green Volkswagen darted in front of him. Joe slammed on the brakes and went from a speed of 120 miles per hour to a stop in 4 seconds, barely avoiding an accident. Joe and his patient finally arrived safely at Hardy Hospital at 11:20.

Copyright © 2008 by John Wiley & Sons, Inc.

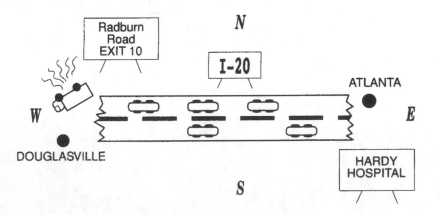

1. What was the speed of the trip from Atlanta to Douglasville? Give your answer in (A) miles/min and (B) miles/hr.

2. What was the speed of the trip from Douglasville back to Atlanta? Give your answer in (A) miles/min and (B) miles/hr.

3. What was the velocity of the trip from Hardy Hospital in Atlanta to Douglasville in miles/hr? Be sure to include both magnitude and direction.

4. What was the velocity of the trip from Douglasville back to Hardy Hospital in miles/hr? Be sure to include both magnitude and direction.

5. What was Joe's acceleration in that 2.5 sec period when he started from the scene of the accident in Douglasville? Give your answer in (A) miles/hr^2 and (B) miles/sec^2.

6. What was Joe's deceleration as he slowed to avoid the accident with the Volkswagen as he returned to the hospital? Give your answer in miles/hr^2.

II. Read the following scenario, consult the drawing, and answer the questions:

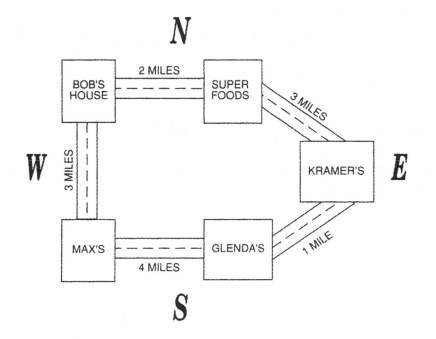

Bob leaves home on his bike at 9:00 A.M. to run some errands. He travels directly from his house to Super Foods to pick up some jelly beans. He leaves Super Foods and pedals to Kramer's Recycling to turn in some plastic bags. He proceeds directly from Kramer's to Glenda's clothing store to purchase some black socks. Finally, he leaves Glenda's and goes to Max's, where he arrives at 11:00 A.M. Now answer the following questions as you look at the map above.

7. What distance did Bob travel?

8. What was the displacement of Bob's journey?

9. What was the average speed of Bob's trip in miles/hr?

10. What was the velocity of Bob's trip in miles/hr? Be sure to include both magnitude and direction.

Copyright © 2008 by John Wiley & Sons, Inc.

III. For the problem below, use this formula to find final velocity:

final velocity = initial velocity + (acceleration due to gravity)(time)

$$V_f = V_i + (g \times t)$$

Remember that the acceleration of an object falling toward the ground due to gravity is 10 m/sec^2.

11. An amateur cliff diver plans to jump off a cliff into the river below. She realizes that injury can result from extremely high dives. To judge the danger of the dive, she needs to know the velocity with which she will strike the water below. The diver does a test to help her: she drops a heavy rock off the cliff to the water below. It takes the rock 2.5 seconds to reach the water. What is its final velocity just prior to striking the water?

IV. For the following questions, use this formula to determine distance traveled:

speed = distance ÷ time

$$S = d/t$$

12. An airplane travels at 250 miles per hour for 90 minutes. What distance did the plane travel in miles?

13. A car travels at 60 miles per hour for 20 miles. How long was the trip time? Give your answer in minutes.

Copyright © 2008 by John Wiley & Sons, Inc.

7-3 THE BALL DROP
Lab on the Energy of Motion

Objectives

Students will drop a tennis ball from a tall structure, then apply the formula relating acceleration, time, and distance to determine the height of that structure.

Teacher Notes

Select a tall structure from which students can drop the ball. Suggestions include the top of the football stadium steps (off the side) and the press box.

The students use tennis balls in this lab, but any object heavy enough to overcome air resistance can be used. It's a good idea to work out some problems in class using the distance formula before conducting this lab.

Extension

Give students the actual value of the structure they measured in the lab and have them calculate their percentage of error. They should use this formula:

percentage of error = [(observed value – accepted value) ÷ accepted value] × 100%

For example, if the student found the stadium to be 225 meters tall, but the administration told you the actual measurement was really 260 meters tall, this formula could be used:

$$[(225m – 260m) ÷ 260m] × 100\% =$$
$$(–35 ÷ 260) × 100\% =$$
$$–0.142 × 100\% =$$
$$–14.2\% \text{ error}$$

You could follow up with a discussion about what caused the error and how to make the measurement more exact.

Copyright © 2008 by John Wiley & Sons, Inc.

THE BALL DROP
Lab on the Energy of Motion

Introduction

The use of formulas is an integral part of physics. It is very important to be able not only to learn formulas and use them in solving word problems but also to apply them to real-life situations. Sometimes distances cannot be easily calculated using basic measurement tools, such as tape measures and rulers, because the measurements can be very inconvenient to take. Let's say you were asked to measure the height of the tallest building in New York. You would look pretty funny using a tape measure to achieve that task. But if you knew a little physics, you could achieve a fairly accurate measurement in a matter of seconds. Let's look at how it might be done.

To measure a tall building, you would need to go to the top of the building with a golf ball or tennis ball, a stopwatch, and a calculator. To conduct your measurement, you would drop the ball off the top of the building and start the stopwatch at exactly the same time. As soon as you see the ball strike the ground below, you would stop the stopwatch. In this way, you could measure the time it took the ball to fall from the top of the building to the ground under the influence of gravity. This quantity can then be used in a physics formula that gives you displacement, the distance the ball fell:

displacement = ½ (acceleration due to gravity)(time)(time)

or $\Delta x = ½ (gt^2)$

In this formula, displacement represents the distance from the top of the building to the ground (the height of the building), and *g* represents acceleration due to gravity. All objects fall toward the earth at the same acceleration due to the pull of gravity (if they can overcome air resistance). This *g* value is always about 10 meters per second squared (10 m/sec^2). Time is the number of seconds it took to complete the fall. When using this formula, your answer will come out in meters.

Here are some sample data to help you learn this formula. Let's say it took 15 seconds for the ball to drop to the ground from the top of the building. You would use the formula like this:

$\Delta x = ½ (10 \text{ m/sec}^2)(15 \text{ sec})(15 \text{ sec})$

$= 5 \text{ m/sec}^2 (225 \text{ sec}^2)$

$= 1125 \text{ m}$

Now you know that the height of the building is 1125 meters. Remember that when performing these experiments, you cannot use objects like feathers or pieces of paper because they are affected by air resistance. If you could eliminate air resistance in a container such as a vacuum, you would see that all objects fall at an acceleration of 10 m/sec^2 toward the earth in response to gravity and the inertia of the object. This value varies on different planets because of the differences in gravity. Now that you know a little more about height, let's practice using this formula.

Copyright © 2008 by John Wiley & Sons, Inc.

Prelab Questions

1. A diver is planning a dive from a cliff into the river below. He knows that dives are safe only from certain heights. He does not know the height of this cliff, but he knows his physics. He drops a large rock from the top of the cliff into the water below. It takes 8 seconds for the rock to hit the water. What is the height of the cliff in meters?

2. Explain why a feather cannot be used in question 1.

3. Explain acceleration.

4. Why is the *g* value different on Earth than on Jupiter?

5. Explain why using this formula is only moderately accurate. What are some problems you might encounter that would cause some error?

6. List three professions that might use this physics formula, and explain how they would use it.

Materials

Stopwatch

Tennis ball or golf ball

Calculator

Procedure

1. Go to the top of a tall structure (such as the top of the stadium steps) with the ball and the stopwatch.

2. Standing on the top step, drop the ball off the side so that it can fall toward the ground without being obstructed during its fall.

3. As you release the ball, start your stopwatch. Stop it when the ball hits the ground below. Enter on the data table the time it took for the ball to reach the ground.

4. Repeat this process three more times and enter each time on the data table.

5. Find the average number of seconds from your four trials and enter it on the data table.

6. Answer the postlab questions.

Copyright © 2008 by John Wiley & Sons, Inc.

DATA TABLE

Trial Number	Number of Seconds Required for Fall
1	
2	
3	
4	
Average	

Postlab Questions

1. Apply your formula to determine the height of your structure using the average number of seconds.

2. Cite any problems you encountered in this lab, and explain how they might have skewed your results.

3. Do you think the use of this formula is more accurate on fairly short structures or on taller structures? Explain why.

4. You are standing at the base of a tree, and you want to know how tall it is. You have a ball, a stopwatch, and a calculator. You toss the ball straight up in the air to almost exactly the height of the tree, and you time the number of seconds it takes to go up and return to the ground below. It took 8 seconds from the time the ball left your hand until the time it returned to the ground. You remember that the time going up will be equal to the time coming down. With this in mind, calculate the height of the tree in meters.

Copyright © 2008 by John Wiley & Sons, Inc.

7-4 TAKE 1
Project on the Energy of Motion

Objectives

Students will apply their knowledge of the three laws of motion to create educational commercials that teach these concepts to the public.

Teacher Notes

Divide students into groups of three or four. To complete this performance assessment, students must be familiar with the three laws of motion. You may want to reserve one or more video cameras for student use. A video camera must be available on the day of presentations. Some suggestions for evaluation have been given, but you may prefer to devise your own evaluation sheet.

This project could be done in two or three class periods or as a project to be completed outside class.

Following is a suggested grading rubric. If you decide to use this rubric, give students a copy.

Copyright © 2008 by John Wiley & Sons, Inc.

SUGGESTED GRADING RUBRIC

Criteria	Star Production (4 points)	Above-Average Production (3 points)	Average Production (2 points)	Below-Par Production (1 point)
Length of commercial	60 to 95 seconds	50 to 59 seconds	30 to 49 seconds	Less than 30 seconds
Everyone on the team played a role in the commercial	All students had roles	Most students had roles	Few students had roles	Only one student played a role
The commercial was interesting	Extremely interesting	Fairly interesting	Slightly interesting	Not very interesting
Props, such as posters and costumes, were used	Several props were used	A few props were used	Props were rare or not well developed	Only one prop was used
The commercial was creative	The commercial was very creative	The commercial had many creative points	The commercial had a few creative points	The commercial lacked any creativity
Students answered questions	The team could answer all questions from the audience	The team could answer most questions from the audience	The team could answer only a few questions from the audience	The team could answer only one question from the audience

Comments: _____

_____

Points possible: 24

Points earned: _____

Copyright © 2008 by John Wiley & Sons, Inc.

TAKE 1
Project on the Energy of Motion

Introduction

You and your team are employed by a company that promotes the importance of science. Currently the company is working to promote physics literacy through the media of television.

Unfortunately, the president of the company does not have a good background in science. In fact, he does not understand basic scientific principles. His sole concern is to develop interesting, flashy presentations that look good to his investors.

In this activity, you and your team will prepare a TV commercial on Newton's three laws of motion for your boss. Your goal is to produce the best possible commercial so that yours will be selected to air on national TV. Your boss has agreed to meet with your team to see what kind of commercial you have developed.

Procedure

1. As a team, write an outline for a one-minute commercial that you will record with a video camera. As you are writing the outline, consider these requirements:

   a. The recorded commercial must last for at least one minute.

   b. The commercial should briefly but very clearly explain the three laws of motion and give examples of each.

   c. Everyone on the team must play a role in the commercial as either an actor, reader, or recorder.

   d. The commercial should be interesting.

   e. Your team should use some props, such as posters and costumes.

   f. The commercial should be creative and imaginative.

2. You can choose to be recorded the day of your presentation, or you can record your presentation prior to the due date and bring your ready-made video with you.

3. Be prepared to answer questions from the teacher and the class after your presentation.

Copyright © 2008 by John Wiley & Sons, Inc.

LESSON 8: ENERGY, WORK, POWER, AND MACHINES

8-1 FULL OF ENERGY
Content on Energy, Work, Power, and Machines

❧❧❧

Going the Distance

Have you ever heard someone described as "full of energy"? Or perhaps you've even said that you "have no energy" on a day that you feel tired. Actually, all persons, places, and things have energy. However, energy is only evident to the observer as work being done. In fact, energy can be defined as the ability to do work.

Work is the transfer of energy during which a force moves an object through a distance. For example, think about step aerobics. Do you think that doing step aerobics is a form of work? Let's take a look at a gym where aerobics is going on. Each participant in the aerobics class moves his or her body weight up and down on a step of about 8 inches. Because moving body weight requires force, and the up-and-down motion of stepping is a distance over which the force is applied, step aerobics accomplishes work!

Let's go to the free weight room and see if work is being done. First, we see a woman doing biceps curls with the free weights. She is lifting 35 pounds. As she curls the bar up and down, she is doing work by supplying force to move the weight a certain distance. Nearby we see a man holding a 200-pound weight bar over his head. You see him grimacing from the load. Is he doing work? Although it looks like work, he is not doing any. This is because he is not moving the object through a distance.

More Power to You

You can calculate the amount of work being done if you know two factors: force and distance. The formula for work is

$$\text{work} = \text{force} \times \text{distance}$$
$$W = F \times d$$

106

Copyright © 2008 by John Wiley & Sons, Inc.

The formula for force is F = mass (m) × acceleration (a). Force is calculated in units of newtons (N or kgm/sec^2), and distance is measured in meters. Thus work is measured in units called newton-meters, or joules. You'll notice that the formula for work says nothing about how long it takes you to perform that task. You do the same amount of work by running up the stadium steps as you do by walking slowly up the steps.

Running up the steps does require more power than walking. Power is the rate at which work is done. Power equals the amount of work done divided by the amount of time during which the work is done. In formula format, it looks like this:

$$P = F \times d \div t$$
$$P = W/t$$

Power is measured in joules per second, or watts. The watt is named after James Watt, the eighteenth-century developer of the steam engine. When Watt was trying to sell his steam engine, he wanted to tell his customers how many horses his engine could replace. To do this, he had to find out how much work a good horse could do. He found that, on an average, a horse could lift 550 pounds a distance of one foot in one second, and this measurement became known as horsepower. One horsepower is the same as 0.75 kilowatts (a kilowatt is 1000 watts). So an engine that is rated as 134 horsepower is also a 100 kW engine. According to the definition for power, engines that are high in horsepower can do work rapidly. This does not mean that these engines do more work or necessarily go faster; they do the work in less time, so they accelerate faster.

Energy Stores and Conversions

Energy is not always performing work; it can be stored. Our bodies stockpile some of the energy from food. Potential energy is energy that is stored and held in readiness. It has the potential for doing work. There are many other ways to store energy.

Would you be willing to walk under a piano suspended 20 meters above the ground by a single rope? Most people would avoid this situation because the piano is loaded with potential energy. With a slight failure of the rope, that energy could be changed into work as the piano moved downward. The piano is an example of an object with gravitational potential energy. The amount of gravitational potential energy it possesses is equal to the work done against gravity in lifting it to that position. The formula for this type of potential energy is

gravitational potential energy = (mass)(acceleration due to gravity)(height)
$$PE = m \times g \times h$$

Mass is measured in kilograms (kg), acceleration due to gravity is always 10 m/sec^2, and height is measured in meters. Look back at the piano example. If the piano has a mass of 2300 kg and is suspended 20 m above the ground, what would its potential energy be?

$$PE = 2300 \text{ kg} \times 10 \text{ m/sec}^2 \times 20 \text{ m} = 460{,}000 \text{ joules}$$

Copyright © 2008 by John Wiley & Sons, Inc.

Once again, the product is in newton-meters, or joules.

After potential energy is set into motion, it is called kinetic energy. Kinetic energy is the energy of motion, and it depends on the mass of the object as well as its velocity. Kinetic energy is equal to half the mass multiplied by the square of the velocity. The formula is written as

$$\text{kinetic energy} = \tfrac{1}{2}\ \text{mass} \times \text{velocity}^2$$
$$KE = \tfrac{1}{2}\ mv^2$$

If the rope holding the suspended piano in the air breaks, then potential energy becomes kinetic energy. To use the kinetic energy formula, you must know the object's velocity. You can find the velocity of an object by using the formula

$$\text{final velocity} = \text{initial velocity} + (\text{acceleration})(\text{time})$$
$$V_f = V_i + a \times t$$

The final answer for kinetic energy is also given in joules.

Lightening the Load with Machines

Work is often performed by machines, devices for multiplying forces or changing the direction of forces. There are six types of simple machines. Each makes work easier for the person doing it. If you don't believe this, think of unscrewing a bolt without a screwdriver or lifting a car without a jack. The six families of simple machines are levers, pulleys, wheels and axles, inclined planes, screws, and wedges.

Copyright © 2008 by John Wiley & Sons, Inc.

Copyright © 2008 by John Wiley & Sons, Inc.

A lever helps you move objects by increasing the distance over which you exert force. A lever is a long, rigid bar with a support that allows it to pivot on the fulcrum, the point of rotation. A seesaw is a lever, and the balance point is the fulcrum. Crowbars and screwdrivers used to pry the tops off of objects are also levers.

Pulleys are machines made of a rope passing over a grooved wheel. You may have seen pictures of fixed pulleys on old water wells. The rope is connected to the bucket and passes over the pulley. You pull down on your end of the rope, and the bucket of water comes up toward you. A fixed pulley does not decrease the force needed to do the job, but it changes the direction and makes work easier. Fixed and movable pulleys can be used together to form a block and tackle.

The wheel and axle is a simple machine made of a wheel and a shaft. As you spin the wheel, the axle turns. Doorknobs and eggbeaters are examples of this type of machine.

An inclined plane is a slanting surface that allows you to lift an object to the desired height with less force than you would use without the devise. Just think of a moving van with pull-down ramps at the back of the truck. These ramps are inclined planes that allow the movers to put furniture into the van. They increase the distance the furniture travels but decrease the amount of force that must be supplied to lift each object. The wedge is a type of inclined plane with either one or two sloping sides. The point of a needle and the blade of a knife are common examples of this machine. A screw is an inclined plane in a spiral form. It makes work easier by pressing against the material around it as it moves into the wood. The ridge that spirals around the screw is called its thread, and the pitch is the number of threads in a given length. When you turn a screw, the direction of force is changed and multiplied. The force you need to apply decreases as the threads get closer together. You have to make a lot of turns with your hands, but the work is much easier than if you did not have the screw.

To evaluate the ability of a piece of machinery to reduce work, you can apply the concept of mechanical advantage (MA). MA is a value that tells you the number of times a machine increases the applied force. For example, if the MA is 4 when you use a lever to pry the lid off of a can of paint, the lever multiplies your force by 4. Each type of simple machine has a formula for calculating its MA. You will see this formula again in Lesson 8-4, *Machines Made Simple*.

Fact or Friction

Simple machines can be combined to form more complex pieces of equipment called compound machines. The value of a compound machine is often based on its efficiency, the amount of useful work obtained from the machine compared to the work put into the machine. It is important to note that no machine has 100 percent efficiency. Why? The culprit is friction, the force that opposes motion. The formula for determining the efficiency of a machine is

efficiency = useful work output ÷ work put in × 100%

For example, if you put 200 joules of work into a machine and the machine did 30 joules of useful work, its efficiency is 30 ÷ 200 × 100% = 15%. This would mean that 85 percent of the work you put into the machine was wasted, probably in over-coming friction.

Many complex machines have very low efficiency ratings. Cars have a low efficiency rating (about 40 percent) because some of the energy is converted to heat. Much of the energy in a car is wasted in friction of the moving parts. Substances like grease and oil reduce friction on moving parts and are important to the efficiency rating of the car.

Copyright © 2008 by John Wiley & Sons, Inc.

ENERGY UNSCRAMBLE—VOCABULARY ACTIVITY ON *FULL OF ENERGY*

After reading *Full of Energy*, unscramble the words below to complete the statements.

1. _____ (oewrp) is work divided by the time it takes to perform that work.

2. A(n) _____ (nnweot), also known as kgm/sec², is the unit used to measure force.

3. _____ (inciket) energy is the energy of motion.

4. The _____ (ipcht) of a screw refers to the number of threads.

5. _____ (rontifci) is one of the major reasons that machines can never reach 100% efficiency.

6. The unit of _____ (tsawt), or joules per second, is used to measure power.

7. Work is measured in newton-meters, which are also called _____ (loseju).

8. _____ (yrgnee) is the ability to do work.

9. James Watt compared his steam engine to the strength of _____ (ressoh) when he was trying to market the new engine.

10. To determine the potential energy of an object, you must know the acceleration due to gravity, the mass of the object, and the object's _____ (iehhgt).

11. To compute kinetic energy, you need to know mass and _____ (yveticol).

12. Devices for multiplying force or changing the direction of a force when moving an object are _____ (ihmnceas).

13. Simple machines that have a fulcrum on which a long, rigid bar rests and pivots freely are called _____ (selerv).

14. A(n) _____ (fnike) is an example of a wedge.

15. James Watson used the unit of _____ (oerhrwsope) to describe his steam engine, and it is still used in car descriptions.

16. A fixed pulley does not increase the force needed to do the job, but it does alter the _____ (ientdrcio) through which the force is exerted.

17. A(n) _____ (eeswas) is an example of a type of lever.

18. To calculate _____ (orkw), multiply the force times the distance an object moves.

19. Mass is calculated in units of _____ (islmoagkr) when determining potential energy.

20. The initial velocity plus acceleration multiplied by time is the _____ _____ (iflan clveotiy).

111

Copyright © 2008 by John Wiley & Sons, Inc.

8-2 GOLF BALLS AND THEIR POTENTIAL
Lab on Potential Energy

Objectives

Students will observe how potential and kinetic energy can perform work. They will evaluate the effect of changing heights on potential and kinetic energy.

Teacher Notes

Golf balls are only one of a variety of balls that can be used in this activity. Paper cups are just one type of container that can be used.

Copyright © 2008 by John Wiley & Sons, Inc.

Copyright © 2008 by John Wiley & Sons, Inc.

GOLF BALLS AND THEIR POTENTIAL
Lab on Potential Energy

Introduction

The potential energy of an object is calculated by multiplying its mass by its acceleration and height. The formula for potential energy is

$$\text{potential energy} = \text{mass} \times \text{acceleration due to gravity} \times \text{height}$$
$$PE = m \times g \times h$$

If the object moves downward due to the pull of gravity, then its acceleration is 10 m/sec^2. In this lab you will be judging the movement of a golf ball down a ramp. The unit to denote potential energy (stored energy) is the newton-meter (joule).

Kinetic energy is the energy of motion. When a stationary object moves, the potential energy of that object changes into kinetic energy. The formula for kinetic energy is

$$\text{kinetic energy} = \tfrac{1}{2}\,\text{mass} \times \text{velocity}^2$$
$$KE = \tfrac{1}{2}\,mv^2$$

The joule is also the unit for this type of calculation. Remember that kg is the unit for mass.

Prelab Questions

1. A ball that has a mass of 2 kg is resting on top of a fence 20 m above the ground. Answer these questions about the ball:

   a. What is its potential energy?

   b. Is the potential energy greater when the ball is sitting on top of the fence or when the ball has fallen 10 m from the fence?

   c. Is the kinetic energy greater near the top or the bottom of the fence? Explain.

2. Create a word problem that addresses work, power, efficiency, kinetic energy, and potential energy. Include a drawing that accompanies that problem. You can write on the back of this page if you do not have enough room below. Be sure to make an answer key to go with your problem.

Materials

Golf ball

Three or four small blocks of wood (to support the meter sticks)

Paper or plastic cup

Platform balance or electronic balance

Two meter sticks or two same-size pieces of wood

Tape

Procedure

1. Tape the underside of two meter sticks together lengthwise so that there is a slit between them that forms a groove. The golf ball can roll down this groove as if it were on a track.

2. Use the small blocks of wood to construct a support for one end of the joined meter sticks. The support should raise one end of the sticks to a distance of 8 cm above the ground (see Figure A). Place a paper cup with the open side facing toward the slit at the other end of the meter sticks.

3. Hold the ball at the top of your ramp. Release it and let it roll down the ramp and into the cup.

4. Measure the distance from the bottom end of the meter sticks to where the cup and ball move along the floor. Record the measurement in the data table.

5. Repeat steps 3 and 4, but vary the height of the ramp each time; indicate the heights in the data table. Complete the data table as you go.

6. Use the balance to determine the mass of the ball.

7. Calculate the potential energy of the ball for each of the heights in the data table. Show your work (be sure to use the units kg, m/sec², and m).

Copyright © 2008 by John Wiley & Sons, Inc.

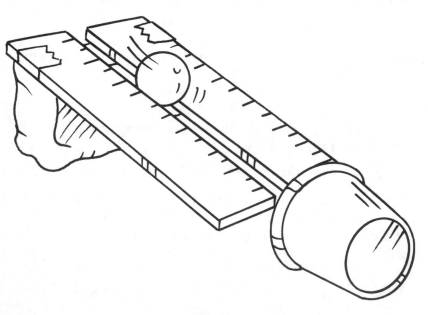

FIGURE A

DATA TABLE

Height of Ramp	Distance Cup Traveled	Potential Energy of the Ball
8 cm		
___ cm		
___ cm		
___ cm		

Postlab Questions

1. As the potential energy of the ball increased, what happened to the amount of work done on the cup? Explain your answer.

2. Explain how potential energy changes into kinetic energy as the ball rolls down the ramp.

3. What type of simple machine was represented in the lab.

4. If you oiled or greased the ramp, what do you think might have happened to your results?

Copyright © 2008 by John Wiley & Sons, Inc.

8-3 PROBLEMS WITH ENERGY
Activity on Energy, Work, Power, and Machines

Objectives

Students will apply their knowledge of formulas to solve problems relating to energy, work, power, and machines.

Teacher Notes

Students should read Lesson 8-1, *Full of Energy*, before they attempt to solve these problems. The following formulas are needed:

$$W = F \times d$$
$$P = W/t$$
$$KE = \tfrac{1}{2}\,mv^2$$
$$PE = m \times g \times h$$
$$\text{efficiency} = \text{useful work output} \div \text{work input} \times 100\%$$

Copyright © 2008 by John Wiley & Sons, Inc.

PROBLEMS WITH ENERGY
Activity on Energy, Work, Power, and Machines

Directions

Read the following problems and solve them using the formulas discussed in *Full of Energy*. You may use the following formulas: $PE = m \times g \times h$; $KE = \frac{1}{2} mv^2$; $W = F \times d$; $P = W/t$; efficiency = useful work output ÷ work input × 100%. Be sure to use the proper units with your answer.

1. The famous barefoot kicker, Rocky Nails, can kick a football 80 m with a force of 20 N. Calculate the work that Rocky does on the ball.

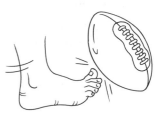

2. Calculate the power Rocky uses in question 1 if he can accomplish this feat in 6 seconds.

3. Hero, the rescue dog, is very fast and can reach speeds of 2 m/sec on a good day. Hero has a mass of 10 kg. Determine his maximum kinetic energy on his good days.

4. Sue Ellen is carrying a present for her boss, who is about to retire. She thought of filling the box with rocks, but she decided on a popcorn popper instead. She is not very anxious to get to her boss's retirement party, so she moves across the floor at a speed of 1.2 m/sec. Sue Ellen weighs 70 kg, and the gift she is carrying weighs about 2 kg. Calculate Sue Ellen's kinetic energy as she travels across the floor.

5. Rover was thrown from his owner's airplane after the owner discovered that Rover was not "plane broken" (house broken on the plane). Luckily, Rover thought to wear his parachute. He opened it as soon as he was hurled out the door. After several seconds, Rover drifted to a position of 200 m above the ground. Compute (if possible) his potential energy at this location above the ground. Rover has a mass of 4 kg. Explain your answer.

Copyright © 2008 by John Wiley & Sons, Inc.

6. Bill, who has a mass of 80 kg, dashes up the stadium steps during football practice. He must travel from the base of the steps to the top, a distance of 70 m. It takes him an average of 3.5 seconds to achieve this.

   a. Calculate the work he does for one trip up the steps.

   b. Calculate the power he uses.

7. Jill lives at the top of a high-rise condo. One day Jill got mad at her husband, Jack, because he forgot to bring home a bucket of fried chicken. It had been a bad day for Jill, so she went a little berserk. She began to throw things out the window at her husband. Find the potential energy of the three objects at the points they are shown suspended in midair in the diagram. Their height and mass are indicated.

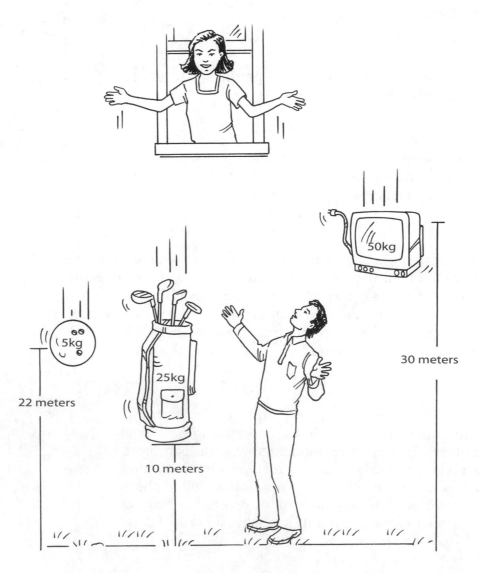

Copyright © 2008 by John Wiley & Sons, Inc.

8. Your lawnmower requires an input of 500 joules of work to make it function. From this you get 100 joules of work. Calculate the lawnmower's efficiency and explain why it seems so low.

Copyright © 2008 by John Wiley & Sons, Inc.

8-4 MACHINES MADE SIMPLE
Performance Assessment on Machines

Objective

Students will evaluate the differences among simple machines.

Teacher Notes

1. Write the names of the six simple machines on slips of paper (one machine per slip). Include enough slips of paper for each student or pair of students in your class. Place these slips of paper into a paper bag.

2. As students enter the room, have them draw a slip of paper from the bag. They will research the simple machine on their slip of paper. After each student receives the name of the machine he or she will examine, distribute the handout explaining this project, which is included at the end of this activity.

3. Provide students with opportunities to go to the library or use the Internet to research their simple machine. They must develop one visual aid and bring in one example of their machine on the day of their presentation.

4. The visual aid should include the following:

   - A definition or description of the simple machine

   - Some examples, such as drawings or photos

   - An explanation of the use of the machine in society, including both everyday and technical uses

   - An explanation of how one calculates the mechanical advantage of that machine and an example of such a calculation

   - Interesting facts or trivia about the machine

5. During the oral presentation, the visual aid should be shared with the class. At the end of the presentation, the example of the simple machine should be displayed and explained.

6. The student should also provide the teacher with five multiple-choice questions that the rest of the class will be able to answer after hearing the presentation.

7. A suggested grading rubric follows. You can use the rubric as it is or tailor it for your needs. Give the students a copy of the rubric before they begin the activity so that they will know how you will assess their work.

Copyright © 2008 by John Wiley & Sons, Inc.

SUGGESTED GRADING RUBRIC

Excellent Quality 4 points	Good Work 3 points	Satisfactory 2 points	Poor Quality 1 point
The visual aid is neat and colorful.	The visual aid is neat, but lacks color.	The visual aid is colorful, but messy.	The visual aid is neither neat nor colorful.
The visual aid contains all the required material.	The visual aid contains most of the required material.	The visual aid contains some of the required material.	The visual aid contains very little of the required material.
All of the information given is accurate.	Most of the information given is accurate.	Some of the information given is accurate.	Very little of the information given is accurate.
Five multiple-choice questions are provided.	Four multiple-choice questions are provided.	Three multiple-choice questions are provided.	One or two multiple-choice questions are provided.
During presentation, material is explained, not read, and presenter is interesting.	During presentation, most material is explained; presenter is fairly interesting.	During presentation, some material is explained; presenter is somewhat interesting.	During presentation, material is read; presenter is not interesting or is difficult to understand.

Comments: _____

_____

Points possible: 20

Points earned: _____

Copyright © 2008 by John Wiley & Sons, Inc.

Name _____ Date _____ (8-4)

MACHINES MADE SIMPLE
Performance Assessment on Machines

Name of simple machine: _____

Due date for presentation: _____ Library research date(s): _____

Directions for Presentation

- You will use library resources, your textbook, and the Internet to research a simple machine. After completing the research, you will create a visual aid that explains the simple machine. The visual aid should include the following components:

- A definition or description of the simple machine

- Some examples of this type of simple machine, with drawings or photos

- An explanation of the use of the machine in society (include both everyday use and technical use)

- An explanation of how you calculate the mechanical advantage (MA) of that machine, and your calculation

- Interesting facts or trivia about the machine

On the presentation date, you will share the visual aid with the class. You should bring in an object that is an example of your simple machine and provide the teacher with five multiple-choice questions that the rest of the class will be able to answer after hearing the presentation.

Copyright © 2008 by John Wiley & Sons, Inc.

Copyright © 2008 by John Wiley & Sons, Inc.

LESSON 9: ELECTRICITY

9-1 DANCING ELECTRONS
Content on Electricity

※↩↩↩※

We Take It for Granted

Look around the room. How many objects, devices, or appliances require electrical energy to operate? How do our daily lives change when there's a power outage? Americans are very dependent on electricity and often take this invisible force for granted. Where does it come from? Who makes it?

Electrical energy is produced by converting some other form of energy into electricity. Some electrical power plants convert the force of steam into mechanical energy, which causes a turbine to rotate. The turbine is connected to an electrical generator that produces a current. This electrical current then travels along wires to our homes and businesses.

Current

An electrical current is the flow of electrons through a wire. Electrons can travel within a wire because they are free to move throughout the atomic network. Electrical current, abbreviated as I, is measured in amperes (A, or amp). One ampere of current equals one coulomb, or 6.25×10^{18} electrons, flowing past a point in one second. Current travels differently in different materials. Some materials are good conductors and allow a current to travel easily through them. Copper, silver, and aluminum are examples of good conductors. Conversely, a current cannot travel through materials known as insulators.

Resistance

The ability of a current to travel through a material depends on that material's resistance to the flow of electrons. Resistance, which is abbreviated as R, is measured in ohms. The resistance of an electrical wire depends on its thickness, length, temperature, and composition. Electrons can travel more easily along a thick wire than a thin one. Long wire offers more resistance than short wire. The filament in a light bulb is a thin wire that is made of tungsten, a material that offers a lot of resistance to the flow of electricity. As electrons attempt to travel through this wire, they produce light and heat. The wire in a lamp cord, in contrast, has very low resistance and remains cool while electricity travels along it.

123

People can be electrocuted or shocked if they are working with electricity and accidentally lower the resistance of their body to the flow of current. When our skin is very dry, our bodies have a resistance of about 50,000 ohms. However, if we are wet, our resistance drops sharply to about 100 ohms. Normal household current can be very dangerous to a person standing in a puddle of water because wet skin conducts current well, and it can travel easily through his or her body to the ground.

Voltage

Not all electrical current has the same amount of push or strength. The amount of electricity available to push electrons along a wire is the voltage (V), also known as the potential difference. When each electron traveling along a wire carries a lot of energy, the voltage is high. However, if each electron is carrying only a little energy, the voltage is low.

The current in a wire can be determined by dividing the voltage of electricity in that wire by the resistance of the wire. This rule, called Ohm's law, is stated as

$$current = voltage \div resistance$$
$$I = V \div R$$

To determine the amount of current flowing through a wire that has a resistance of 25 ohms when voltage is 50, divide 50 volts by 25 ohms:

$$I = 50 \text{ volts} \div 25 \text{ ohms}$$
$$I = 2 \text{ amps}$$

Notice that current is expressed in amperes, or amps.

Types of Current

Electrical currents are generated in various ways. Direct current, or DC, is produced by dry-cell batteries, wet-cell batteries, and thermocouples. Flashlight batteries and other types of dry-cells change chemical energy to electrical energy. A zinc casing around the battery surrounds a paste made of various chemicals. The zinc serves as a negative pole for the battery. A carbon post in the center serves as a positive pole. Chemical reactions between the paste and the zinc cause electrons to build up around the zinc pole. If the two poles are connected by a wire, electrons will flow from the negative to the positive pole. If the wire connects to a small light, electrons will flow through that light bulb filament and cause it to give off heat and light.

A wet-cell battery like the one in a car operates in a similar fashion. A wet-cell battery is composed of two metal poles (electrodes) and an acid (electrolyte). The chemical reaction between the acid and the metal at the negative pole causes an accumulation of electrons. A wire between the two poles allows electrons to flow, producing an electrical current.

Alternating current, or AC, changes direction 60 times per second. This type of electricity is produced by power plants and runs into our homes on long transmission wires. Most homes, businesses, and industries rely on alternating current.

Copyright © 2008 by John Wiley & Sons, Inc.

Thermocouples

Heat energy can be changed to electrical energy. When two different kinds of wire, such as iron and copper, are connected to form a loop, a current can be produced by heating the wires at one junction and cooling them at another. Such devices are called thermocouples, and they are used as thermostats on car engines. By placing one junction inside the engine and the other junction on the outside, a temperature difference is created when the engine becomes hot, and a small electrical current is generated. This current operates the temperature gauge on the car's dashboard.

Circuits

Electrons flow along a path called a circuit. The parts of a circuit include the source of electrons (such as a battery or power plant), the load (such as a light or radio), the wires, and a switch. The switch opens and closes the circuit.

In order for electricity to flow, electrons must have a closed path to follow. In other words, electrons can only travel along a circuit that begins at a negative pole and ends at a positive pole. In Figure A, both wires are connected to the battery, so electrons can flow along the path of the wire and operate the stereo headset, which represents the load. However, when one wire is not connected to the battery, as in Figure B, the circuit is incomplete, and electrons will not move. Removing one wire from the battery has the same effect as opening a switch.

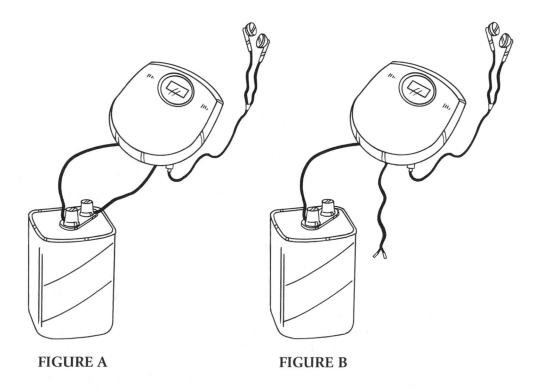

FIGURE A　　　　　　　　**FIGURE B**

Copyright © 2008 by John Wiley & Sons, Inc.

There are two types of circuits, series and parallel, defined by how the components are connected. In a series circuit (see Figure C), there is only one path for electrons to follow. If there is a break anywhere in the circuit, current cannot travel through it. The older strings of Christmas tree lights were often in series circuits, so if one light bulb was defective, none of the lights in the string would work. Household light circuits, however, are wired in parallel (see Figure D). If the bulb in one lamp burns out, other lights on that same circuit continue to burn.

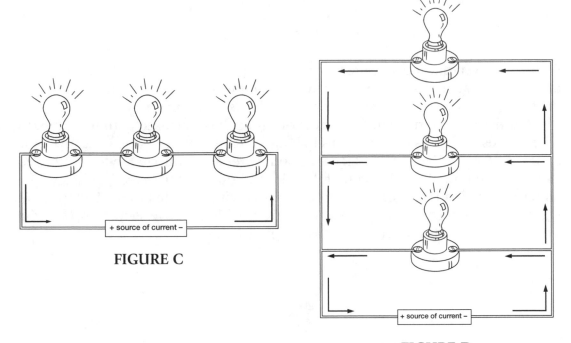

FIGURE C

FIGURE D

Copyright © 2008 by John Wiley & Sons, Inc.

Electrical Power

Each month, homes and businesses receive bills for the electrical power they use. Electrical power is a measure of the rate at which electricity does work or provides energy. Electrical power can be calculated by multiplying voltage used by the amount of current:

$$\text{power} = \text{voltage} \times \text{current}$$
$$P = V \times I$$

Power is expressed in watts (W) and kilowatts (kW). A kilowatt is 1000 watts and is used to measure large amounts of power.

To determine how many watts of power are used by a light bulb on a 120-volt circuit with 0.5 amps of current, multiply voltage by amps.

$$P = V \times I$$
$$P = 120 \text{ volts} \times 0.5 \text{ amps}$$
$$P = 60 \text{ watts}$$

Different appliances have different power ratings. The higher the rating, the greater the amount of electricity needed to run the appliance. Some common appliances and the power (watts) they use are as follows:

Clock:	3 watts (W)
Radio:	100 W
Hair dryer:	1000 W
Dishwasher:	2300 W
Clothes dryer:	4000 W

Our electricity bills are based on the total amount of energy a household uses. This amount depends on the total amount used by all appliances multiplied by the time they were used.

$$\text{energy} = \text{power} \times \text{time}$$
$$E = P \times t$$

Electrical energy is expressed in kilowatt-hours (kWh). One kWh equals 1000 watts used for one hour. To get an idea of how much energy 1 kWh represents, imagine ten 100-watt light bulbs burning for one hour. Or think about the power used to operate a 500-watt TV for two hours.

The Cost of Electricity

When we pay our electricity bills, we multiply the amount of energy used in kilowatt-hours by the cost of energy per kilowatt-hour. An average household might use 1000 kWh in a month. If the local utility company charges \$0.07/kWh, one would multiply 1000 kWh by \$0.07/kWh to determine the family's power bill.

$$1000 \text{ kWh} \times \$0.07/\text{kWh} = \$70.00$$

Copyright © 2008 by John Wiley & Sons, Inc.

AC-DC—VOCABULARY ACTIVITY ON
DANCING ELECTRONS

Directions

After reading *Dancing Electrons,* review the following list of terms. Put terms that relate to alternating current (AC) in the circle. Put terms that relate to direct current (DC) in the box. Put terms that relate to either AC or DC in the area where the circle and box overlap.

Word List

CIRCUIT	THERMOCOUPLE	TURBINE
APPLIANCE	FLASHLIGHT	WET-CELL BATTERY
GENERATOR	CAR THERMOSTAT	POWER PLANT
OHMS	TRANSMISSION LINES	CURRENT
LIGHT BULB	VOLTAGE	WATTS
POWER	ELECTRICITY	CONDUCTOR

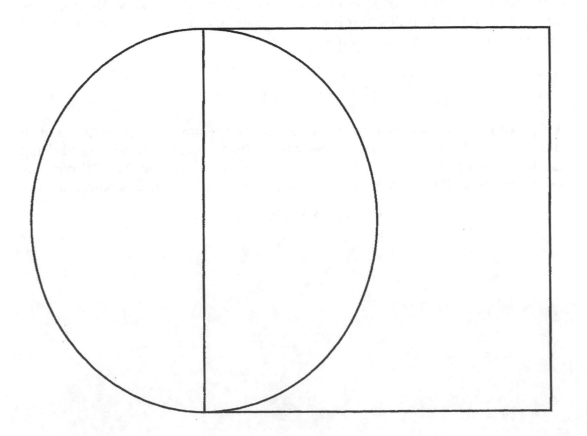

Copyright © 2008 by John Wiley & Sons, Inc.

9-2 PAYING THE BILLS
Activity on Calculating the Cost of Electric Power

Objectives

Students will calculate the cost of electricity and analyze the way utility companies charge customers for use of electricity.

Teacher Notes

Rates in this lesson are generalized from information gathered from local utilities and from the Energy Administration Web page, www.eia.doe.gov/cneaf/electricity/epm/table5_6_a.html. You may prefer to get exact rates from your local utility.

Copyright © 2008 by John Wiley & Sons, Inc.

Paying the Bills
Activity on Calculating the Cost of Electric Power

Background Information

Customers receive monthly bills from their utility companies based on how much electrical power they have used. Utilities charge different rates for winter (October through April) and summer (June through September) seasons. In the summer months, customers are charged an escalating rate and in winter a declining one. Examine the following chart:

kWh	Summer	Winter
First 650 kWh	$.0693	$.0704
Next 350 kWh	$.0756	$.0590
Over 1000 kWh	$.0797	$.0559

For example, in June, a customer is charged $.0693 for the first 650 kWh of electric power. The next 350 kWh (651 to 1000 kWh) is charged at the rate of $.0756. Charges on the remaining electricity used, anything over 1000 kWh, are calculated at the rate of $.0797. So if a customer used 1200 kWh of electricity, charges would be:

First 650 kWh = 650 × $.0693 = $45.045
Next 350 kWh = 350 × $.0756 = $26.46
Last 200 kWh = 200 × $.0797 = $15.94
Total charges = $87.445

The base rate each month is $7.50 whether customers use any electricity or not. Customers also pay 5% sales tax on their entire electric bill as well as a fuel recovery cost of $.015 per kWh.

Questions

1. In December, the Kendrix family stayed at home for two weeks to celebrate the Christmas season with family and friends. The regular group of two adults and three teenage children was increased by visiting grandparents and plenty of friends spending the night. They cooked meals at home and did laundry daily. At the end of the month, Mr. Kendrix was surprised to see his electric bill, which stated that they had used 3233 kWh of electricity.

   Calculate the Kendrix family's power bill using the sample bill shown here and the rates listed in the background information section.

2. In June, the entire Kendrix family took a trip to Washington State, and the house was empty for three weeks. The monthly power bill stated that they had used only 630 kWh of electricity. Calculate their power bill.

3. In July, the heat wave and summer drought brought daily temperatures into the nineties. Mrs. Kendrix set the air conditioner at 76°F. The power bill stated that the family used 2995 kWh of electricity. Calculate the Kendrix power bill for July.

Copyright © 2008 by John Wiley & Sons, Inc.

4. During which season is electricity more expensive to use? Does the amount of electricity one uses affect the cost of this energy to the customer?

5. How could a family conserve electricity in the summer?

6. Do utilities encourage or discourage customers to use a lot of electricity in the summer? Explain your answer.

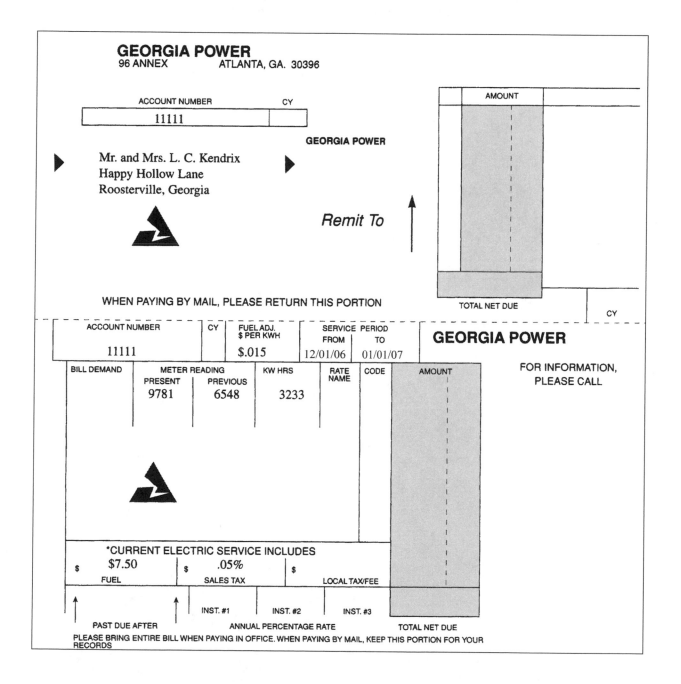

Copyright © 2008 by John Wiley & Sons, Inc.

9-3 SHOCKING SOLUTIONS
Math Problems Involving Electricity

Objectives

Students will use formulas related to electricity to solve written problems.

Teacher Notes

Calculators are optional; students should be able to solve these problems without them. You may want to write relevant electrical formulas on the board.

Copyright © 2008 by John Wiley & Sons, Inc.

SHOCKING SOLUTIONS
Math Problems Involving Electricity

1. Brad has a new flashlight that runs on one 8-volt battery. How much current flows through this circuit if the bulb has 2 ohms of resistance?

2. If your fingers are damp and offer a resistance of only 1200 ohms, how much current will pass through them if you touch the terminals of a 6-volt battery?

3. If your hair dryer draws 10 amps of current on a 120-volt circuit, how much power does it use?

4. Shane's 100-watt radio draws 7 amps of current on a 120-volt circuit. What is the resistance in the radio?

5. It is Lisa's night to clean up the kitchen, but she's anxious to get started on her physics homework. While loading the dishwasher, she calculates how many amps of current it uses on a 120-volt circuit. What did she find?

6. Audrey fell off her horse during riding lessons and got all her clothes dirty. How much energy does an 1800-watt washing machine use if it runs for 30 minutes? What about a 4000-watt clothes dryer that runs for 1 hour? If electricity costs $0.06/kWh, how much did it cost Audrey to wash and dry her clothes?

Copyright © 2008 by John Wiley & Sons, Inc.

9-4 WIRED FOR ACTION
Lab on Parallel and Series Circuits

Objectives

Students will experiment with different ways to create circuits and differentiate between series and parallel circuits.

Teacher Notes

Use batteries that are 9 volts or larger. Use small lamps (light bulbs) that can be lit by batteries.

Copyright © 2008 by John Wiley & Sons, Inc.

WIRED FOR ACTION
Lab on Parallel and Series Circuits

Copyright © 2008 by John Wiley & Sons, Inc.

Background Information

Electricians plan the circuits they will build and then draw their plans as schematics. In a schematic, a straight line represents a wire. Electricians use the symbols in Figure A to represent resistors (such as light bulbs) and batteries.

This is a resistor

This is a battery

FIGURE A

The schematic in Figure B shows a battery that is attached to wires leading to three resistors (labeled R_1, R_2, and R_3). The arrows in this schematic show you the direction in which electrons flow through the circuit. Notice that electrons flow from the negative terminal of the battery, through the wires and resistors, and back to the positive terminal. An electrical circuit must be complete for electricity to flow through it. If the circuit is broken, the path of electrons from the battery's negative terminal to the positive terminal is broken.

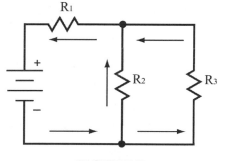

FIGURE B

Materials

Battery in holder (9 volts or larger)

Three light bulbs

One piece of string (about the same length as the wires)

Several pieces of insulated wire (with the ends stripped or with alligator clips on the ends)

Procedure, Part A: Create Your Own Circuits

1. Examine the materials provided by your teacher.

2. Use these materials to make an electrical circuit that lights one of the light bulbs.

3. Draw a schematic for the circuit you just created.

4. Rearrange your circuit to see how many different ways you can get the bulb to light. (You may need to use additional pieces of wire.) Draw a schematic for each arrangement.

Procedure, Part B: Follow a Schematic

1. Build the circuit shown in Figure C.

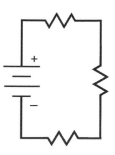

FIGURE C

135

2. Take out one of the light bulbs. Observe the circuit and record your observations.

3. Replace the light bulb. Take one of the wires out of the circuit and substitute the piece of string. Observe the circuit and record your observations.

4. Build the circuit shown in Figure D.

5. Take out one of the light bulbs. Observe the circuit and record your observations.

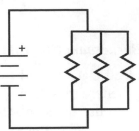

FIGURE D

Postlab Questions

1. In steps 1 through 4 of Procedure A, you built several electrical circuits. In your own words, define an electrical circuit.

2. What provided the energy for your electrical circuits? What offered resistance to the flow of electricity in your electrical circuits?

3. The circuit you built in step 1 of Procedure B is described as a series circuit. Using what you learned in this experiment, define a series circuit.

4. In step 2 of Procedure B, what happened when you removed a light bulb? Why did this occur?

5. In step 3 of Procedure B, what happened when you replaced a wire with a string? Why did this happen?

6. In step 3 of Procedure B, the wire is a conductor and the string is an insulator. Define these two terms in your own words.

7. The circuit you built in step 4 of Procedure B is a parallel circuit. Using what you learned in this experiment, define a parallel circuit.

8. In step 5 of Procedure B, what happened when you removed a light bulb? Why did this occur?

9. Which type of circuit would you prefer to have in your house: series or parallel? Explain your answer.

Copyright © 2008 by John Wiley & Sons, Inc.

SECTION 3

Astronomy

LESSON 10: PLANETS

10-1 PLANETARY FAMILY
Content on the Planets in Our Solar System

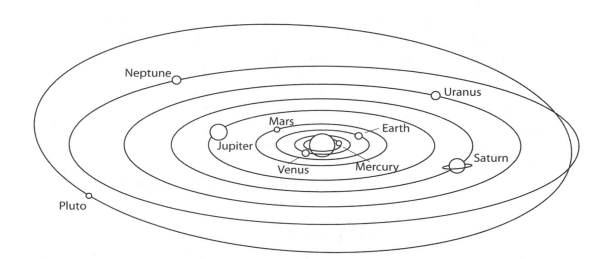

Siblings of the Solar System

Earth is a member of a family of planets that rotate around our nearest star, the sun. Our solar system includes eight major planets, a dwarf planet, and thousands of asteroids. Most asteroids are less than a few miles in diameter, and many scientists believe they are chips broken from the major planets. The solar system also includes comets, masses of frozen gases and rocks that travel around the sun in long, narrow orbits. As comets near the sun, they heat up and create bright glows that we can see from Earth. Scattered among the planets and asteroids are meteoroids, tiny particles of matter, often less than one gram, that travel at high speeds.

Inner and Outer Space

The eight planets of our solar system can be divided into two categories: the inner, or terrestrial, planets and the outer, or gaseous, planets. The inner, earthlike planets include the four closest to the sun. The outer planets and the dwarf planet move in orbits of vastly greater diameter than the inner planets.

Copyright © 2008 by John Wiley & Sons, Inc.

139

The planets all rotate in a uniform direction, with the exception of Uranus. They revolve about the sun in the same direction, and all have orbits within a few degrees of each other. Gravitational attraction pulls the planets toward the sun and keeps them moving through space.

A Close-Knit Family

The planet closest to the sun is Mercury, at about 36 million miles away. The sunward side of Mercury can reach temperatures of up to 770°F; its shaded side can drop to absolute zero. No other planet has such an extreme temperature range. The heat is so extreme that scientists believe that pools of molten metal might exist on the surface. This planet takes about 88 days to revolve once around the sun, and it has no satellites. The terrain of Mercury is very much like that of Earth's moon. No discernable atmosphere exists on Mercury. The average density of Mercury is similar to that of Earth, which suggests that it may have a core made of iron.

Venus is the second planet from the sun, at about 67 million miles away. This planet is often called the morning or evening star because it is the brightest object in our sky after the sun and our moon. Venus requires about 225 days to revolve once around the sun. It is much like Earth in mass, size, and density, but its temperatures can soar to a blistering 570°F. The atmosphere of Venus is extremely dense because it is composed primarily of carbon dioxide with very little oxygen. In addition, the air is filled with pale yellow clouds composed of corrosive sulfuric acid. The air pressure on the surface is about 90 times that of Earth.

Earth is the third planet from the sun and the fifth-largest planet in size. More than 75 percent of its surface is covered with water. One revolution of Earth around the sun requires 365 days. Earth is tilted on its axis, a position that causes the change in seasons. The atmosphere of the earth is 79 percent nitrogen, 20 percent oxygen, and 1 percent trace elements. Temperatures are variable but moderate. Earth is the only planet known at this time to be capable of supporting life.

Mars is the fourth and last of the inner planets. The length of a Martian day is about the same length as that of a day on Earth, but a year on Mars is about twice as long as Earth's. Air pressure on Mars is extremely low, about 166 times less than that on Earth. The little air that does exist is primarily carbon dioxide. Mars has cold and warm seasons like those on Earth, but with much greater temperature extremes than those to which we are accustomed. Temperatures at night can dip to −170°F. The terrain of Mars includes soil that has a red tint due to iron oxide (rust) found on the surface of the planet. Sand dunes, craters, mountains, and volcanoes can all be found on Mars.

Distant Relatives

Jupiter is the largest planet in our solar system, with 125 times the surface area of Earth. Despite its size, the density of Jupiter is just one quarter of Earth's density. Sixteen moons orbit Jupiter. A day on Jupiter lasts only about 10 hours, but a year

Copyright © 2008 by John Wiley & Sons, Inc.

Copyright © 2008 by John Wiley & Sons, Inc.

is about 12 times as long as a year on Earth. The planet is composed primarily of two gases, hydrogen and helium. Its atmosphere consists of ammonia and methane but no oxygen. Winds blow constantly, whipping white clouds around the surface of this planet. Scientists believe that Jupiter consists of a rocky metallic core surrounded by a thick layer of ice.

Saturn, the second-largest planet, is orbited by 20 moons. Its distinctive rings have intrigued people for many years. These rings are probably composed of ice particles. Saturn's atmosphere is composed of hydrogen and helium. The temperature on Saturn is much colder than that on Jupiter, and strong winds blow across the planet, constantly forming storm systems. A day on Saturn lasts about 17 hours, and a year is about 29 times longer than on Earth.

Uranus has an atmosphere composed mostly of hydrogen and helium. This planet is less dense than water and is surrounded by rings similar to those around Saturn. An interesting feature of Uranus involves its axis of rotation. Unlike the other seven planets, Uranus does not rotate in a uniform direction. A day on Uranus lasts about 13 hours, but a year is equivalent to 84 Earth years.

Neptune shows little or no surface marking and is almost identical to Uranus. A day on Neptune lasts only 16 hours, but a year is 165 Earth years. Neptune has an icy, rocky surface and one large moon. Its atmosphere is like that of Uranus, hydrogen and helium.

Orbiting outside of Neptune is Pluto, which was considered to be a true planet until August 2006. At that time, the International Astronomical Union reclassified Pluto as a dwarf planet. It is an icy, rocky structure and is located the farthest from the sun in our solar system. One year on Pluto is about 248 Earth years, and a day is only 6 hours long.

PLANET UNSCRAMBLE—VOCABULARY ACTIVITY ON
PLANETARY FAMILY

After reading *Planetary Family,* unscramble the words to complete the following sentences.

1. The earthlike planets are called the _____ (resretrtlai) planets.

2. The planet that does not rotate in a uniform direction is _____ (arusun).

3. The planet closest to the sun is _____ (yrcuemr).

4. The dwarf planet and the member of the solar system that is most distant from the sun is _____ (toulp).

5. The planet with the icy rings around it is _____ (natsur).

6. The gas that makes up the greatest percentage of the Earth's atmosphere is _____ (itnogrne).

7. Sulfuric acid makes up the clouds of the planet _____ (evsun).

8. A great number of _____ (sertcar), volcanoes, and mountains are found on the surface of Mars.

9. Jupiter has clouds of ammonia and methane, and constant _____ (insdw) occur on this planet.

10. _____ (moecst) are bright objects with glowing tails that travel in long and narrow orbits.

Copyright © 2008 by John Wiley & Sons, Inc.

10-2 BRINGING THE SOLAR SYSTEM DOWN TO EARTH
Activity on the Size of Our Solar System

Objectives

Students will develop a scale model of the solar system.

Teacher Notes

Math skills are required to calculate the distances and diameters. You may want to give younger students a completed chart to do this activity. Older students can compute the distances and diameters and fill in the chart for themselves. The class should be divided into groups of four or five. Parts A and B (mathematical computations) of the lab activity can be done indoors. Part C of the activity can be done outdoors on the second day. You could award the best solar system creation with bonus points or a special prize.

Copyright © 2008 by John Wiley & Sons, Inc.

BRINGING THE SOLAR SYSTEM DOWN TO EARTH
Activity on the Size of Our Solar System

Materials

Apparatus for measuring length in meters

Calculator

Pencil

Outdoor materials (such as stones, twigs, pine cones, and leaves)

Part A: Calculating the Scaled-Down Diameter of the Planets

1. Look at Chart 1, which gives the diameter of the planets, Pluto, and the sun (in kilometers).

2. The sun is 1,380,000 km in diameter. In this experiment, arbitrarily assign the sun a diameter value of 1.

3. Compare the diameter of Mercury to the diameter of the sun. To do so, divide 1,380,000 km by 4989. Write the answer, 277, in the column of the chart marked Number of Times Smaller Than the Sun. Repeat this procedure for the other planets. For instance, Venus would be 1,380,000 km divided by 12,392 km. Record this value in Chart 1.

4. For the last column in Chart 1, you will assign a scaled-down value for the size of each object. Begin with the sun and assign the sun a value of 1 meter (1000 mm). Calculate the scaled value of the other planets by dividing 1000 by the number of times smaller than the sun you calculated that planet to be. For instance, Mercury's size is calculated by dividing 1000 by 277. The answer is 3.6 mm. This number has already been entered in the chart. Repeat this procedure for each of the planets.

5. When the chart is complete, the last column will represent the diameter your group will use to represent each planet in the activity.

Copyright © 2008 by John Wiley & Sons, Inc.

CHART 1

Object	Diameter (km)	Number of Times Smaller Than the Sun	Scaled-Down Diameter (mm)
Sun	1,380,000	—	1000
Mercury	4989	277	3.6
Venus	12,392		
Earth	12,757		
Mars	6959		
Jupiter	142,749		
Saturn	120,862		
Uranus	51,499		
Neptune	44,579		
Pluto	2414		

Part B: Calculating the Scaled-Down Distance of the Planets from the Sun

1. Chart 2 lists the distance of the planets and Pluto from the sun in millions of miles. Your group will convert these distances to astronomical units (AUs). An AU represents the distance of the Earth from the sun, or 93 million miles. In Chart 2 you will see the number 1 under AU for Earth. To find the AUs for the other planets and Pluto, divide each object's distance from the sun by 93 million. For instance, Venus is 0.7 AU. To arrive at that figure, you divide the distance of Venus from the sun, 67.27 million miles, by 93 million. The number for Venus is already entered in Chart 2. Follow this procedure for the remaining planets and Pluto.

2. In the last column of Chart 2, record the relative distance of the celestial body from the sun. To do so, assign a value of 1 meter (1000 mm) to represent the distance of the Earth from the sun, or 1 AU. That value (1000 mm) has been written in the last column on Chart 2, as has the distance from Venus to the sun, which is 700 mm. Use the same procedure to find the distance of the other objects from the sun.

Copyright © 2008 by John Wiley & Sons, Inc.

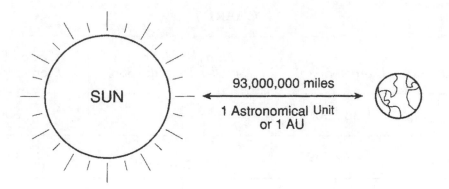

CHART 2

Object	Distance from the Sun (in millions of miles)	AU Equivalent (astronomical unit)	Scaled-Down Distance (mm)
Mercury	36		
Venus	67.27	0.7	700
Earth	93	1	1000
Mars	141.7		
Jupiter	483.9		
Saturn	887.1		
Uranus	1783.98		
Neptune	2795.5		
Pluto	3675.3		

Copyright © 2008 by John Wiley & Sons, Inc.

Part C: Creating a Scaled-Down Model

1. With your group, take completed Charts 1 and 2 and a meter stick or metric tape measure outdoors.

2. Use the data in the last column of Chart 1 to assign objects of appropriate diameters the roles of the sun, the eight planets, and Pluto. For example, you might find a small rock that is about 700 mm in diameter that can represent Venus. Rocks, twigs, straw, pine cones, and other natural objects can be used to build each planet and the sun.

3. The sun should be at one end of the model, and the planets and Pluto should be placed in the proper order away from the sun. To determine the appropriate distance of each object from the sun, use the meter stick and information from the last column of Chart 2. Measure the appropriate distance from the sun in meters or millimeters for each planet and Pluto.

4. Make a model of the entire solar system by arranging the sun, the planets, and Pluto in the appropriate scaled-down diameter and at the appropriate distance from the sun.

5. When you are finished, show your solar system to your teacher.

6. Visit and view the solar systems created by other groups.

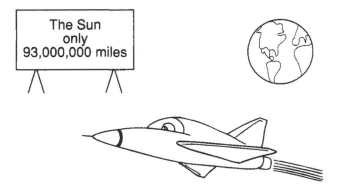

Postlab Questions

1. What is a scale model?

2. What is an AU?

3. Why is a scale model of the solar system useful?

4. On your scale model, which two planets are closest together?

5. If you wanted to create a scale model of the solar system inside your classroom, you would need to use a smaller scale than the one you used in this activity. What would be the diameter of the sun, planets, and Pluto if you reduced the size of each by 10? What would be the diameter of each if you reduced their size by 100? Write your calculations in Chart 3. The reduced sizes of the sun and Mercury have been calculated and entered for you.

Copyright © 2008 by John Wiley & Sons, Inc.

CHART 3

Object	Scaled-Down Diameter (mm)	Size Reduced by a Factor of 10 (mm)	Size Reduced by a Factor of 100 (mm)
Sun	1000	100	10
Mercury	3.6	.36	.036
Venus			
Earth			
Mars			
Jupiter			
Saturn			
Uranus			
Neptune			
Pluto			

Copyright © 2008 by John Wiley & Sons, Inc.

6. In the space below, draw a sun with a diameter of 100 mm. Then draw the planets (to scale) inside the sun.

Copyright © 2008 by John Wiley & Sons, Inc.

10-3 ASTONISHING PLANETARY DISCOVERY
Performance Assessment on Designing
Life Forms for the Planets

Objectives

Students will evaluate information about a planet in our solar system, then design and create an imaginary creature that can exist on this planet.

Teacher Notes

This activity can be adapted for all grade levels. You can require students to build models of their creatures, draw pictures or diagrams, or describe them in writing. The ability level and age of the student can dictate the approach you use. This activity can be taken further by integrating math skills for older students. It works best in cooperative learning groups. Oral presentations are recommended when each group has completed a description of a creature.

Write the names of the planets (except for earth) and Pluto on eight different slips of paper. Put these in a paper bag. Divide students into groups of three or four. A member of each group will select one slip of paper from the bag to begin the activity. The slip of paper will indicate the orbiting body the group will research.

Give students access to the Internet and resource materials from the library.

A grading rubric follows. You can use the rubric as it is or tailor it for your needs. Give the students a copy of the rubric before they begin the activity so that they will know how you will assess their work.

Copyright © 2008 by John Wiley & Sons, Inc.

SUGGESTED GRADING RUBRIC

	1 point	2 points	3 points	4 points
Worksheet section with information on the heavenly body	Less than 25% of the information is completed.	25% of the information is completed.	50% of the information is completed.	All of the information is completed.
Worksheet section with information on the creature	Less than 25% of the information is completed.	25% of the information is completed.	50% of the information is completed.	All of the information is completed.
Creature drawn on poster board or modeled with art materials	Model (drawing) does not meet the requirements stated on worksheet.	Model (drawing) meets some of the requirements stated on worksheet.	Model (drawing) meets most of the requirements stated on worksheet.	Model (drawing) perfectly reflects the requirements stated on worksheet.
Creature presented to class	Presentation is difficult to understand, leaves off important details.	Presentation is not completely clear, does not include all details.	Presentation is clear and understandable, but some information omitted.	Presentation is clear and interesting, and includes all details.

Comments: _____

_____

Points possible: 16

Points earned: _____

Copyright © 2008 by John Wiley & Sons, Inc.

ASTONISHING PLANETARY DISCOVERY

Performance Assessment on Designing
Life Forms for the Planets

Background Information

Before doing this activity, read *Planetary Family* for background on the solar system. Read the following scenario:

> *Congratulations! Your team is one of only eight in the world that has been selected to work on a NASA space project to conduct detailed research on a planet (or Pluto). Upon completion of this research, your team will use the information you gathered to design a creature that could exist on that heavenly body.*
>
> *Each exploration team will randomly select a slip of paper that denotes which space structure they will research. Each team will then decide what characteristics a creature must have to exist on the designated structure. Access to library materials and Internet articles written by space experts will be provided to aid in your work. Your team will design a perfect creature for the structure.*
>
> *When the class is finished with its designs, NASA and the heads of the government will determine which creature is best suited for its heavenly body. The winning design team will be given a special award. Good luck in your work. Remember, good research is extremely important.*

Materials

The background information, *Planetary Family*

Library and Internet resources on the planets and Pluto

Poster board and markers

Various art materials (to make a model of your creature)

Procedure

1. Draw a slip of paper to find out which heavenly body you are researching.

2. Use the library and Internet resources to complete the section of the Scientist Worksheet titled "I. Information on Your Heavenly Body."

3. Analyze the information you gathered on the worksheet and come up with a design for a creature that could survive on this heavenly body. As you work, complete the part of the worksheet titled "II. Information on Your Creature."

4. Either draw a picture of your creature on poster board or create a model of your creature with art supplies.

5. Present your creature, and the information you have developed, to your class.

Copyright © 2008 by John Wiley & Sons, Inc.

Scientist Worksheet

Exploration team members:

_____

_____

I. Information on Your Heavenly Body

Heavenly body explored: _____

Distance of heavenly body from the sun: _____

Diameter of the structure: _____

Distance from Earth: _____

Composition of the atmosphere (gases and their percentages): _____

_____

Temperature range: Low _____ High _____

    Average temperature: _____

    Do seasonal temperatures exist? _____

    Average humidity (if any): _____

    Average barometric pressure: _____

Describe the surface terrain:

_____

_____

_____

Gravity on this structure compared with Earth: _____

Storms or other climatic conditions that might exist:

_____

Period of one revolution around the sun (length of a year): _____

Period of one rotation on the structure's axis (length of a day): _____

Is there evidence of volcanoes? _____

Copyright © 2008 by John Wiley & Sons, Inc.

Number of satellites that orbit the structure: _____

Is there evidence of wind? Explain how much: _____

_____

Describe the geology of the interior of the structure. Indicate the layers and the composition of each layer:

_____

_____

_____

Describe any special features and interesting information about the structure not included in the material above:

_____

_____

_____

_____

_____

_____

II. Information on Your Creature

Describe in detail the special features of your creature:

_____

_____

_____

_____

_____

_____

Copyright © 2008 by John Wiley & Sons, Inc.

What will your creature eat?

_____

_____

Describe how your creature will metabolize its food source for energy:

_____

_____

Describe the process of respiration for your creature:

_____

_____

List some dangers the creature will face:

_____

_____

Explain the adaptations of your creature that will help it deal with the following factors:

Temperature extremes: _____

Food intake: _____

Gravity: _____

Atmospheric conditions: _____

Recreation: _____

Climatic conditions: _____

How old will your creature be if it was 1 year old when taken to the heavenly body and retrieved 10 Earth years later? _____

Copyright © 2008 by John Wiley & Sons, Inc.

LESSON 11: STARS

11-1 STAR LIGHT, STAR BRIGHT
Content on Stars

Where Are We?

The night sky is filled with sparkling lights, some bright and bold, others faint and difficult to see. How many stars are there? What are they made of?

Galileo answered some of our questions when he determined that the sun and its planets make up only a small part of a huge system, the galaxy we call the Milky Way. As such a small part of this galaxy, we find it difficult to get an idea about the appearance of the entire system. From our position on Earth, we can see that the stars in or near the constellation Sagittarius are the brightest in the sky, and the faintest ones are in the opposite direction near Auriga and Cassiopeia. The brightness we see near Sagittarius is due to the large number of stars in that area; in the early days, this led astronomers to believe that the center of the galaxy is in that direction.

Copyright © 2008 by John Wiley & Sons, Inc.

Copyright © 2008 by John Wiley & Sons, Inc.

We now know that our solar system is near the edge of the Milky Way, a huge galaxy that is about 100,000 light years in diameter. (A light year is the distance light travels in a year, which is 5.87×10^{12} miles or 9×10^{12} kilometers.) The Milky Way has a spiral shape, and its stars are arranged in long, curved arms. The entire galactic system revolves around its center at a rate of 612,000 miles per hour. Even at this speed, it takes our sun and its planets 220 million years to make one trip around the entire galaxy.

Bright Stars and Black Holes

There are billions of stars in the Milky Way, and no two of them are exactly the same. Some stars appear bright, others very dim. Some are blue, others yellow. Many of the brightest stars in the heavens are novas, stars that are giving off enormous amounts of mass in huge explosions of light and energy. Early observers gave these stars the name *nova* ("new star") because they believed that they were witnessing the birth of a star. Novas typically flare brightly for a few days and then recede to their original brightness. Scientists now believe that novas may be shedding mass before dying of old age.

A supernova, an even more spectacular event than a nova, is a star that actually blows itself apart. Supernovas flare up millions of times brighter than the sun and can be seen over enormous distances. Only three supernova sightings have been recorded in the last thousand years. Chinese and Japanese literature of 1054 C.E. record a supernova that could still be seen two years later. The remains of that historic explosion make up the Crab Nebula.

The ultimate star is a black hole. A black hole begins its existence as a regular star. Eventually the star burns up all of its nuclear fuel and begins collapsing. The star matter becomes condensed into such a small volume that atomic structure no longer exists. The gravity on this dead star is incredibly strong, and nothing, not even light, can escape. There are no particles in black holes due to their excessive gravitational forces. The radius of a black hole is extremely small; a black hole with the mass of our sun would have a radius of only 1.9 miles. Astronomers estimate that there are at least one million black holes in our galaxy.

Stardust

Nebulae are vast clouds of cosmic dust. Some nebulae form swirling, bubbling shapes that eventually condense into new stars. Other nebulae are bright remnants of supernovas, such as the Crab Nebula. The Great Nebula is the only spiral nebula in the night sky that is visible to the naked eye; it is found in the constellation Orion along with the Horse's Head Nebula. The latter is dark because there are no nearby stars to illuminate it. Dark nebulae are huge clouds of matter that have not yet formed into stars. Nebulae vary from the size of our solar system to thousands of light years in width.

Brightness and Distance

When you look carefully at the night sky with the unaided eye, some stars seem very bright, whereas others are faint. Two thousand years ago, astronomers used a magnitude system to compare star brightness. The Greek astronomer Hipparchus divided the stars into six magnitudes of brightness. The brighter a celestial body, the lower its magnitude on the magnitude scale. A star of the first magnitude is about 2.5 times brighter than a star of the second magnitude. Thus a first-magnitude star is 6.4 times brighter than a third-magnitude star, 16 times brighter than a fourth-magnitude star, and 40 times brighter than a fifth-magnitude star. There are about 20 first-magnitude, 50 second-magnitude, 150 third-magnitude, 450 fourth-magnitude, 1350 fifth-magnitude, and 4000 sixth-magnitude stars in the sky. Modern astronomers have extended this system to include all bright objects as well as objects too dim for Hipparchus to see.

The magnitude of a star depends not only on its brightness but also on its distance from Earth. To compare the brightness of two bodies, you must compare their absolute magnitudes. The absolute magnitude of a body is defined as the magnitude that body would have if it were situated 10 parsecs from Earth, a distance of about three light years. Thus, we can see that the brightest star in the sky, Sirius, is really less bright than Rigel (see Chart 1).

To compare the light that two stars actually radiate, astronomers do not rely on their appearance; they measure the stars' luminosity. The luminosity of a star is the total amount of energy radiated into space every second. This can be determined by multiplying the amount of light received on Earth by the distance of the star from Earth. When we compare the luminosity of Sirius and Rigel, Rigel is 2000 times more luminous than Sirius. Sirius simply appears brighter because it is 90 times closer to us.

Copyright © 2008 by John Wiley & Sons, Inc.

CHART 1: THE MAGNITUDES OF SOME FAMILIAR OBJECTS IN THE SKY

Star	Location	Apparent Magnitude	Absolute Magnitude	Distance in Light Years
Rigel	Orion	+0.11	–7.0	660
Sirius	Canis Major	–1.45	+1.41	8.64
Canopus	Carina	–0.73	+0.16	190

STAR PUZZLE—VOCABULARY ACTIVITY ON
STAR LIGHT, STAR BRIGHT

Directions

Complete the following puzzle using terms from *Star Light, Star Bright.*

Copyright © 2008 by John Wiley & Sons, Inc.

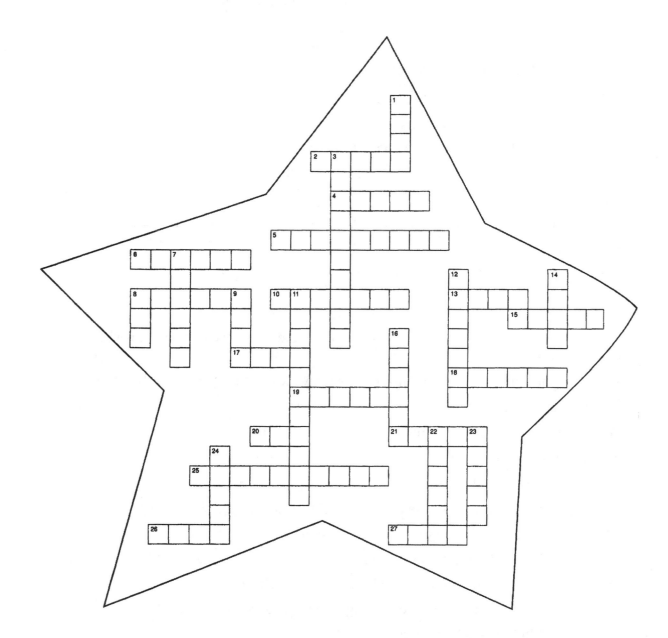

Across

2. Light cannot escape from the gravitational pull of a(n) _____ hole.

4. Our galaxy is the _____ Way.

5. The brighter a star, the lower its _____ on the magnitude scale.

6. There are about 50 _____ magnitude stars.

8. The solar _____ is on the edge of the Milky Way.

10. _____ was an early astronomer who determined that our solar system is only a small part of the Milky Way.

13. In a black _____, matter is so dense that atomic structure collapses.

15. The distance light can travel in 2 years is 2 light _____.

17. Sirius is the brightest _____ in the sky.

18. The Milky Way has a _____ shape.

19. The Crab _____ is a remnant from a supernova.

20. Modern astronomers can see stars too _____ for Hipparchus.

21. A parsec is 3.626 light _____.

25. The astronomer _____ divided the stars into six magnitudes of brightness.

26. Stars burn nuclear _____.

27. Rigel is a _____ in the constellation Orion.

Down

1. The Horse's Head Nebula is _____ because there are no stars close by to provide illumination.

3. The _____ of a star is the total amount of energy radiated into space each second.

7. Nebulae are formed from clouds of _____ dust.

8. The Greeks divided the stars into _____ magnitudes of brightness.

9. A black hole with the sun's _____ has a radius of only 1.9 miles.

11. Scientists who study the heavenly bodies are _____.

12. In _____ and Japanese literature from 1054 C.E., a supernova event was recorded.

14. The _____ Nebula is a remnant from a supernova.

16. Our _____ is 100,000 light years in diameter.

22. The faintest stars are near the constellations Cassiopeia and _____.

23. Our _____ system consists of one star, eight planets, and Pluto.

24. _____ is 660 light years from Earth.

Copyright © 2008 by John Wiley & Sons, Inc.

11-2 STAR CHAMBER
Class Project on Constellations

Objectives

Students will use computational, graphing, and measuring techniques to recreate the positions of constellations.

Teacher Notes

In this activity, students create a large bag that can be inflated with air. If space is a problem, the size of the bag can be varied, as long as it is large enough for a few students to enter the bag and lie on their backs. Directions in the Procedure section enable students to create a bag that can hold 10 or 15 students.

Star charts for autumn and winter are provided. Enlarge pages to 11 inches by 17 inches.

Copyright © 2008 by John Wiley & Sons, Inc.

Star Chamber Activity
Class Project on Constellations

Constellations Are Star Patterns

People have seen patterns formed by stars in the night sky for thousands of years. The arrangement of the stars has been credited with determining the course of events on Earth. Early astronomers who could "read" stars were important members of their communities.

We know today that the patterns seen in the stars have no influence on our lives, and that visualizing constellations is just one way of studying the arrangement of heavenly bodies. Whether stars are viewed with the naked eye, a low-power telescope, or a stronger one, they can be beautiful and fascinating. One of the most famous star patterns, or constellations, is Ursa Major (the Great Bear), whose "tail" is known as the Big Dipper. Two stars in the Great Bear are alpha and beta Ursae Majoris; these are called the pointer stars because they point to Polaris, the North Star. The North Star indicates the position of the north celestial pole, the point around which all the heavens seem to rotate. Polaris is also the last star in the "tail" of Ursa Minor (the Little Bear).

A King, a Queen, and a Dragon

Several other easily identifiable constellations are near Polaris. Cepheus (named for Cepheus the Monarch) is a circumpolar constellation, which means that it is near the north pole. Ursa Major and Cepheus are exactly opposite Polaris. Draco (the Dragon) is made up of several fairly faint stars that form a long path between the tails of the Big and Little Dippers and then curve northeast around the bowl of the Little Dipper before winding southwest to form the easily recognizable quadrilateral, Dragon's Head. Cassiopeia (named for a queen in Greek mythology) is easily recognizable because it forms a widespread W in the sky. It is the same distance from Polaris as is Ursa Major.

A Dog, a Horse, and a Servant

Aquarius (the Water Carrier) is a faint but wide constellation. Its most prominent feature is the Water Jar, a group of four stars that form a Y. In ancient times, people saw the water jar as being inverted so that water poured into the mouth of the Southern Fish (Pisces). Pegasus (the Flying Horse) is most famous for the so-called Great Square of Pegasus formed by four stars, one of which actually belongs to the constellation Andromeda. This star is Beta-Pegasi, one of the largest known stars; if it were in the sun's location in our solar system, its size would extend beyond the orbit of Venus.

Canis Major (the Great Dog) includes Sirius, the brightest star in the sky. The Little Dog, or Canis Minor, forms an equilateral triangle with Sirius and one of the stars in Orion. Orion is generally believed to be one of the most beautiful and imposing constellations in the heavens. Four bright stars form a large rectangle, and three smaller, evenly spaced stars within the rectangle form the belt. No other constellation has so many bright stars. Orion also contains two nebulae, which we discussed in *Star Light, Star Bright.* One of these, the Great Nebula,

Copyright © 2008 by John Wiley & Sons, Inc.

162

STARS OF AUTUMN

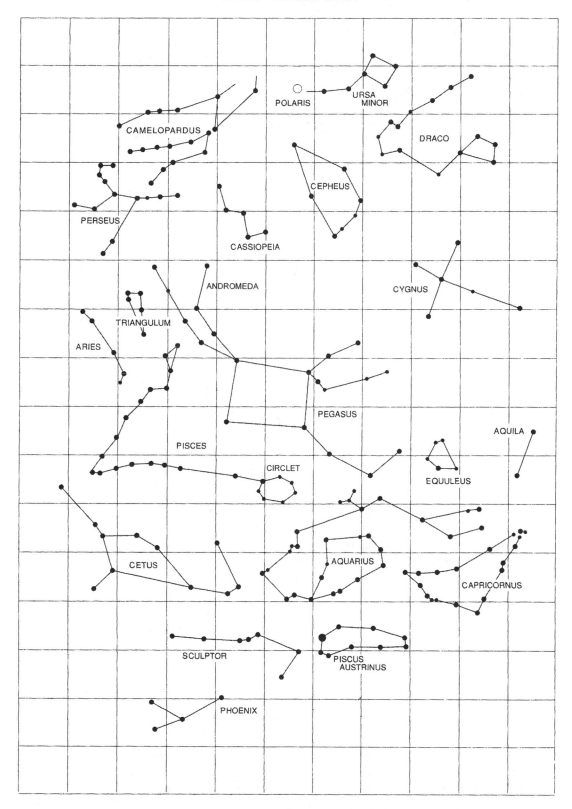

Copyright © 2008 by John Wiley & Sons, Inc.

STARS OF WINTER

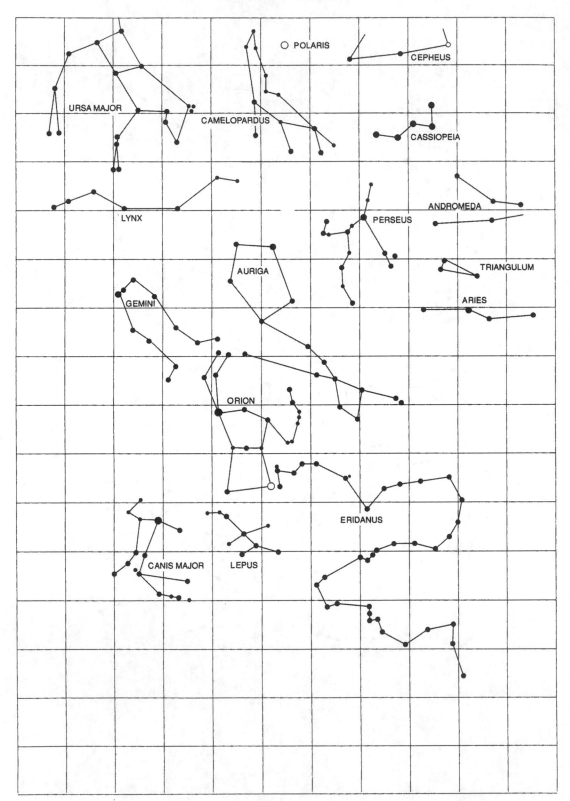

Copyright © 2008 by John Wiley & Sons, Inc.

can be seen with the naked eye. It is a diffuse nebula, a great cloud of dust 26 light years in diameter and 1625 light years from Earth. The other nebula in Orion is the Horse's Head Nebula, a dark cloud silhouetted against a glowing cloud of cosmic dust. Long photographic exposures are required to reveal this beautiful object.

In this lab activity, you will form a star chamber and model some of the constellations.

Materials

Star charts enlarged on 11-by-17-inch paper

Ice pick or knife

A sheet of black plastic, 80 feet by 40 feet

Meter sticks or measuring tapes

Duct tape

Large fan

Narrow masking tape

Procedure

1. Spread out the black plastic.

2. Use masking tape to create 4-by-4-foot grids on half of the black plastic (see Figure A).

3. The grid on each paper star chart represents one 4-by-4-foot grid on the black plastic. Using a knife or ice pick, recreate the constellation patterns depicted on the star chart on the plastic.

4. For example,

    a. On the Stars of Autumn star chart, find the constellation Cassiopeia.

    b. On the star chart, Cassiopeia falls within the fifth grid from the left and the fourth and fifth grids from the top.

    c. Find the corresponding grids on the plastic, and punch holes to re-create the Cassiopeia design.

    d. Do not try to connect the stars with cuts in the plastic.

5. When you have placed all the constellations on one of the star charts on the plastic, fold the plastic in half. With the duct tape, tape the two sides of the plastic together. Tape part of the third side, leaving enough room for the fan and for students to enter the star chamber. The fourth side is formed by the fold (see Figure B).

6. Place the fan in the open area and turn it on. After the bag is inflated with air, enter and lie down on your back. Constellations should be visible in the chamber.

7. Use the chamber to memorize constellations or as a place to read and study astronomy.

Copyright © 2008 by John Wiley & Sons, Inc.

FIGURE A. BLACK PLASTIC WITH MASKING TAPE GRID

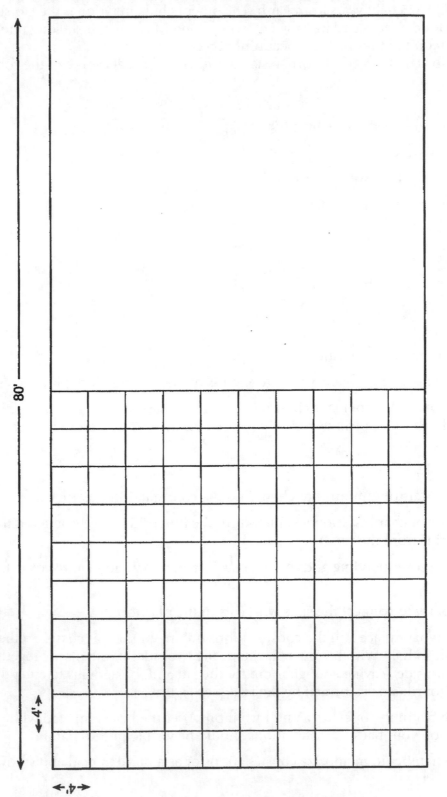

Copyright © 2008 by John Wiley & Sons, Inc.

STAR CHAMBER ACTIVITY (*continued*)

FIGURE B. FOLD THE PLASTIC IN HALF AND TAPE THE SIDES.

Bottom
Sheet

Top
Sheet

Postlab Questions

1. What is Polaris? Why does locating Polaris help lost people find their way home?

2. Why do we study constellations?

3. Look at the star patterns created in the star chamber. See if you can create your own constellation. Draw it and give it a name.

4. Fill in the blanks with the following words. (Some are used more than once.) Put the corresponding letter in the space to the left of each number.

a. Sirius   b. Orion   c. Ursa Major

d. Draco   e. Andromeda   f. Cassiopeia

g. Pegasus   h. Cepheus

_____ 1. _____ is a constellation that contains two nebulae.

_____ 2. The Big Dipper is the tail of _____.

_____ 3. Canis Major includes _____, the brightest star in the sky.

_____ 4. Many believe that _____ is the most beautiful constellation in the sky.

_____ 5. _____ has more bright stars than any other constellation.

_____ 6. _____ is a long constellation that winds between the Big and Little Dippers.

_____ 7. _____ forms a wide W across the sky.

_____ 8. _____ contains the Horse's Head Nebula, one of the dark nebulae.

_____ 9. The pointer stars in _____ point to the North Star.

_____ 10. Beta-Pegasi, one of the largest stars known, is in the constellation _____.

167

Copyright © 2008 by John Wiley & Sons, Inc.

LESSON 12: THE MOON

12-1 THE MAN IN THE MOON
Content on the Moon's Surface

Moon Tales

Because it is the largest object in our night sky, the moon has been the source of wonder and speculation for centuries. Legends and tales about the moon, its possible inhabitants, and its influence on Earth abound. For example, at one time farmers feared the "red moon," which legend says begins after Easter and continues through part of April and May, a period of time in which young plants can be reddened.

Nearly all countries have a story about a thief who was sent to the moon as punishment. An ancient German fable tells of a man who was exiled to the moon because he had stolen cabbages from poor people. This thief acquired the power to influence people's behavior on Earth. The word *lunatic,* from the word *lunar,* is derived from these tales as a description of those who behaved strangely because they had been exposed to moonlight.

In the second century B.C.E., Lucian of Samosata wrote two widely read books about his "trips" to the moon. Lucian met the "moonites," whom he described as large and hairless except for beards that hung down below their knees. Moonites had the unique ability to pluck out their eyes when they needed to see around corners. A typical moonite evening meal consisted of the fumes produced by roasting frogs, accompanied by a drink of water obtained by melting the hailstones that grew on household vines.

In 1638, Bishop Francis Godwin penned *The Man in the Moon,* the story of a traveler who was accidentally carried to the moon by his flock of trained birds. Godwin wrote about the reduced gravity of the moon, even though Newton had not yet formulated his theory of gravitational attraction. The "lunars" who lived on Godwin's moon had the ability to jump long distances, and they always spoke in song.

Craters and Maria

One of the oldest lunar legends refers to the man in the moon. If you look closely, you can see facial features on the moon's surface. When the moon is full, dark areas look like a person's eyes and mouth, and light areas define a nose. In reality, these light and dark areas are created by the craters, valleys, and flatlands on the moon's surface.

168

Copyright © 2008 by John Wiley & Sons, Inc.

In 1647, Hinelius of Danzig used an early telescope to describe lunar features and published the first good map of the moon. Later, the astronomer Riccioli started naming features on the moon's surface after great men, a custom that still exists today. When Galileo (1564–1642) viewed the moon, he thought that the smooth, dark areas were seas, so he named them *maria* (the plural of *mare,* meaning "seas"). The largest "sea" is Mare Serenitatis, which has a diameter of 430 miles. We now know that these seas are smooth parts of the landscape covered with a dark dust (see Figure A).

The moon is covered with about 30,000 large craters and countless small ones. Clavier is a huge crater with a diameter of 146 miles. Tycho and Copernicus are craters of equally impressive size. Light-colored streaks radiating from craters are called rays. The origins of lunar craters have long captured the attention of selenographers, scientists who study the moon's physical features. An early hypothesis was that the craters were extinct volcanoes and that the seas were beds of lava.

Copyright © 2008 by John Wiley & Sons, Inc.

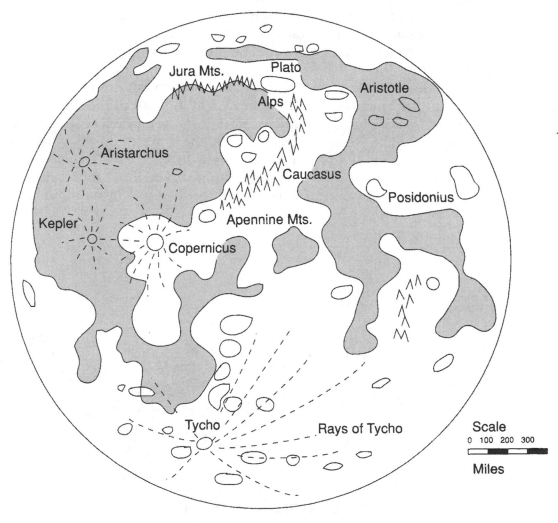

FIGURE A. THE MOON

This theory fell into disfavor for many reasons, one of which was the central peak found inside each crater. The American geologist G. K. Gilbert (1874–1936) first suggested that craters are formed from meteoritic impacts. This hypothesis was easy to demonstrate because similar craters are formed by falling raindrops on a muddy or sandy surface. Meteoroids were much more numerous in our solar system in the past, so meteoritic impacts were more frequent and of greater intensity than they are today. Earth probably received a similar bombardment, but the processes of erosion and deposition have erased most of our craters.

Most craters on the moon are round, and indicate a direct strike from above the surface. A few are elliptical, suggesting that they were formed by meteorites that struck the lunar surface from low angles. Scientists believe that the tremendous kinetic energy of a moving meteorite was converted to heat energy, raising the temperature of the meteorite to millions of degrees and vaporizing it. This enormous heat resulted in an explosion, blowing out the crater and dispersing the contents as tiny fragments far over the surrounding surface. The force of the explosion threw rock out to form a rim, but a peak remained below the center of the exploding mass, which is characteristic of explosions (see Figure B). The crater rays are believed to be streaks of rock fragments shot outward from the meteoritic explosion. Such explosion particles can travel hundreds of miles because the moon has a small force of gravity and no atmosphere.

Much of the moon's face is covered in fine dust in which billions of stones are embedded. The dust in the Swamp of Putrefaction at the foot of the Apennines (mountains where *Apollo 15* landed) is finely textured; it is somewhat coarser at the *Apollo 14* landing site in the Ocean of Storms. Under the carpet of dust is a layer of broken rocks that varies from 2 to 20 meters in depth.

The six Apollo space missions to the moon brought 2200 lunar rock samples, weighing 400 kilograms (882 pounds), back to Earth. Most of the elements found in

Copyright © 2008 by John Wiley & Sons, Inc.

Crater rim

Crater peak

Crater floor

FIGURE B. CROSS SECTION OF A CRATER

these rocks are original to the moon's formation 4.6 billion years ago. Oxygen is the most abundant element on the moon's surface, as well as on Earth. The presence of a few elements, especially iron, can be ascribed to meteorites and solar wind. There are just 75 varieties of minerals on the moon, as opposed to more than 2000 on Earth. Three of these minerals had never been seen on Earth before the moon rocks arrived: tranquillitite, phroxyferroite, and armalcolite (which has since been discovered in the diamond mines of South Africa).

Copyright © 2008 by John Wiley & Sons, Inc.

LUNAR MESSAGE—VOCABULARY ACTIVITY ON
THE MAN IN THE MOON

Directions

After reading *The Man in the Moon,* fill in the blanks using the clues provided. When you have completed the puzzle, your answers will spell out a three-word message.

Clues

1. *Mare* means _____.

2. Falling meteors have a lot of _____ energy.

3. Godwin wrote a book about fictional moon inhabitants whom he called _____.

4. Legends say that the man in the moon is a _____ who was exiled for punishment.

5. The largest sea on the moon is Mare _____.

6. In the second century B.C.E., Lucian wrote about meeting _____ on his two lunar trips.

7. Meteors striking the moon's surface at a low _____ will produce an elliptical crater.

8. Galileo named dark areas on the moon _____.

9. At one time, astronomers believed that the dark areas on the moon were made of _____.

10. Inside a meteor crater, there is a central _____.

11. The kinetic energy of a meteor is changed to _____ energy on impact.

12. Lines leading away from craters are called _____.

13. The edge of a crater is the _____.

14. Maria are covered with a layer of dark _____.

15. Craters were once believed to be old _____.

16. _____ once meant "crazy due to exposure to moonlight."

17. _____ is a large crater.

18. The moon has a small force of _____ compared to the Earth.

19. The heat energy produced by a meteor's impact is capable of _____ the meteor and surrounding rock.

Copyright © 2008 by John Wiley & Sons, Inc.

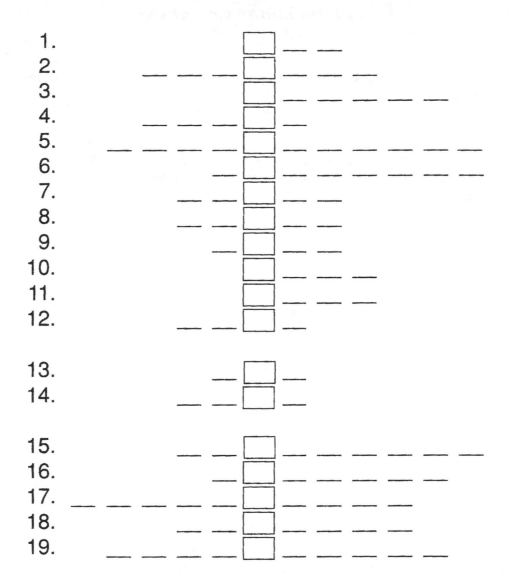

Copyright © 2008 by John Wiley & Sons, Inc.

12-2 MOON MADNESS
Lab on Lunar Craters

Objectives

Students will create craters and study their shapes, examine crater rays, and determine the relative ages of craters.

Teacher Notes

Peas and beans are only one type of material that can be used to form craters. Any small objects that are available in different shapes will do as well. Sand can be used in place of flour. This is a good activity for outdoors.

Copyright © 2008 by John Wiley & Sons, Inc.

MOON MADNESS
Lab on Lunar Craters

Introduction

The moonscape is remarkably different from any landscape on Earth. We can see two distinct types of lunar terrain, one dark and one light. The light areas are called highlands or continents, and the dark areas are called maria (the Latin word for "seas"). The name *maria* is somewhat misleading because there are no seas on the moon.

Most of the geographical features of the moon are associated with craters. A conspicuous depression is the crater Copernicus, named for the famous astronomer. Copernicus is 92 km wide and features a depression with a central peak and walls that appear to be a series of terraces. The outside rim of Copernicus is light colored and is believed to be made of material thrown out of the crater. This rock is called the ejecta blanket, and it forms deposits of white material called rays.

Some lunar geographical features are found only on the maria, such as mare ridges. These wrinkled ridges are several kilometers wide and hundreds of kilometers long. Chain craters are rows of small craters that are only a few kilometers wide. They are found everywhere: in the maria, inside larger craters, and in the highlands. Rilles are another unusual feature of the moon's landscape. These ridges are generally thought to be bounded by faults.

The surface material of the maria is soil that is crumbly but firm. The craters were once believed to have been formed from volcanoes but are now known to be the result of meteoritic impacts. There are a few meteor craters on Earth, and they have the same general shape as the craters on the moon. With a width of only 1.6 km, Meteor Crater in Arizona is small compared to some lunar craters, but it has many traits similar to those on the moon, including a rim and rays.

Materials

White flour	Butter beans
Whole wheat flour	Aluminum pans or pie plates
Kidney beans	Ruler
Peas	Paper and pencil

Procedure

1. Pour 2 to 3 inches of white flour in your aluminum pan.

2. Sprinkle a thin layer of whole wheat flour on top of the white flour. This represents the moon's surface.

3. The peas and beans represent meteors of different sizes and shapes. Designate one person in the lab group as the "thrower." This person must always throw with about the same amount of force. The thrower will toss beans and peas into the pie plate.

Copyright © 2008 by John Wiley & Sons, Inc.

a. Trial 1. To begin the lab, have the thrower toss a pea into the pie plate from directly above the plate with enough force to make a crater. Leave the pea in place. Have the thrower squat beside the plate and throw another pea into the flour, leaving it in place.

b. Trial 2. Repeat these two throws with two butter beans.

c. Trial 3. Repeat these two throws with two kidney beans.

4. Measure the diameter of each crater from three different starting points so that you know the shape of each crater produced. Record your measurements in the data table. Also describe and sketch each crater to answer postlab question 1.

5. Remove the peas and beans very carefully, without disturbing the craters. Observe the craters.

6. Answer the postlab questions.

DATA TABLE: CRATER MEASUREMENTS

Trial	Pea from Above	Pea from Angle	Butter Bean from Above	Butter Bean from Angle	Kidney Bean from Above	Kidney Bean from Angle
1						
2						
3						

Postlab Questions

1. Describe and draw the craters formed by the following throws. Use the back of this sheet if you need more space.

   a. Pea from above

   b. Pea from an angle

   c. Butter bean from above

   d. Butter bean from an angle

   e. Kidney bean from above

   f. Kidney bean from an angle

2. Which craters were formed by peas or beans with the lowest angle of impact: those thrown from above or those thrown from a squat?

3. Were all the craters the same size and shape? Explain your answer.

Copyright © 2008 by John Wiley & Sons, Inc.

4. Why was it important for one student in a lab group to be the only one who threw?

5. After all the beans and peas were removed, could you tell which crater was the oldest (formed first) and which was the youngest (formed last)? How could you tell?

6. Most craters on the moon have a circular shape. Do you think they were formed by the impact of a meteor striking the moon's surface? Explain your answer.

7. Do the craters created in flour have rays? If so, how were these formed?

Copyright © 2008 by John Wiley & Sons, Inc.

12-3 DEAR MOON
Performance Assessment on the Moon's Phases

Objectives

Students will observe the moon for a month and keep a diary describing its appearance.

Teacher Notes

The first part of this experiment requires students to work with others to keep a diary of the moon's phases over 29 days. The second part asks students to develop their own method of demonstrating the way the moon's phases develop. You can use the following rubric to evaluate this activity. Give the students a copy of the rubric before they begin the activity so that they will know how you will assess their work.

Copyright © 2008 by John Wiley & Sons, Inc.

SUGGESTED GRADING RUBRIC

Tasks	4 points	3 points	2 points	1 point
Answered prelab questions correctly	Answered all questions	Answered 3 questions	Answered 2 questions	Answered 1 question
Worked with group to observe moon	Took full responsibility to help observe the moon	Was somewhat helpful in observing the moon	Was not very helpful in observing the moon	Took little responsibility to help observe the moon
Completed Figure B	Completed entire figure	Completed 75% of figure	Completed 50% of figure	Completed 25% of figure
Participated in developing a plan for showing moon phases	Participated completely	Participated some	Participated occasionally	Participated very little
Participated in carrying out the plan to show moon phases	Participated completely	Participated some	Participated occasionally	Participated very little
Answered postlab questions correctly	Answered all questions	Answered 3 questions	Answered 2 questions	Answered 1 question

Comments: _____

_____

Points possible: 24

Points earned: _____

Copyright © 2008 by John Wiley & Sons, Inc.

DEAR MOON
Performance Assessment on the Moon's Phases

Background Information

When you think of the night sky, you most likely envision the moon and stars. Stars are distant, fiery masses of burning gases. Like our sun, stars produce their own light. The moon, in contrast, cannot generate light. We can see the moon because it reflects sunlight. The moon is Earth's only natural satellite, and it revolves around our planet on a path that takes 27.3 days (about a month) to complete. During this time, the moon travels about 240,000 miles (384,000 kilometers)

Going Through a Phase

Because only one-half of the moon is facing the sun, the moon always has a night side and a day side, depending on the sun's position. The amount of sunlit moon visible to us here on Earth depends on the positions of the moon and sun. As the moon travels around Earth, its position relative to the sun changes. As a result, the amount of the sunlit surface that we can see also changes. We describe these changes as moon phases.

When the moon passes between the sun and Earth, the lunar surface nearest us does not receive any sunlight, so it is dark. We describe this phase as a new moon. On the night after the new moon, a thin crescent of the moon can be seen. Each night, the crescent grows larger until it has reached full size almost 28 days later (see Figure A). When the entire surface is lit, the phase is called a full moon. The term *waning* refers to a gradual decrease in size. The opposite of waning is *waxing*, a gradual increase in size. *Gibbous* means that an object has a shape that is larger than a semicircle, but smaller than a circle.

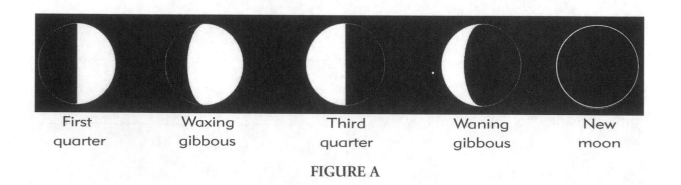

First quarter   Waxing gibbous   Third quarter   Waning gibbous   New moon

FIGURE A

Copyright © 2008 by John Wiley & Sons, Inc.

Prelab Questions

1. The moon does not produce its own light. Why can we see it from Earth?

2. How long does it take the moon to orbit Earth?

3. What causes the phases of the moon?

4. On some nights, there does not seem to be a moon in the sky. Explain why.

Materials

Figure B, the Moon Phase Diary

Flashlight

Styrofoam ball

Stick or ruler (about 12 inches long)

Procedure A: Keep a Moon Diary

1. Work with a group of three or four other students.

2. Each member of the group needs a copy of Figure B, the Moon Phase Diary.

3. Your group will observe the appearance of the moon for 29 nights. As a group, develop a schedule for watching the moon. For example, one person might want to observe and sketch the moon for the first seven days, then let another person take over for the next seven days. Or your group might prefer a schedule in which each member of the group observes for one night out of every four.

4. Write the dates of the next 29 days on the Moon Phase Diary.

5. Each night, the person who is observing the moon should draw its appearance on the Moon Phase Diary.

6. At the end of the 29-day observation period, share your observations with the other students in your group so that everyone can fill in the entire Moon Phase Diary.

Procedure B: Inquiry into Phases

1. Work with the same group of three or four other students.

2. Your group needs a flashlight, Styrofoam ball, and stick or ruler.

3. As a group, devise a plan for using these materials to demonstrate how the moon goes through its phases.

4. Write your plan on a piece of paper and show it to your teacher. If your teacher approves of your plan, carry it out. If not, revise your plan and resubmit it.

5. Answer the postlab questions.

Copyright © 2008 by John Wiley & Sons, Inc.

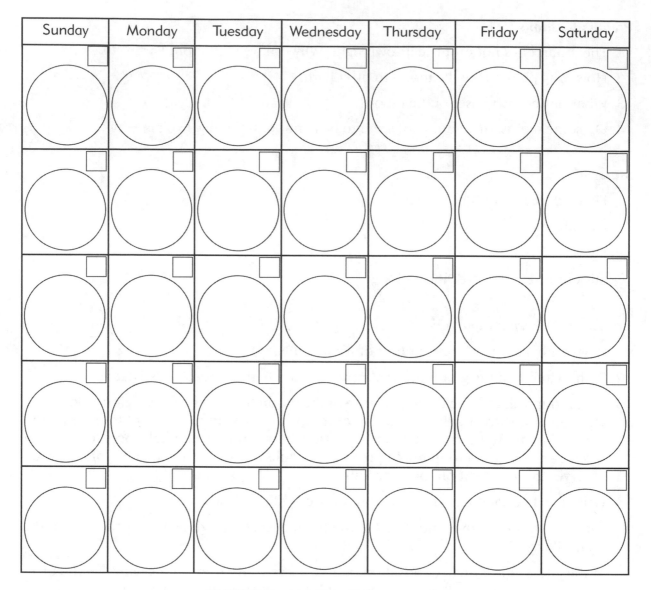

FIGURE B. MOON PHASE DIARY

Postlab Questions

1. Explain how the amount of sunlight on the moon's surface changes during its orbit.

2. Why can't you see the new moon? During what phase can you see one entire side of the moon?

3. On the basis of your observations, predict what kind of moon we will have tonight. What kind of moon will we have for the next five evenings?

4. What did you use to represent the moon? What did you use to represent the sun?

Copyright © 2008 by John Wiley & Sons, Inc.

Copyright © 2008 by John Wiley & Sons, Inc.

LESSON 13: SPACE TRAVEL

13-1 THE SPACE SHUTTLE
Content on Space Travel

❧❧❧

Early Flight

For centuries, humans have dreamed of traveling into space. The technology to make those dreams come true did not evolve until the mid-1900s. Manned space travel developed in stages. Early spacecraft were unmanned missiles that arced through the upper atmosphere. Later, rockets were launched into orbit around Earth. The next step was to send animals into space to see how travel would affect them.

By the 1960s, human travelers took the place of animals. The Mercury program was the first U.S. attempt at human travel in space. In May 1961, astronaut Alan B. Shepard Jr. was launched from Cape Canaveral in the *Freedom 7* Mercury craft. During his 15-minute suborbital mission, he traveled 116 miles into space, then splashed down in the ocean 300 miles from his launch site. In February 1962, John H. Glenn Jr. became the first American to orbit Earth, circling it three times in *Friendship 7*. Glenn's craft was about 95 feet tall and used RP-1 (refined kerosene) and liquid oxygen for fuel.

The Gemini program was developed to send two-man crews on longer trips. A Gemini spacecraft consisted of a two-part ship: a reentry module containing a life-support cabin and an adapter module. Only the reentry module returned to Earth, where it crash-landed into an unoccupied location in the sea. The *Gemini 11* mission reached a record altitude of 853 miles. Gemini ships were 108 feet tall and used UDMH (unsymmetrical dimethylhydrazine) and nitrogen tetroxide for fuel.

The Apollo program sent the first manned spacecraft to the moon. Between 1968 and 1972, eleven manned Apollo flights took place. The first man to walk on the moon, Neil Armstrong, did so on the 1969 Apollo mission. The U.S. Skylab program began in 1973 and put a space station in place. This relatively large space environment permitted three astronauts to remain in space for weeks at a time.

Reusable Spacecraft

Space shuttles, the first reusable manned space craft developed in the United States, appeared on the scene in 1981. The shuttles can take off like rockets, orbit Earth like spaceships, and land like airplanes. Shuttles were designed to deliver heavy payloads, such as satellites, to space and to repair objects already orbiting Earth. Each

183

space shuttle has three components: two solid rocket boosters, an external tank, and a winged orbiter. In the solid rockets, the propellant is a mixture of aluminum powder, aluminum perchorate powder, and iron oxide catalyst held together by a polymer binder. This fuel produces a thrust of 3.1 million pounds for the first few seconds, and it burns out completely in 2 minutes. Fuel tanks store 140,000 gallons of liquid oxygen and 380,000 gallons of liquid nitrogen. These tanks feed into the main engines during the 8-minute ascent into orbit, and then they are discarded. The fuel tanks are the only disposable parts of the space shuttle.

Each orbiter has a size and shape similar to a DC-9 jetliner and is intended to last for about 100 flights. The first orbiter, *Enterprise,* was designed for atmospheric flight tests. Since that time, five other orbiters have been built: *Columbia, Challenger, Discovery, Atlantis,* and *Endeavour.* Each orbiter is covered with a special silicon-based insulation in the form of 100-square-inch tiles. These lightweight tiles can survive temperatures of up to 1260 degrees Celsius, and they protect the orbiter during reentry into Earth's atmosphere. Although most space shuttle flights have been safe and successful, there have been serious problems. The *Challenger* and its crew were lost in an accident in 1986.

The space shuttle can carry a crew of two to eight people. Space flight no longer requires intensively trained, physically perfect astronauts. The low-acceleration launch and low-deceleration reentry produce forces that normal, healthy people can tolerate (1.5 *g* to 3 *g*). Scientists and technicians now fly along with the pilot and crew.

In a space shuttle, astronauts live in a two-floor, pressurized cabin in the nose section. The top floor consists of the flight deck and a work area, and the bottom floor houses living quarters, the galley, and bathrooms. The cabin is maintained with microgravity, a condition that seems weightless because the astronauts are in free fall all the time.

Problems in Space Travel

Microgravity produces special problems for travelers. For example, food and beverage particles cannot be allowed to escape because they float around the craft. Food trays have clasps that hold dishes in place. Astronauts dine on food that is preserved by dehydration, because a heavy refrigerator cannot be carried into space. A convection oven makes it possible for astronauts to warm a variety of foods to maintain their diet of 3000 calories per day.

Because the shuttle cabin is small, people are close together, and microbes find plenty of opportunity to grow. Dirty clothes are sealed in airtight plastic bags to avoid bacterial infection. To minimize the number of water droplets floating in the shuttle, sponge baths are the only form of bathing permitted. Men shave with shaving cream and water to prevent loose whiskers from floating away. Toilets on the shuttle are similar to gravity toilets but depend on air to force wastes into plastic bags.

Crew members must exercise to maintain muscle strength. One of the special problems of weightlessness is mineral loss from bones due to lack of force exerted on them. Some astronauts suffer from space adaptation syndrome, a form of motion sickness.

Copyright © 2008 by John Wiley & Sons, Inc.

The Travelers

Shuttle crew members include the commander and pilot, who are responsible for the safety of the crew and the success of the mission. A mission coordinator plans the crew activities, keeps track of use of consumables, and performs experiments. Payload specialists are often technicians or scientists who have specialized duties on each flight.

Copyright © 2008 by John Wiley & Sons, Inc.

LANDING SPACECRAFT—VOCABULARY ACTIVITY ON
THE SPACE SHUTTLE

Directions

After reading *The Space Shuttle,* draw a circle around the shuttle in each group that *cannot* land on the air strip because it carries a term that is different.

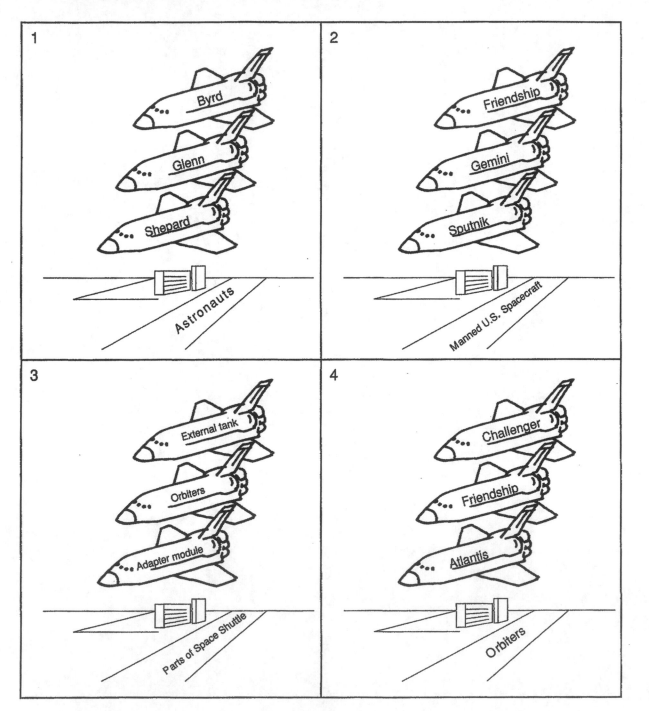

Copyright © 2008 by John Wiley & Sons, Inc.

Copyright © 2008 by John Wiley & Sons, Inc.

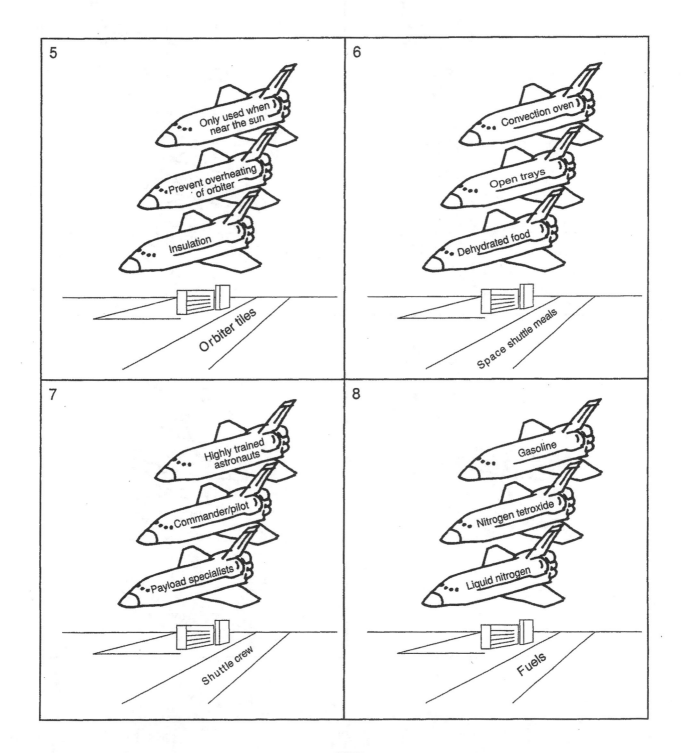

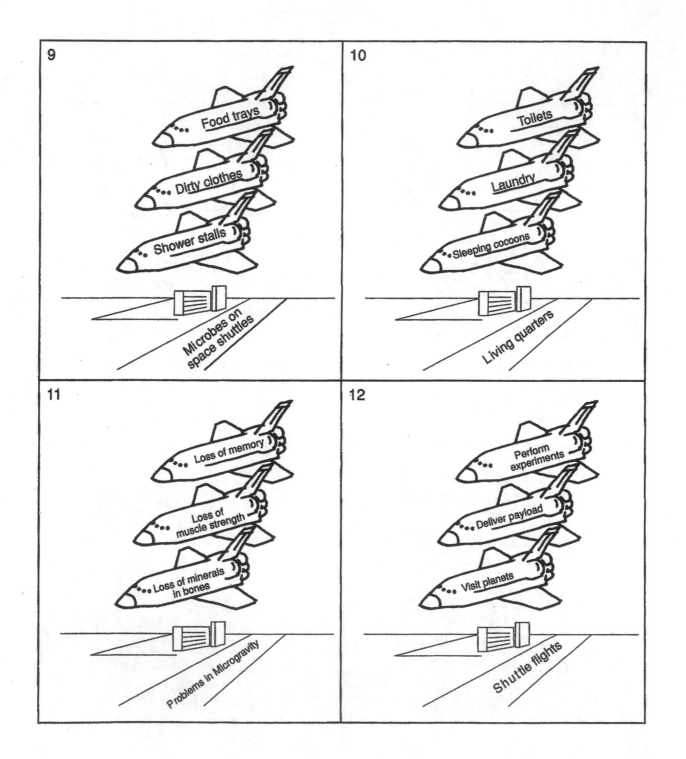

Copyright © 2008 by John Wiley & Sons, Inc.

13-2 DESIGN A SPACECRAFT
Performance Assessment on Designing an Original Space Vehicle

Objectives

Students will design an original spacecraft that could theoretically carry out the following tasks:

1. Travel in space

2. Land on the moon

3. Depart from the moon

4. Land on Mars

5. Depart from Mars

6. Return to Earth and land

Students will describe the needs of the crew (materials or conditions that are necessary for the crew during space travel) and will design their living quarters.

Teacher Notes

Students may want to have a competition for the best spacecraft. Students, teachers, or parents might be asked to act as judges. Students can extend this activity by doing research in the library and on the Internet on spacecraft, the moon, and Mars. If you want to study all the planets and Pluto with this unit, ask students to design spacecraft that can visit Mercury, Venus, Jupiter, Saturn, Uranus, Neptune, and Pluto.

An optional checklist to help evaluate student progress follows.

Requirements	Not Yet (0 points)	Some Evidence (1 point)
Type of fuel selected and explanation for this choice		
Size and shape of spacecraft and explanation for these choices		
Design features to protect craft from heat and cold and explanation for these choices		
Supplies required by crew and explanation for these choices		
Location and means of storing supplies and explanations for these choices		
Projected length of trip and explanation for this projection		
Possible hazards and problems and explanation for how these will be handled		

Comments: _____

Points possible: 7

Points earned: _____

189

Copyright © 2008 by John Wiley & Sons, Inc.

DESIGN A SPACECRAFT
Performance Assessment on Designing an Original Space Vehicle

Background Information

Space travel in the future will take humans to places they only dream about today. As the space program advances, more and more people will be able to enjoy space flight, and ships will become more comfortable and faster.

We can only guess what the fuels of the future will be. Solar energy seems like a viable option for flights near the sun. Solar wind, which is made of charged particles from the sun, may be another source of energy for spaceships. Nuclear energy and solid rocket fuel are the two methods that we currently use, and they may still be practical fuel choices in the future.

The moon is the most likely place for us to visit. Traveling to the moon will require special considerations for the crew and ship. Visits to Mars may even be an option one day. See Table 1 for a description of characteristics of the moon and Mars.

TABLE 1. CHARACTERISTICS OF THE MOON AND MARS

Characteristic	Moon	Mars
Distance from Earth	239,000 miles	48,600,000 miles
Diameter	¼ Earth's diameter	½ Earth's diameter
Gravity	⅙ Earth's gravity	⅓ Earth's gravity
Atmosphere	None	Thin carbon dioxide; 1% air pressure of Earth
Day length	29 Earth days	24 hours, 37 minutes
Trip time	3 days	1.88 Earth years
Communication time	2.6-sec. round trip	10- to 41-minute round trip

Copyright © 2008 by John Wiley & Sons, Inc.

Materials

Art supplies (such as paper, scissors, glue, modeling clay, aluminum foil)

Procedure

1. The job of your group is to design a spacecraft that will allow a crew to travel to the moon, to Mars, then back to Earth. When designing your spacecraft, consider these key issues:

    a. What type of fuel will be needed?

    b. What is the shape and size of the spacecraft?

    c. What special design features will protect the craft from heat and cold?

    d. What supplies will the crew need?

    e. How and where will the supplies be stored on the spacecraft?

    f. How long will the trip last?

    g. What environmental hazards or special problems might the crew encounter along the way?

2. Use the Internet or resource books from the library to help you design the spacecraft. As you work, record your design plans on the table.

3. On the table, draw an illustration of the inside and outside of your craft.

4. Make a model of this spacecraft using various art supplies.

Copyright © 2008 by John Wiley & Sons, Inc.

SPACECRAFT WORKSHEET

Feature	Reason/Explanation
Fuel used by your spacecraft	
Shape and size of craft	
Special environmental protective devices	
Crew size	
Crew requirements	
Supplies required by crew	
Other necessary supplies	
Method of storing supplies	
Time required for trip	

Illustrations

Sketch of Interior	Sketch of Exterior

Copyright © 2008 by John Wiley & Sons, Inc.

SECTION 4

Chemistry

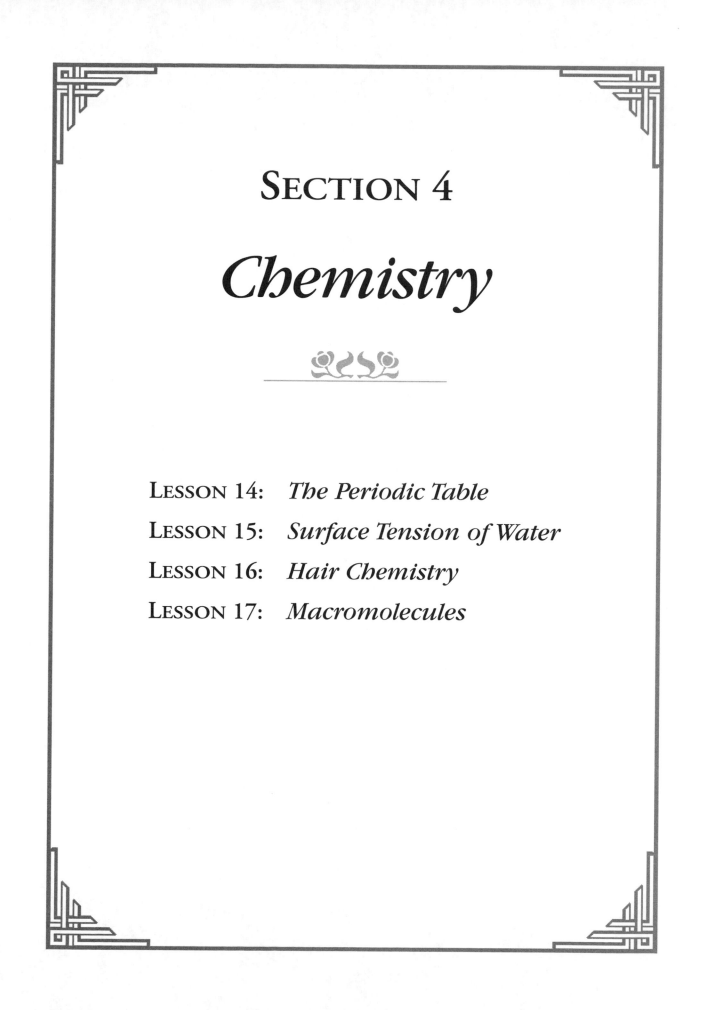

LESSON 14: THE PERIODIC TABLE

14-1 PERIODIC PROPERTIES
Content on Periodicity of Elements

Elements

Most science classrooms display a large chart with symbols and numbers, the periodic table of elements (see Figure A). On the table, the elements are represented by abbreviations made of one or two letters. An element is composed of just one type of atom. An atom of an element contains a specific number of protons, represented by its atomic number, and an equal number of electrons. The combined number of protons and neutrons in an atom is that element's atomic mass. There are 112 known elements today. Elements whose atomic numbers range from 1 to 92 are naturally occurring; those with atomic numbers 93 through 112 were produced during experiments.

Periodic Table

In the mid-1800s, only about half the elements on today's periodic table had been discovered. Dmitry Mendeleev, a Russian scientist born in 1834, tried to organize the elements. Mendeleev arranged the elements in several rows, or periods, according to atomic mass. In this arrangement, he noticed that he had three missing elements, so he left blank spaces for them. He saw that some elements had similar chemical and physical characteristics, such as boiling point, melting point, density, atomic mass, and bonding power. He arranged the elements so that those with similar properties were close to each other. Mendeleev recognized repeating or periodic patterns in the properties of the elements in each row. On the basis of the characteristics of elements adjacent to the blank spaces, he predicted the properties of the missing elements. Within sixteen years, the elements were discovered and analyzed, and Mendeleev's predictions proved correct.

Periodic Trends

Mendeleev discovered an important concept that is still true today: elements on the periodic table show periodicity, regularly occurring chemical and physical traits. The trends can be understood by analyzing the arrangements of electrons of elements.

Copyright © 2008 by John Wiley & Sons, Inc.

The Modern Periodic Table of Elements

Average relative masses are 2001 values, rounded to two decimal places.

All average masses are to be treated as measured quantities, and subject to significant figure rules. Do not round them further when performing calculations.

Element name →
Atomic number →

Mercury
80
Hg
200.59 ← Average mass
1.9 ← Electronegativity

Symbol →

1																	18
Hydrogen 1 **H** 1.01 2.1	2											13	14	15	16	17	Helium 2 **He** 4.00 —
Lithium 3 **Li** 6.94 1.0	Beryllium 4 **Be** 9.01 1.5											Boron 5 **B** 10.81 2.0	Carbon 6 **C** 12.01 2.5	Nitrogen 7 **N** 14.01 3.0	Oxygen 8 **O** 16.00 3.5	Fluorine 9 **F** 19.00 4.0	Neon 10 **Ne** 20.18 —
Sodium 11 **Na** 22.99 0.9	Magnesium 12 **Mg** 24.31 1.2	3	4	5	6	7	8	9	10	11	12	Aluminium 13 **Al** 26.98 1.5	Silicon 14 **Si** 28.09 1.8	Phosphorus 15 **P** 30.97 2.1	Sulfur 16 **S** 32.07 2.5	Chlorine 17 **Cl** 35.45 3.0	Argon 18 **Ar** 39.95 —
Potassium 19 **K** 39.10 0.8	Calcium 20 **Ca** 40.08 1.0	Scandium 21 **Sc** 44.96 1.3	Titanium 22 **Ti** 47.88 1.5	Vanadium 23 **V** 50.94 1.6	Chromium 24 **Cr** 52.00 1.6	Manganese 25 **Mn** 54.94 1.5	Iron 26 **Fe** 55.85 1.8	Cobalt 27 **Co** 58.93 1.8	Nickel 28 **Ni** 58.69 1.8	Copper 29 **Cu** 63.55 1.9	Zinc 30 **Zn** 65.39 1.6	Gallium 31 **Ga** 69.72 1.6	Germanium 32 **Ge** 72.61 1.8	Arsenic 33 **As** 74.92 2.0	Selenium 34 **Se** 78.95 2.4	Bromine 35 **Br** 79.90 2.8	Krypton 36 **Kr** 83.80 3.0
Rubidium 37 **Rb** 85.47 0.8	Strontium 38 **Sr** 87.62 1.0	Yttrium 39 **Y** 86.91 1.2	Zirconium 40 **Zr** 91.22 1.4	Niobium 41 **Nb** 92.91 1.6	Molybdenum 42 **Mo** 95.94 1.8	Technetium 43 **Tc** (98) 1.9	Ruthenium 44 **Ru** 101.07 2.2	Rhodium 45 **Rh** 102.91 2.2	Palladium 46 **Pd** 106.42 2.2	Silver 47 **Ag** 107.87 1.9	Cadmium 48 **Cd** 112.41 1.7	Indium 49 **In** 114.82 1.7	Tin 50 **Sn** 118.71 1.8	Antimony 51 **Sb** 121.76 1.9	Tellurium 52 **Te** 127.60 2.1	Iodine 53 **I** 126.90 2.5	Xenon 54 **Xe** 131.29 2.6
Cesium 55 **Cs** 132.91 0.7	Barium 56 **Ba** 137.33 0.9	57–70 *	Lutetium 71 **Lu** 174.97 1.1	Hafnium 72 **Hf** 178.49 1.3	Tantalum 73 **Ta** 180.95 1.5	Tungsten 74 **W** 183.84 1.7	Rhenium 75 **Re** 185.21 1.9	Osmium 76 **Os** 190.23 2.2	Iridium 77 **Ir** 192.22 2.2	Platinum 78 **Pt** 195.08 2.2	Gold 79 **Au** 196.97 2.4	Mercury 80 **Hg** 200.59 1.9	Thallium 81 **Tl** 204.38 1.8	Lead 82 **Pb** 207.20 1.9	Bismuth 83 **Bi** 208.98 1.9	Polonium 84 **Po** (209) 2.0	Astatine 85 **At** (210) 2.2	Radon 86 **Rn** (222) 2.4
Francium 87 **Fr** (223) 0.7	Radium 88 **Ra** (226) 0.9	89–102 **	Lawrencium 103 **Lr** (262) —	Rutherfordium 104 **Rf** (261) —	Dubnium 105 **Db** (262) —	Seaborgium 106 **Sg** (263) —	Bohrium 107 **Bh** (262) —	Hassium 108 **Hs** (265) —	Meitnerium 109 **Mt** (266) —	Ununnilium 110 **Uun** (271) —	Unununium 111 **Uuu** (272) —	Ununbium 112 **Uub** (277) —	Ununtrium 113 **Uut** (284) —	Ununquadium 114 **Uuq** (289) —	Ununpentium 115 **Uup** (289) —	Ununhexium 116 **Uuh** (291) —	Ununoctium 118 **Uuo** (294) —

*lanthanides

Lanthanum 57 **La** 138.91 1.1	Cerium 58 **Ce** 140.12 1.1	Praseodymium 59 **Pr** 140.91 1.1	Neodymium 60 **Nd** 144.24 1.1	Promethium 61 **Pm** (145) 1.1	Samarium 62 **Sm** 150.36 1.1	Europium 63 **Eu** 151.97 1.1	Gadolinium 64 **Gd** 157.25 1.1	Terbium 65 **Tb** 158.93 1.1	Dysprosium 66 **Dy** 162.50 1.2	Holmium 67 **Ho** 164.93 1.2	Erbium 68 **Er** 167.26 1.2	Thulium 69 **Tm** 168.93 1.3	Ytterbium 70 **Yb** 173.04 1.1

**actinides

Actinium 89 **Ac** (227) 1.1	Thorium 90 **Th** 232.04 1.3	Protactinium 91 **Pa** 231.04 1.5	Uranium 92 **U** 238.03 1.4	Neptunium 93 **Np** (237) 1.4	Plutonium 94 **Pu** (244) 1.3	Americium 95 **Am** (243) 1.3	Curium 96 **Cm** (247) 1.3	Berkelium 97 **Bk** (247) 1.3	Californium 98 **Cf** (251) 1.3	Einsteinium 99 **Es** (252) 1.3	Fermium 100 **Fm** (257) 1.3	Mendelevium 101 **Md** (258) 1.3	Nobelium 102 **No** (259) 1.3

FIGURE A

Copyright © 2008 by John Wiley & Sons, Inc.

Copyright © 2008 by John Wiley & Sons, Inc.

Atoms are stable when their valence electrons, the ones in the outermost orbits, are in the octet formation. An octet is a set of eight electrons, which is a full outer orbit. Some atoms reach the octet formation by losing a few electrons; other atoms get there by gaining electrons. The elements that naturally have stable octets make up the far right-hand side column of the periodic table. These inert gases are described as noble gases because of this electron configuration.

The number of protons, neutrons, and electrons in an atom determines the size of the atom's nucleus. Moving from left to right across a row of the periodic table, the number of electrons increases. As this occurs, the electrons in the outermost orbits are attracted to the nucleus with increasing strength. As a result, electrons are bound closer and closer to the center of the atom as their number increases. Consequently, the atomic radius gets smaller as you move from left to right across a period.

As you move down through any column, which is also called a group, the number of valence electrons in atoms remains constant. However, the number of filled inner levels of electrons increases. These inner levels shield the nucleus, reducing the pull on electrons and increasing the diameter of the atoms. As a result, the atomic radius gets larger as you move down a column.

Bonding Power

The energy needed to remove an electron from a gaseous atom or ion is called its ionization energy. The closer and more tightly an electron is held to an atom, the harder it is to remove, so the higher its ionization energy. On the periodic table, ionization energy increases from left to right across a period (as atomic radius decreases). As you look down a column, ionization energy decreases (as atomic radius increases).

Electronegativity is related to ionization energy. Atoms that have high electronegativity have a lot of energy for attracting electrons that form chemical bonds. The higher the electronegativity of an atom, the stronger its ability to attract bonding electrons. Moving across a period, electronegativity increases. Moving down a group, electronegativity decreases. The trends on the periodic table are summarized below.

Moving left to right on the periodic table,

- Atomic radius decreases.

- Ionization energy increases.

- Electronegativity increases.

Moving top to bottom on the periodic table,

- Atomic radius increases.

- Ionization energy decreases.

- Electronegativity decreases.

PERIODIC CROSSWORD—VOCABULARY ACTIVITY ON PERIODIC PROPERTIES

Across

4. Atoms have the same number of protons and _____.

6. Formation of stable electrons

9. Energy for attracting bonding electrons

14. There are _____ electrons in an octet.

15. Electrons in the outermost electron level of an atom

16. Moving left to right across the periodic table, the number of electrons in atoms _____.

Copyright © 2008 by John Wiley & Sons, Inc.

Vocabulary Activity on Periodic Properties (*continued*)

Down

1. Moving left to right across the periodic table, atomic radius _____.

2. Column on the periodic table

3. Energy needed to remove an electron from an atom

5. Number of protons in an atom (2 words)

7. Developed the first periodic table

8. Row on the periodic table

10. Elements are arranged by characteristics on the periodic _____.

11. Number of protons and neutrons in an atom (2 words)

12. Group of gases that naturally have stable octets

13. Smallest particle of an element

Word List

ATOM	EIGHT	INCREASES	OCTET
ATOMIC MASS	ELECTRONEGATIVITY	IONIZATION	PERIOD
ATOMIC NUMBER	ELECTRONS	MENDELEEV	TABLE
DECREASES	GROUP	NOBLE	VALENCE

Copyright © 2008 by John Wiley & Sons, Inc.

14-2 TREND SETTERS
Lab on Density Trends in Family 14

Objectives

Students will experimentally determine the density of three elements in Family 14, then use their results to make predictions about the density of other elements in the family.

Teacher Notes

Make a copy of the answer sheet for each student or for each lab group. Each lab group will need 2.0 to 5.0 grams each of silicon, tin, and lead.

Copyright © 2008 by John Wiley & Sons, Inc.

Copyright © 2008 by John Wiley & Sons, Inc.

TREND SETTERS
Lab on Density Trends in Family 14

Introduction

The periodic table contains a wealth of information for those who know how to interpret it. The placement of horizontal rows, called series or periods, indicates how many energy (or electron) shells are located in the elements in that row. The position of columns, called families or groups, holds clues as to how many outer shell electrons, or valence electrons, the elements contain. Therefore, knowing the series and the family to which an element belongs reveals some of the properties of that element.

Certain trends occur throughout a series or a family. If you know the properties of one or two elements in a row, you can make predictions about the properties of other elements in that row. For example, potassium belongs to series 4 and family 1. This tells us that potassium has four energy shells and that the last shell has only one electron. Because of the arrangement of its electrons, potassium is constantly trying to give away that one lone electron on the last shell, so it is very reactive. When you go from the top to the bottom of family 1, the elements increase in reactivity. These are all metals, and when placed in water they react to produce heat and light. Lithium, at the top of family 1, is the least reactive element in the family. As you move down the family, the reactivity with water increases.

In this lab, you will study the trends in another property of elements: density, a measure of mass per unit volume. By performing a series of experiments, you will be able to determine how density changes as you move from the top to the bottom of family 14.

Prelab Questions

1. Explain the difference between a period and a family.

2. What kinds of information on elements can you derive from the periodic table?

3. Elements in family 1 have one electron in their outer orbits. How many electrons would you expect to find in the outer orbits of elements in family 2? Why?

4. The term *periodic* means "recurring in a predictable, regular pattern." Why is *periodic* a good descriptor of the periodic table?

5. Make a prediction as to how you think the density of elements will change as you move down a family on the periodic table.

Materials

10 ml graduated cylinder	Pieces of tin (Sn)
Weighing boats	Pieces of lead shot (Pb)
Metric ruler	Pieces of silicon (Si)
Electronic balance	Graph paper

Procedure

1. Use the weighing boat to collect between 2.0 and 5.0 grams of silicon. Use the electronic balance to determine the exact mass of the silicon pieces you collect. The silicon you collect must be small enough to fit inside a 10 ml graduated cylinder. Record the exact mass of your silicon on the data table on the answer sheet. Place this sample to the side for later use.

2. Use the weighing boat to collect between 2.0 and 5.0 grams of tin. Use the electronic balance to determine the exact mass of the tin pieces you collect. The tin you collect must be small enough to fit inside a 10 ml graduated cylinder. Record the exact mass of your tin on the data table on the answer sheet. Place this sample to the side for later use.

3. Use the weighing boat to collect between 2.0 and 5.0 grams of lead. Use the electronic balance to determine the exact mass of the lead pieces you collect. The lead you collect must be small enough to fit inside a 10 ml graduated cylinder. Record the exact mass of your lead on the data table on the answer sheet. Place this sample to the side for later use.

4. Pour exactly 6 ml of water into a graduated cylinder. Add your sample of silicon to the graduated cylinder. Examine the graduated cylinder to determine the water level of the water and silicon. The difference between the new water level and the original water level is the volume of the silicon sample. Record this volume on the data table. Pour off the water and dry your wet pieces of metal. Return them to the supply area.

6. Repeat step 5 for tin and record your answer on the data table on the answer sheet.

7. Repeat step 5 for lead and record your answer on the data table on the answer sheet.

8. Calculate the density of each element by dividing the mass of each element sample by the volume each element sample occupied. Record these values on the data table on the answer sheet.

Postlab Questions

1. Which sample had the greatest volume?

2. Which sample had the greatest density?

3. What units are used to express density in this lab?

4. Make a bar graph that compares the density and atomic number of the three elements on the data table. Place atomic numbers on the x-axis and density on the y-axis. Make an equal number of divisions between your numbers.

5. How does density change as you go down a group in the periodic table?

6. Use your graph to estimate the density of germanium (Ge, atomic number 32) and carbon (C, atomic number 6).

7. Calculate the percentage of error of the density you determined for each of the three elements. Show your work and circle your final answer. Your teacher will give you the actual

Copyright © 2008 by John Wiley & Sons, Inc.

(accepted or correct) density of each of these elements to use in your calculation. Use the following formula:

Percentage of error = [(observed density – accepted density) ÷ accepted density] × 100%

8. What were some possible sources of error in this lab?

9. Write a paragraph using all of the following words to explain what you learned in this lab. Underline each word as you use it in context in the paragraph. Words: *density, family 14, valence electrons, increase, atomic number, trend* or *pattern, periodic table, silicon, lead, tin.*

Copyright © 2008 by John Wiley & Sons, Inc.

LAB ON DENSITY TRENDS IN FAMILY 14
Student Answer Sheet

Name _____ Date _____

Partners _____ Lab area _____

Prelab Questions

1. _____

_____

2. _____

_____

3. _____

_____

4. _____

_____

5. _____

_____

DATA TABLE

Measurement	Silicon	Tin	Lead
Mass of each element (g)			
Volume of the element (ml)			
Density of each element (g/ml)			

Postlab Questions

1. _____

2. _____

Copyright © 2008 by John Wiley & Sons, Inc.

3. _____

4. Answer on graph paper.

5. _____

6. _____

7. Density calculations. Show your work and circle your final answers.

Silicon	
Tin	
Lead	

8. _____

_____

9.

Copyright © 2008 by John Wiley & Sons, Inc.

14-3 BERTH OF A PERIODIC TABLE
Activity on What the Periodic Table Reveals to Scientists

Objectives

Students will use the modern periodic table, clues, and technology to develop a periodic table for the fictitious planet Berth that mirrors Earth's periodic table.

Teacher Notes

Give each lab group a set of Berth element cards and a copy of the Blank Template for Berth Elements and the Elements from Earth's Periodic Table.

Copyright © 2008 by John Wiley & Sons, Inc.

Balloonium (Bl)	Gasite (Gt)	Rockite (R)	Sandide (Sd)	Medicon (M)
Atomic #: _____	Atomic #: _____	Atomic #: _____	Atomic #: _____	Atomic #: _____
Atomic mass: _____	Atomic mass: _____	Atomic mass: _____	Atomic mass: _____	Atomic mass: _____
Series: _____	Series: _____	Series: 2	Series: _____	Series: 3
Group: _____	Group: _____	Group: _____	Group: _____	Group: _____
State: _____	State: Gas	State: _____	State: _____	State: _____
Fact: Lightest noble gas on planet	Fact: Most chemically active of all nonmetals	Fact: This element is classified as a metalloid.	Fact: This metalloid is a common component of the metallic oxide, sand.	Use: Metal used to make Epsom salts
	Use: _____	Use: _____	Use: _____	

Atmospherium (A)	Universium (U)	Toxigas (Tg)	Malleabium (Ma)	Nocorrodium (Nc)
Atomic #: _____	Atomic #: _____	Atomic #: _____	Atomic #: _____	Atomic #: _____
Atomic mass: _____	Atomic mass: _____	Atomic mass: _____	Atomic mass: _____	Atomic mass: _____
Series: 2	Series: _____	Series: 3	Series: 3	Series: _____
Group: _____	Group: _____	Group: _____	Group: 13	Group: 2
State: _____	State: _____	State: _____	State: _____	State: _____
Fact: During electrical storms, this element can form ozone.	Fact: Heaviest noble gas on planet	Fact: In its diatomic form, this element becomes a toxic green gas.	Fact: _____	Fact: Weight per weight, this metal is stronger than steel.
		Use: _____	Use: _____	

Floatium (Ft)	Coatide (Ci)	Explosium (Ex)	Bonine (Bn)	Saltium (Sa)
Atomic #: _____	Atomic #: _____	Atomic #: _____	Atomic #: _____	Atomic #: _____
Atomic mass: _____	Atomic mass: _____	Atomic mass: _____	Atomic mass: _____	Atomic mass: _____
Series: 1	Series: _____	Series: _____	Series: _____	Series: _____
Group: _____	Group: _____	Group: _____	Group: 2	Group: _____
State: _____	State: _____	State: _____	State: _____	State: _____
Fact: This element has 1 proton.	Fact: This element has 50 electrons.	Use: When combined with nitrate, this alkali metal is used for explosives.	Use: Most abundant mineral in the human body	Use: Alkali metal found in table salt
Use: _____	Use: _____			

Copyright © 2008 by John Wiley & Sons, Inc.

Lightemupium (Lp)

Atomic #: _____

Atomic mass: _____

Series: _____

Group: _____

State: _____

Use: Noble gas used in electric light bulbs

Ammonite (Ae)

Atomic #: _____

Atomic mass: _____

Series: _____

Group: _____

State: _____

Fact: This element composes 79% of the Earth's atmosphere.

Use: _____

Reactium (R)

Atomic #: _____

Atomic mass: _____

Series: _____

Group: 1

State: _____

Fact: _____
_____

Pyrotechnium (Py)

Atomic #: _____

Atomic mass: _____

Series: _____

Group: _____

State: _____

Fact: Heaviest of the alkaline earth metals

Use: Commonly used in pyrotechnics

Glowium (G)

Atomic #: _____

Atomic mass: _____

Series: _____

Group: _____

State: _____

Use: Noble gas commonly used in glowing signs

Hotium (Ho)

Atomic #: _____

Atomic mass: _____

Series: 5

Group: _____

State: _____

Fact: Has properties very similar to Changium but has almost twice its atomic mass

Covalentite (Cv)

Atomic #: _____

Atomic mass: _____

Series: _____

Group: 15

State: _____

Fact: Metalloid

Use: _____

Organican (Or)

Atomic #: _____

Atomic mass: _____

Series: _____

Group: _____

State: _____

Fact: Has four electrons in its outer energy shell. It has the lowest atomic mass in its family.

Use: _____

Liquidite (Ld)

Atomic #: _____

Atomic mass: _____

Series: _____

Group: _____

State: _____

Fact: The only nonmetal that is liquid at room temperature

Use: _____

Semicondite (Sm)

Atomic #: _____

Atomic mass: _____

Series: _____

Group: _____

State: Solid

Fact: Mendeleev predicted the discovery of this element, which he called ekasilicon.

Use: _____

Painteon (Pa)

Atomic #: _____

Atomic mass: _____

Series: 3

Group: _____

State: _____

Fact: This element needs two more electrons in its outer shell to reach an octet.

Use: _____

Redpowderite (Rd)

Atomic #: _____

Atomic mass: _____

Series: _____

Group: 16

State: _____

Fact: The heaviest of the elements in this family

Use: _____

Matchium (Mc)

Atomic #: _____

Atomic mass: _____

Series: _____

Group: _____

State: _____

Fact: This element has properties similar to Ammonite.

Use: This element is used to make the head of matches.

Sparkese (Sp)

Atomic #: _____

Atomic mass: _____

Series: 2

Group: _____

State: _____

Fact: Very reactive metal with only two energy shells

Changium (Cg)

Atomic #: _____

Atomic mass: _____

Series: _____

Group: 13

State: _____

Fact: Solid at room temperature but becomes liquid when heated slightly

Copyright © 2008 by John Wiley & Sons, Inc.

BLANK TEMPLATE FOR BERTH ELEMENTS

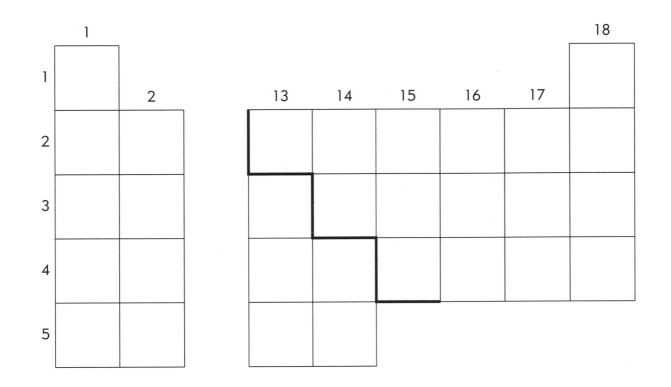

Copyright © 2008 by John Wiley & Sons, Inc.

ELEMENTS FROM EARTH'S PERIODIC TABLE

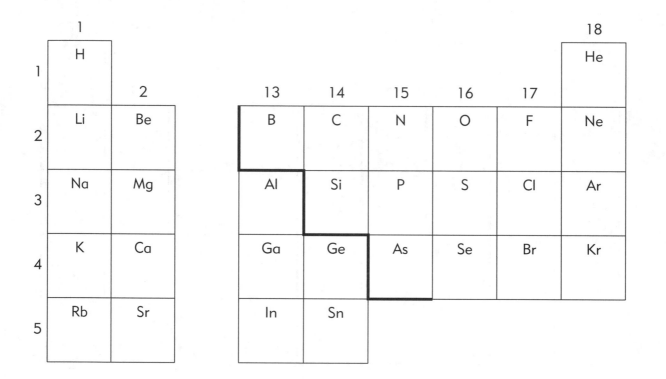

Copyright © 2008 by John Wiley & Sons, Inc.

Berth of a Periodic Table
Activity on What the Periodic Table Reveals to Scientists

Introduction

In the mid-nineteenth century, chemists were faced with a challenge. New elements were being discovered, and scientists were performing experiments on the elements to determine their properties. Valuable scientific data were accumulating at a fast pace, and scientists needed a way to organize and interpret them.

Dmitry Mendeleev set out to find a way to lend order to the chaos of information that existed about these elements. Mendeleev, an avid card player, wrote information about each of the 63 elements known at that time on a separate playing card. He spent countless hours arranging and rearranging the cards in columns and rows, looking for a pattern in the elemental properties.

Eventually Mendeleev found that when he arranged the cards in order of increasing atomic weight, the elements lined up naturally into groups with similar properties. When there was no known element to fit into a particular slot, he left the slot blank. He left three blank spaces or gaps on his periodic table and predicted the properties and masses of these undiscovered elements. Within 16 years all three were discovered, and he was proven correct.

In a few cases, the recurring patterns of properties did not match the order of atomic weights. Mendeleev insisted that the weights were wrong and switched the order of certain elements so that they stayed in their columns with similar properties. Mendeleev was not wholly correct, because he based his periodic table on increasing atomic mass, but his system was a tremendous advance. Today the periodic table has been revised and is based on increasing atomic number rather than atomic mass. But the work of Mendeleev established the foundation for our modern periodic table and all it reveals about the properties of the elements.

In this activity, you will use the modern periodic table; 30 cards of elements from a planet in another galaxy, Berth; and Internet or other references to help you devise a periodic table for Berth's elements.

Prelab Questions

1. Why was it important to Mendeleev to devise a periodic table in the nineteenth century?

2. On what did Mendeleev base the order of his elements, and how does this differ from the way the modern periodic table is organized?

3. What did Mendeleev say about gaps he found in this periodic table organization?

4. What did Mendeleev say about inconsistencies he found when developing his periodic table?

5. Look at the modern periodic table and write down five things that it tells you.

Copyright © 2008 by John Wiley & Sons, Inc.

Materials

Sheet of 30 elements from Planet Berth

Rulers

Modern periodic table of Earth elements that corresponds to
the new periodic table of Berth

Glue or clear tape

Blank periodic table to use as a template for making your own

Crayons

Construction paper or butcher paper

Procedure

1. Read the following scenario:

   A mirror galaxy to our Milky Way has been discovered. One of the planets in this mirror galaxy is identical to our Earth in composition. The name of this matching planet is Berth. Scientists have collected samples of 30 elements on Berth and are convinced that these elements are identical in properties to 30 of our elements here on Earth. Scientists have identified the sections of our periodic table that match the Berth elements. They have provided you with a blank template for the Berth periodic table as well as a copy of the applicable section of Earth's periodic table. In honor of Mendeleev, scientists have named the elements and listed clues they have thus far about each on 30 separate cards. In cases where elements are not known, they have left blanks for you to fill in with predictions. Your job is to use the blank template and develop a table that places each of the Berth elements in the proper location based on where each mirror element is found on Earth's periodic table.

2. Cut out the 30 Berth elements so that you have 30 cards.

3. Use construction paper or butcher paper to make an enlarged version of the blank periodic table template so that each card can be glued in the appropriate slot.

4. Use Earth's periodic table, your knowledge of periodic properties, the clues on the cards, and the Internet or other references to determine the appropriate location of each element from the mirror galaxy.

5. Fill in any blanks on the cards.

6. Once you have placed each card in its proper slot, glue or tape the cards down.

7. Lightly shade the element cards using this color scheme:

   Alkali metals—light blue

   Alkaline earth metals—light red

   Halogens—light green

   Noble gases—light yellow

8. Answer the postlab questions.

Copyright © 2008 by John Wiley & Sons, Inc.

Postlab Questions

1. What does the series tell you about an element? What does the group tell you about an element?

2. Based on the Berth periodic table, what is the formula for table salt on Berth?

3. Based on the Berth periodic table, what is the formula for water on Berth?

4. If sand is called silicon dioxide on Earth, what would you call it on Berth?

5. Which four elements on Berth would be the most likely to react violently with water? How do you know?

6. Name two elements on Berth that were the most difficult to classify properly. Explain how you made your final determination about their placement.

Copyright © 2008 by John Wiley & Sons, Inc.

LESSON 15: SURFACE TENSION OF WATER

15-1 WALKING ON THE WATER
Content on the Surface Tension of Water

Water Has a Thick Skin

How do some bugs walk across the top of a pond without sinking or even getting their feet wet? The answer is surface tension. The word *tension* means "tightening force." When a liquid displays this property, its surface acts like a stretched elastic membrane or a skin. Surface tension is due to the pull exerted on the molecules at the surface. Molecules in the middle of the liquid are attracted and pulled equally from all directions by surrounding molecules, as shown in Figure A. However, surface molecules of the liquid are pulled in a sideward and downward direction by other water molecules, but not upward. This unequal tugging action causes the surface molecules to be pulled downward and squeezed together, creating the tight skin that allows the pond critters to walk on the water.

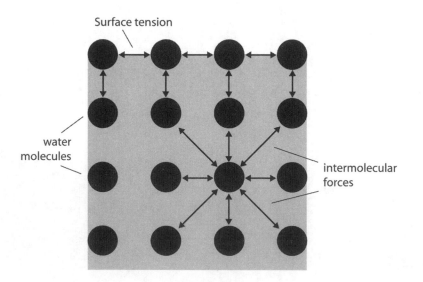

FIGURE A

214

Copyright © 2008 by John Wiley & Sons, Inc.

Cohesion and Adhesion

Surface tension results from forces of attraction between the particles within a liquid. The attraction of liquid molecules to each other is called cohesion. However, molecules of liquids can also experience adhesion, the attraction to other kinds of molecules. For example, water molecules adhere to molecules of glass that make up beakers and graduated cylinders. The adhesion of water molecules to glass molecules is greater than the cohesion of water molecules to each other. That is why water rises up the sides of a glass test tube or graduated cylinder and takes a concave shape, as shown in Figure B.

When cohesion of a liquid is greater than the adhesion to other molecules, the liquid will adopt a spherical shape. Raindrops are a good example of this. Water droplets are nearly spherical because the cohesion of the water molecules is greater than the adhesion of the water molecules to the air molecules. The downward pull of gravity distorts raindrops slightly and prevents them from being perfect spheres.

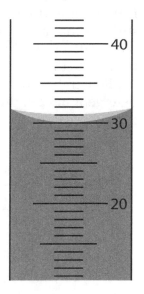

FIGURE B

Breaking Through the Skin

When your hands are really dirty, you probably reach for the soap. That's because plain water is not a very good cleaner. If you wash your hands with plain water, the water will tend to roll off in drops. Your skin produces oily molecules that do not break the water's surface tension. But there are ways to reduce the surface tension of water to get the dirt off your hands. The easiest way is by using soap.

Soap and other detergents weaken the surface tension of water. Molecules of soap or detergent move between the water molecules and reduce the attraction of water molecules to each other. Such substances as soap and other cleansers that reduce surface tension are called surfactants (surface-active agents). Surfactants increase the spreading and wetting properties of a liquid. A surfactant has molecules shaped like tadpoles, with long tails that have fatty properties and are described as hydrophobic. These tails are water insoluble, so they do not interact with, or dissolve in, water. Surfactant molecules also have small, electrically charged heads that are hydrophilic, or water soluble. The charge on the head of a surfactant molecule can be either negative or positive. Negative molecules are called anions, and positive charges are cations. Anionic detergents are very efficient at cleaning glass. The surface of glass normally carries a slightly negative charge, so anionic detergents do not bind to glass and can be used to clean it. Cationic surfactants are strongly attracted to glass. Their charged heads adhere to the glass, leaving their long hydrophobic (fatty) chains facing outward, making the glass look greasy. Cationic surfactants are more useful in cleaning plastic because plastic has a slightly positive charge on the surface.

Copyright © 2008 by John Wiley & Sons, Inc.

During the cleaning process, surfactant molecules tend to concentrate on the surface layer of water because the hydrophobic portion of the molecules moves away from the interior of the water. This arrangement makes it possible for water to wet surfaces that are normally nonwettable. Some of the cleaning power of the surfactant results from the enhanced ability of water to wet the hydrophobic surface and lift off the dirt.

Remember that bug that can walk on water? If you were to drop some soap or detergent near it, the insect would sink into the pond. The soap would reduce the surface tension and destroy the water's skin.

Copyright © 2008 by John Wiley & Sons, Inc.

Word Find—Vocabulary Activity on
Walking on the Water

Directions

After reading *Walking on the Water*, fill in the blanks with the correct answer. Each of the answers appears in the word find puzzle that follows. Find the words vertically, horizontally, and diagonally, backward or forward. Circle these words in the puzzle to make sure you chose the correct terms.

Clues

1. The attraction of water molecules to other water molecules is called _____.

2. One type of cleaner that weakens the surface tension of water is _____.

3. A molecule with a positive charge is also called a(n) _____.

4. Cationic detergents do a better job of cleaning _____ containers than anionic detergents.

5. Materials that interact with water are _____.

6. Materials that do not interact with water are _____.

7. The force of _____ keeps raindrops from being perfectly spherical.

8. The attraction of molecules in a liquid to the molecules of another substance is _____.

9. Cationic detergents leave a thin, greasy film on _____ containers.

10. Another name for a surface cleaning agent is a(n) _____.

11. A molecule with a negative charge is called a(n) _____.

12. The surface of water often resembles a tight _____ because of the inward-pulling force exerted on the surface molecules.

13. Water forms a _____ shape where it adheres to glass.

14. Due to cohesion, water will tend to assume a nearly _____ shape unless acted on by gravity.

15. The force exerted on surface water molecules by _____ molecules is always less than the force exerted by adjacent water molecules.

16. Detergents and soaps tend to _____ the surface tension of a liquid.

17. Substances that tend to avoid water and will not dissolve in water are called _____ substances.

Copyright © 2008 by John Wiley & Sons, Inc.

```
K P R C R Y T I V A R G V R I G H K
M C S O B L D H Q M D R R T L L N T
O O T H F G P Q Y F K C G B J A O R
J N U E H K P S R D V B E F E S I S
F C B S A E O L S L R N L G L S S N
T A L I R A C A O U B O D T B K E O
Z V U O P I A C K V M I P F U T H I
M E K N T T N I Z N T N E H L V D T
J V D S B I B R D D U A F E O L A A
K D A C K M F E N E K A E W S B M C
R L B S L Q J H D K R I A M N J I K
P R H Y D R O P H I L I C I I J S C
S M D B R L V S T N A T C A F R U S
```

Copyright © 2008 by John Wiley & Sons, Inc.

15-2 SURFACE TENSION
Lab on the Effect of Detergents on the Surface Tension of Water

Objectives

Students will demonstrate the property of surface tension in pure water and in water to which detergent has been added.

Teacher Notes

In Part 1, you can substitute other materials for gem clips. Thumbtacks, small nails, and pennies are a few possible substitutions. You will want to emphasize that the cup should be filled up to the rim with water before beginning this activity. Be sure to have plenty of paper towels available for overflows.

In Part 2, you can use various materials to construct the water bugs. Pipe cleaners for legs, a straw for the body, and candle wax on the feet work well. Rather than dictating the specific materials they should use, let the students be inventive in designing their water bugs. When each student group has completed the design for their bug, you might consider having them present their bug to the class. You could hold a competition between the bugs in a large tub of water to see which one stays on top of the water the longest without sinking. A special prize or grade could be given to the winning group.

Copyright © 2008 by John Wiley & Sons, Inc.

SURFACE TENSION

Lab on the Effect of Detergents on the Surface Tension of Water

Introduction

Like many forms of matter, water consists of molecules. Water molecules are attracted to one another by cohesive forces. The molecules in the middle of a container of water have molecular forces exerted on them by water molecules on all sides. Molecules on the surface of the container have molecular forces exerted on them by water molecules underneath and air molecules above them. The force of attraction produced by air molecules is much weaker than the force exerted by water molecules. The water molecules beneath the surface exert an inward-pulling force on the surface of the water that tightens the surface of the water. If you slowly add water to an already full glass of water, the tension on the water's surface produces a skin-like dome above the top of a glass.

Certain conditions can lower the surface tension of water and break the skin. An increase in temperature will lower surface tension because the density of the vapor above a liquid increases as the liquid gets hotter. These vapor molecules have a stronger attraction for the surface molecules in the liquid, and the tightness of the surface skin of the water is decreased.

The addition of surfactants, such as soap and detergent, can reduce the surface tension by increasing the spreading and wetting properties of water. A surfactant molecule looks like a tadpole. The tail of a surfactant molecule is composed of a fatty material that prevents it from dissolving in water but allows it to stick to greases, oils, and fats. This property of being insoluble in water is referred to as being hydrophobic. The head of the surfactant molecule is hydrophilic, or water soluble. The surfactant molecules possess the ability to break the surface tension of water and allow water to contact the dirt molecules on materials being cleaned. Dirt contains grease and oil. Detergents enable water to penetrate the surface skin of water and interact with hydrophobic molecules. This is the chemistry behind all cleansers. You will examine the effect of surfactants on water in Part 1 of this lab.

Surface tension also allows insects such as water striders to walk on the surface of ponds and rivers. Hypothetically, any object whose density is greater than water will sink when placed in water. What property allows these insects to stride across the water even though their density is significantly greater than that of water? Once again, surface tension accounts for this feat.

Small hairs are located on each of the water strider's feet. These hairs are equipped with a special material that prevents water from wetting them. The inability of water to wet these hairs allows the water strider to rest on the surface of the water. What would happen to the water strider if it tried to walk on the surface of a pond that laundry detergent had polluted? Would it sink, or could it still stride freely? In Part 2 of this lab, you will examine that question.

Copyright © 2008 by John Wiley & Sons, Inc.

Prelab Questions

1. Define *surface tension.*

2. Name two factors that lower surface tension. Explain the reason behind each.

3. Explain why water striders can stay on top of the water.

4. Define *cohesion.*

5. What is a surfactant? Discuss the effect it has on water and cleaning.

Part 1: Studying Surface Tension

Materials, Part 1

Four small clear plastic cups

Liquid dishwashing detergent (a few drops per group)

Water

Paper towels

Hand mitts for the hot glassware

Hot plate and a large beaker

Two boxes of clips per group

Black pen for labeling

Procedure, Part 1

1. Label the four cups A, B, C, and D. (See Figure A for the proper setup of the four cups.)

2. Place a beaker of water on the hot plate and heat it on High until the water begins to boil.

3. While you are waiting for the water to boil, fill cup A to the brim with tap water from the faucet. Do the same for cup B. Be sure that the water level in each of these cups is exactly to the rim of the cup without spilling over the side.

4. Carefully drop one paper clip at a time into cup A until you see the water begin to seep over the side of the cup. Count the number of paper clips it takes to cause water to overflow. Record this number in the lab chart, and describe the shape of the water in cup A.

5. Now add five drops of dishwashing detergent to cup B and allow about a minute for it to disperse in the water. Repeat the process you used with cup A. Count the number of paper clips required to cause the water to seep over the side of the cup. Record this in the lab chart, and describe the dome of water on top of cup B.

6. Fill cups C and D to the top with the water you have been heating on the hot plate. Be very careful not to burn yourself with the hot water or the hot container. Make sure you get the water level to the rim as you did with cups A and B.

Copyright © 2008 by John Wiley & Sons, Inc.

7. Add paper clips to cup C until water overflows. Observe the shape of the water in the cup and record its appearance in the lab chart.

8. Add five drops of dishwashing detergent to cup D and allow about a minute for it to disperse in the water. Repeat the process for cup D and record your results in the chart.

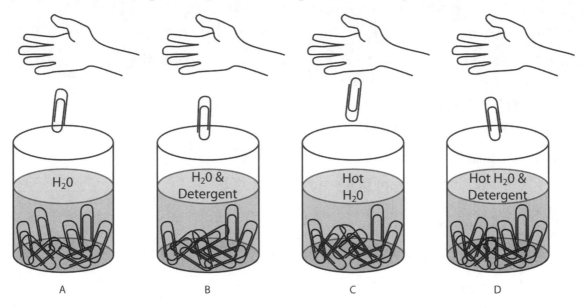

FIGURE A

		Lab Chart
Cup	Number of Paper Clips Added	*Description of Top of Water in Cup*
A		
B		
C		
D		

Copyright © 2008 by John Wiley & Sons, Inc.

Postlab Questions, Part 1

1. Which container had the least surface tension? Explain why.

2. Which container had the greatest surface tension? Explain why.

3. What effect does heat have on surface tension?

4. What effect does detergent have on surface tension?

5. Why was a dome able to form on top of the containers of water?

Part 2: Making a Water Strider

Materials, Part 2

Your teacher will let you know what materials are available, but the following are some suggestions.

Drinking straws	Pipe cleaners
Glue	Thin wire
Hot glue	Popsicle sticks
Candle wax	Matches
Garbage bag ties	Lard or other types of grease
Toothpicks	Cardboard
A bowl of water	Five drops of liquid detergent

Procedure, Part 2

1. Work with a lab partner.

2. Examine Figure B, a drawing of a model of a water strider. Your group will design your own water strider. It must have six legs, a central body, and two antennae.

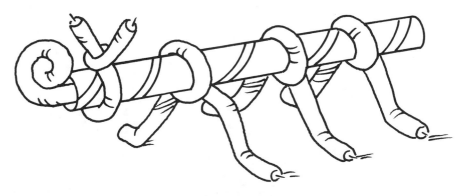

FIGURE B

Copyright © 2008 by John Wiley & Sons, Inc.

3. Your job is to make a water strider that is able to stand on top of the water. This may require some trial-and-error construction on your part. You may use any of the materials available, but you do not have to use all of them.

4. Remember that in nature, the feet of this insect have fine hairs that are coated with a waxy substance that prevents them from getting wet. You will want to use some candle wax or other fatty material on the feet of your insect to accomplish this.

5. Once you have designed and built a water strider, test it in the bowl of water to check your design.

6. When you have completed your model, show it to your teacher and demonstrate its ability to stand on water.

7. Remove your strider from the bowl. Add five drops of detergent to the bowl and wait 1 minute. Place the strider back in the bowl of water. Observe what happens.

8. Answer the postlab questions and then be prepared to show your creation to your classmates when each group is finished.

Postlab Questions, Part 2

1. Draw a sketch of your water strider in the box provided. On the back of this sheet, list the materials you used to design your creature and your reasons for this design.

Copyright © 2008 by John Wiley & Sons, Inc.

2. Why did you place a fatty substance on the feet of the insect?

3. What would have happened if you had not added the fatty substance to the water strider's feet?

4. What happened when the strider was placed in water with detergent?

5. Explain why this occurred.

6. What effect would adding detergent to a pond have on the water striders in the pond?

Copyright © 2008 by John Wiley & Sons, Inc.

LESSON 16: HAIR CHEMISTRY

16-1 HAIR CARE CHEMISTRY
Content on the Chemical Nature of Hair and Hair Products

ℛℯℒℯ

Hairy Bodies

As mammals, humans are covered with hair. Hair serves various functions. The long hair that grows on top of our heads helps us conserve body heat. The hair that forms our eyebrows may keep sweat out of our eyes, and eyelash hairs protect the eyes from dust and other particles. Pubic and armpit hairs help trap body odors, a function that was important in the society of early humans. Human hair is also an important expression of personality. In some cultures, the length and condition of hair indicate social status.

Hair's Structure

Hair contains keratin, a tough protein. This is the same protein that creates the calluses on our hands and feet and that makes up our nails. Like all proteins, keratin is composed of the elements hydrogen, oxygen, carbon, nitrogen, phosphorous, and sulfur. Keratin has more sulfur than any other protein. The presence of sulfur in a protein allows it to form cross-links, a characteristic that gives it strength. Because keratin can form extensive cross-links, hair is chemically and biologically resistant to decay, digestion, and decomposition.

Layers of Hair

Hair has three parts: the cuticle, the cortex, and the medulla.

The cuticle. The protective covering on the outside of a hair shaft is the cuticle. It is arranged in overlapping scales along the length of the hair (see Figure A). One function of the cuticle is to protect the inner cortex. At the ends of hair, there is no cuticle, and the cortex is exposed to air. This causes the cortex to dry and the ends of the hair to split. Cuticle scales give hair strength and flexibility. One hair can support 5 to 7 ounces of weight.

Copyright © 2008 by John Wiley & Sons, Inc.

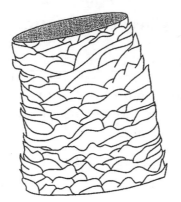

FIGURE A. HAIR CUTICLE

Cuticle scales vary with different types of hair. Some hair is very porous because it has loose, open scales; other hair has closed, tight scales. Hair with porous scales is easier to treat because chemicals can easily reach the cortex. In contrast, hair with tight scales is somewhat resistant to chemical treatment. Cuticle scales also function as traps that hold oil produced by cells on the scalp. This oil gives hair its natural luster. Unfortunately, the cuticle scales also trap dust or dirt.

The cortex. Beneath the cuticle scales is the cortex, the layer of hair that composes 75 to 90 percent of each strand. The cortex is composed of millions of protein fibers arranged in a parallel fashion. Occasional twists in the fibers add to hair's strength. The color of hair is due to the presence of pigment granules in the cortex. These granules are originally in cells that produce melanin, our body's color molecule. As the hair lengthens and melanin-producing cells die, granules of melanin are left in the cortex.

The medulla. The innermost layer of hair is the medulla, which is also known as the pith or marrow. It is made up of only two to four rows of round cells and is often filled with soft keratin. Thick hair usually has a medulla, but the structure is missing in thin and in blond hair. The role of the medulla is not clear.

Changing the Bonds Within Hair

Chemical services by cosmetologists primarily alter the cortex of the hair. Permanent waves, permanent colors, and hair straightening are achieved with chemicals that penetrate the cuticle layer. There are two types of chemical bonds that normally connect the protein fibers in the cortex: hydrogen bonds and sulfur bonds. Hydrogen bonds are weak bonds formed by the attraction of negative charges (anions) and positive charges (cations). Even though these bonds are weak, there are thousands of them within the cortex. Sulfur bonds are stronger than hydrogen bonds and are formed between two different parts of a protein. Hydrogen bonds and sulfur bonds give hair its natural shape: straight, wavy, curly, or kinky.

Copyright © 2008 by John Wiley & Sons, Inc.

Basic Chemicals Penetrate Hair

The hair cuticle can be penetrated and bonds in the cortex can be broken by chemicals that are basic, or alkaline. The pH scale is used to represent the acidity or alkalinity of a substance. This scale ranges from 1 to 14, with 7 as the neutral point. Substances with a pH below 7 are acidic, and those with a pH above 7 are basic (see Table 1).

TABLE 1. pH SCALE

1	2	3	4	5	6	7	8	9	10	11	12	13	14
	Acidic					Neutral						Basic	

Many foods are acidic: coffee has a pH near 6, cola has a pH of about 5, and vinegar has a pH close to 4. Substances with a pH in the 1 to 3 range are considered to be strong acids; those with a pH in the 4 to 7 range are mild acids. Strong bases are those in the 10 to 14 range; mild bases are in the 7 to 10 range. Some cleaners and antacids are mild bases. Hair is damaged at a pH below 3 or above 10. Table 2 summarizes how products with various pHs affect hair.

TABLE 2. EFFECTS OF VARIOUS pH LEVELS ON HAIR

pH	Hair Treatment	Effect on Hair
1–3	None made at this pH level	Would dissolve hair
3–6	Neutralizers, antidandruff shampoos, conditioners, lightening agents	Have an astringent (shrinking) effect, harden cuticle
7–10	Semipermanent colors, soap shampoos, permanent waving solutions	Remove oil, swell and soften hair
10–14	Depilatories	Swell hair to as much as 10 times original size; may dissolve hair

Copyright © 2008 by John Wiley & Sons, Inc.

Copyright © 2008 by John Wiley & Sons, Inc.

Basic Permanent Wave and Hair Relaxer Solutions

Ammonium thioglycolate, a permanent waving solution, has a pH of 9. Sodium hydroxide, another moderately strong base, is used as a hair relaxer. These basic hair solutions break sulfur bonds in the hair's cortex. Mild acids (such as acetic acid, citric acid, and tartaric acid) and oxidizers (such as hydrogen peroxide and bleach) reform sulfur bonds in the cortex (see Figure B).

FIGURE B. SULPHUR BONDS ARE BROKEN, HAIR IS RESHAPED, AND SULFUR BONDS ARE REFORMED TO PRODUCE PERMANENT CURLS.

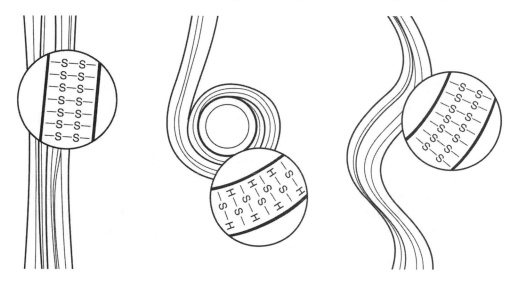

Acidic Hair Colors

Temporary hair colors, or rinses, are mildly acidic and leave the hair in good condition. The effect of an acid on hair is to harden the cuticle so that no color can enter the hair cortex. Only a small amount of color is absorbed on the hair surface. Because rinses are water soluble, the color left on the cuticle is easily rinsed out upon washing.

Mildly Basic Temporary Hair Colors

Semipermanent hair colors are mildly alkaline and cause the cuticle to swell somewhat, allowing a limited number of large, tinted hair color molecules to enter the cortex. Once the molecules are inside the cortex, the alkaline solution is washed off the hair, and color molecules are trapped. However, because shampoos are mildly alkaline, some swelling of the cuticle takes place with every shampoo, and some color escapes.

Basic Permanent Hair Colors

Permanent hair colors use small, colorless molecules that can pass easily into the cortex. Once they are inside, a developer, such as hydrogen peroxide, combines the small, colorless molecules into giant, colored molecules. These large molecules are trapped in the cortex. They are stable and insoluble, giving hair a permanent color. Therefore, permanent hair colors cannot be shampooed out of the hair. Because permanent hair colors do not combine with the hydrogen and sulfur bonds in the cortex, these bonds are still free for various other hair treatments.

Conditioners

Hair that has undergone several chemical treatments may have a damaged cuticle. Consequently, hair may look dry and be hard to manage. In this case, conditioners can be applied to the hair that even out the cuticle and add oil. Many conditioners are made of protein fillers plus lanolin or cholesterol. Lanolin (a fat from sheep's wool) and cholesterol replace the natural oil produced by the scalp. Protein fillers are made from cheap waste protein, such as scrap leather, animal hooves, and turkey feathers. These protein sources are chopped and cooked under pressure in a strong alkaline solution. They are then neutralized with an acid to a pH of 7. The resulting solution is almost pure protein. These protein molecules have positive and negative charges on them, just like the protein molecules that make up hair. The negatively charged filler proteins bond to the positively charged hair proteins, and the positively charged filler proteins bond to the negatively charged hair proteins so that the conditioner joins with the hair.

Hair Chemists

Today, the hair care industry is growing in importance in our economy. Millions of dollars are spent annually on hair and its care. The beauty and barber industries employ thousands of workers, who must be knowledgeable about the effects of chemicals on hair as well as on the skin.

Copyright © 2008 by John Wiley & Sons, Inc.

A Tri-ing and Hairy Experience— Vocabulary Activity on *Hair Care Chemistry*

Introduction

Dr. Colorfast, a professor at a prominent cosmetology school, likes to give his tests in an original manner. He takes a full-size mannequin and cuts a puzzle in the hair on the back of the mannequin's head. He then tapes the clues and word choices to the mannequin's back.

Directions

After reading *Hair Care Chemistry,* read puzzle clues 1 through 15 and match them to a vocabulary word. The letter next to the correct vocabulary word corresponds to a letter in the triangle puzzle. Place the number of the clue above this letter on the triangle. The first one is done for you. Repeat this until all 15 blocks have been filled in with numbers.

   You can check to see if you have the correct answers by adding the numbers on the HUMAN side of the triangle and entering that number in the box above this word. Do the same thing for the numbers on the SPLIT side of the triangle and for the numbers on the COVER side. If all your choices are correct and you have added correctly, the three boxes will contain the same number.

Copyright © 2008 by John Wiley & Sons, Inc.

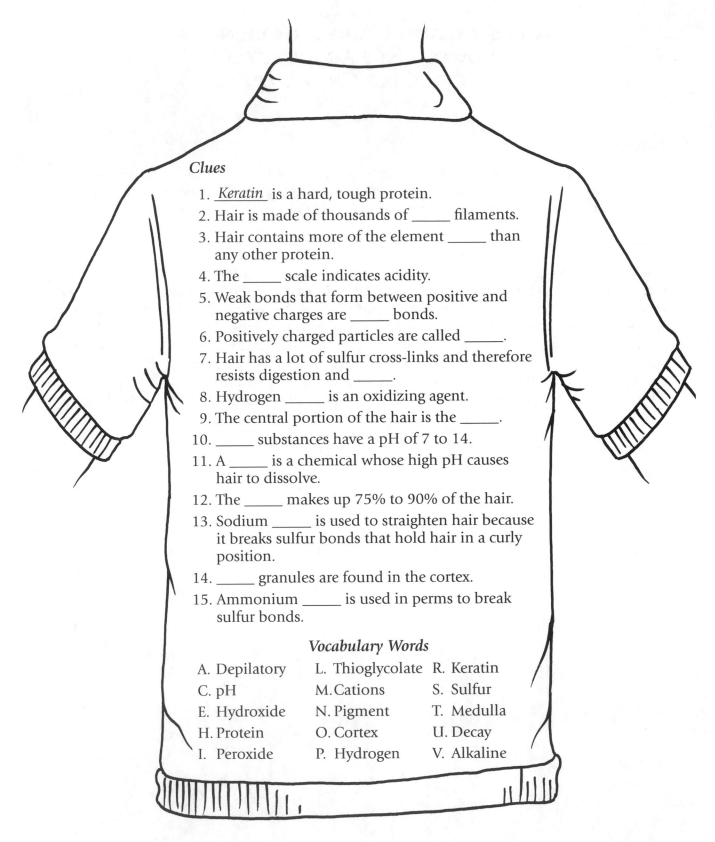

Clues

1. _Keratin_ is a hard, tough protein.
2. Hair is made of thousands of _____ filaments.
3. Hair contains more of the element _____ than any other protein.
4. The _____ scale indicates acidity.
5. Weak bonds that form between positive and negative charges are _____ bonds.
6. Positively charged particles are called _____.
7. Hair has a lot of sulfur cross-links and therefore resists digestion and _____.
8. Hydrogen _____ is an oxidizing agent.
9. The central portion of the hair is the _____.
10. _____ substances have a pH of 7 to 14.
11. A _____ is a chemical whose high pH causes hair to dissolve.
12. The _____ makes up 75% to 90% of the hair.
13. Sodium _____ is used to straighten hair because it breaks sulfur bonds that hold hair in a curly position.
14. _____ granules are found in the cortex.
15. Ammonium _____ is used in perms to break sulfur bonds.

Vocabulary Words

A. Depilatory	L. Thioglycolate	R. Keratin
C. pH	M. Cations	S. Sulfur
E. Hydroxide	N. Pigment	T. Medulla
H. Protein	O. Cortex	U. Decay
I. Peroxide	P. Hydrogen	V. Alkaline

Copyright © 2008 by John Wiley & Sons, Inc.

Copyright © 2008 by John Wiley & Sons, Inc.

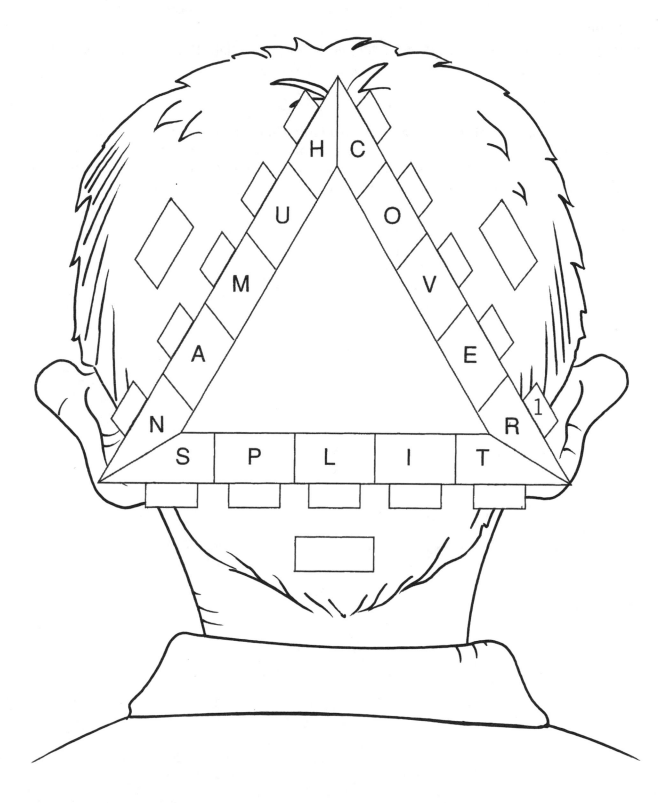

16-2 HOMEMADE PERMS
Lab on Hair Chemistry

Objectives

Students will demonstrate the effects of different solutions on hair. They will also observe untreated and treated hair under the microscope.

Teacher Notes

A week or two before this lab, ask a local cosmetologist or the cosmetology department in your school to save you some long hair (2 to 5 inches). Hair samples should be bundled together with a rubber band for easy handling by students. Students should wear goggles and take extreme caution when working with NaOH.

Copyright © 2008 by John Wiley & Sons, Inc.

HOMEMADE PERMS
Lab on Hair Chemistry

Introduction

Most of the permanent treatments for hair affect the inner layer of the hair, the cortex. That means that the outside protective layer, the cuticle, must be opened so that hair chemicals can enter and alter the arrangement of the sulfur and hydrogen bonds.

Hair is a fibrous protein made up of thousands of polypeptide chains twisted around each other into long strands. Sulfur bonds link the fibers together. Other fibrous proteins are animal hair, natural silk, and the horns of some animals.

All proteins are composed of chains of amino acids. There are 22 amino acids, some of which are positively charged, some negatively charged, and some neutral. Four of these amino acids, including cysteine, contain sulfur ions. The sulfur in one cysteine is capable of forming strong bonds with other cysteines in nearby proteins. These bonds are extremely durable and give hair its strength.

In this lab, you will expose hair to sodium hydroxide, a strong base, and acetic acid, a mild acid, to demonstrate the breaking and reforming of sulfur bonds. This mimics the process of creating a permanent wave in hair.

Materials

Lab apron	2 large test tubes
Goggles	Clock or timer
Hair sample	Microscope, slide, and coverslip
Pencil	Hair dryer
20 ml NaOH (pH about 10)	Rubber bands
Vinegar	

Procedure

1. Put on your goggles and lab apron.

2. Take one strand of hair and make a wet-mount slide by placing the hair and a drop of water on the slide and placing a coverslip on top. Observe the hair on low, medium, and high power. Sketch what you see in the spaces provided in Postlab Question 1.

3. Wrap several strands of hair around a pencil and secure with rubber bands. Submerge the hair and wrapped portion of the pencil in a large test tube that contains NaOH.

4. After 15 minutes, rinse the sample with water and carefully remove one strand of hair to examine under the microscope. Wash your hands after handling NaOH. Sketch the appearance of the strand of hair under the microscope in Postlab Question 2.

5. Rewrap the strands of hair around the pencil and return them to the NaOH.

6. Repeat step 4 after another 15 minutes. Answer Postlab Question 3.

Copyright © 2008 by John Wiley & Sons, Inc.

7. Remove the hair sample from NaOH and rinse it in vinegar to neutralize it. Dry the strands of hair with a hair dryer for 10 minutes. Unroll the hair. Answer Postlab Question 4.

8. Answer the postlab questions.

Postlab Questions

1. Sketch of hair before treatment

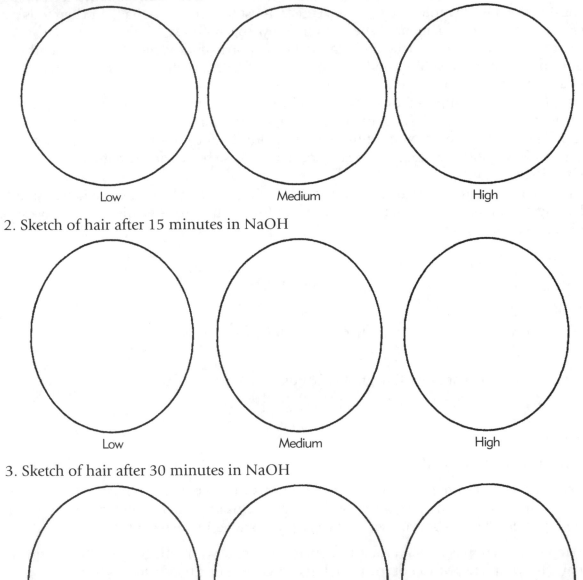

2. Sketch of hair after 15 minutes in NaOH

3. Sketch of hair after 30 minutes in NaOH

Copyright © 2008 by John Wiley & Sons, Inc.

4. Sketch of hair after 10 minutes of drying

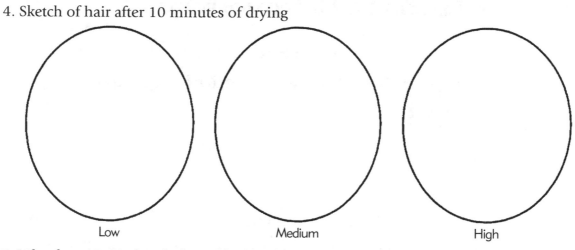

| Low | Medium | High |

5. Why does NaOH break the sulfur bonds in hair?

_____

_____

_____

6. What is the purpose of the vinegar?

_____

_____

_____

7. Did your samples become permanently curled?

_____

_____

_____

Copyright © 2008 by John Wiley & Sons, Inc.

LESSON 17: MACROMOLECULES

17-1 FATS
Content on the Structure and Roles of Fat

❧❧❧

Concentrated Energy

Lipids, which include fats and oils, are an essential part of everyone's diet. Fats occur in several different forms. Most of the lipids in our foods and in our bodies are made of triglycerides, and the balance consists of phospholipids and sterols.

Lipids serve several important roles in the body. Fat is a calorie-rich food that delivers more than twice as much energy as the same amount of carbohydrate. Fat surrounds and pads all the vital organs, protecting them from injury and temperature variations. Cell membranes contain fat. Some essential nutrients, such as linoleic acid and vitamins A, D, E, and K, are soluble in fat and are found in fatty foods. In addition, fat is the component of food that gives it aroma and flavor.

Triglycerides

Triglycerides are molecules formed of three hydrocarbon chains (called fatty acids) that are attached to a backbone of glycerol. The following is the general formula for a triglyceride. In this figure, notice the short chain of carbon atoms that form the basic structure of glycerol.

$$CH-O-\underset{\underset{O}{\|}}{C}-R$$
$$CH-O-\underset{\underset{O}{\|}}{C}-R$$
$$CH-O-\underset{\underset{O}{\|}}{C}-R$$

Each R in this formula stands for "radical" and represents a variety of hydrocarbon groups. In triglycerides, the hydrocarbon groups are either saturated fatty acid chains or unsaturated fatty acid chains.

Fatty acids differ primarily in two ways: chain length and degree of saturation. Chain length affects the solubility of a lipid in water. Shorter fatty acid chains are more

238

Copyright © 2008 by John Wiley & Sons, Inc.

soluble than longer ones. Saturation refers to the chemical structure of the fatty acid and reflects the number of hydrogen atoms in the chain. If every available bond for carbon is attached to a hydrogen atom, the chain is said to be saturated, or filled with hydrogen atoms. Many animal fats are saturated. If there is a hydrogen atom missing, then the fatty acid is described as unsaturated. When two or more hydrogen atoms are missing, it is known as a polyunsaturated fat. Most polyunsaturated lipids are found in plants, where they form the protective coating on leaves and the skin of seeds.

A saturated fatty acid chain:

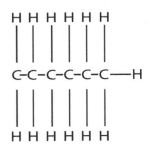

An unsaturated fatty acid chain:

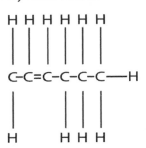

The presence of unsaturated fatty acid chains in lipids affects the temperature at which the fats melt. Fats that are highly unsaturated are liquids at room temperature. The more saturated a fat, the firmer its texture. Therefore, animal fats tend to be solids at room temperature and plant fats or oils tend to be liquids. Hydrogenation (adding hydrogen atoms) of liquid fats causes them to become firmer. Some margarine manufacturers hydrogenate their liquid product to produce a firmer, more spreadable food.

For years, scientists have advised consumers to select vegetable oils and to avoid eating saturated fats, such as butter and the fats in meats, because such foods are most likely to lead to high levels of cholesterol in the blood and contribute to heart disease. Research also indicates that the process of hydrogenating plant oils creates an artificial class of fats called trans fatty acids. Trans fatty acids can raise blood cholesterol levels, even though the vegetable oil itself contains no cholesterol. Therefore, hydrogenated vegetable oils are as unhealthy as saturated fats.

Phospholipids

Phospholipids, another form of fat, play key roles in cell membrane structure. A phospholipid molecule is amphipathic; that is, one end is attracted to water molecules, and the other end is attracted to organic molecules (lipids). The lipophilic

Copyright © 2008 by John Wiley & Sons, Inc.

("lipid-loving") end of a phospholipid is the long fatty acid chain. The hydrophilic ("water-loving") end contains a phosphate group, which has a positive and a negative charge. Because of their amphipathic nature, phospholipids tend to form bilayers in which the fatty acids are forced together and the hydrophilic groups are exposed (see Figure A). The basic structure of a cell membrane is the phospholipid bilayer.

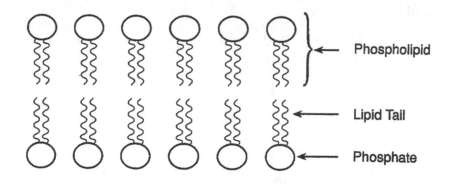

FIGURE A. PHOSPHOLIPID BILAYER

Sterols

Sterols are fats found in both plants and animals. In animals, sterols are components of cholesterol and steroid hormones. Cholesterol, which has many functions in the body, is a component of bile acids and is necessary in the digestion of fats. In addition, cholesterol is involved in the formation of sex hormones, and it is important in the structure of brain and nerve tissue. Even though many tissues require cholesterol, the compound causes problems when it forms deposits in arteries and thus constricts the flow of blood.

Because Americans consume a large amount of fat in their diets, many people suffer from obesity and atherosclerosis, a condition in which blood vessels become clogged with deposits of fatty substances. The amount of cholesterol circulating in the blood can be used to forecast heart and artery disease. Because blood cholesterol is made primarily from saturated fats, a person can lower his or her blood cholesterol levels by following three strategies: reducing total fat intake, increasing the proportion of polyunsaturated fat relative to saturated fat, and reducing cholesterol intake.

Copyright © 2008 by John Wiley & Sons, Inc.

FAT CROSSWORD—VOCABULARY ACTIVITY ON
FATS

Copyright © 2008 by John Wiley & Sons, Inc.

Across

3. Linoleic acid and vitamins are essential _____.

4. Fat _____ organs and protects them from injury.

5. _____ is one component of triglycerides.

6. _____ and oil are two examples of lipids.

8. Cholesterol is important in the structure of _____ tissue.

10. Fats are also known as _____.

13. The length of a fatty acid chain affects its _____ in water.

14. _____ acids are chains of carbohydrates in triglycerides.

15. _____ are a type of food that supplies a little less than half as much energy as fat.

17. _____ acids are important in digestion of fats.

19. All cell membranes are made of a _____ of phospholipids.

20. _____ can change liquid fats to solids at room temperature.

Down

1. Lipids are an important structural part of cell _____.

2. *Hydrogenation* means adding _____ to a chain of carbon atoms.

4. Lipids in _____ are usually oils.

7. Most of the fat in our bodies is in the form of _____.

9. In a chemical formula, a(n) _____ group represents several hydrocarbon variations.

11. _____ molecules are attracted to water on one end and to lipids on the other end.

12. _____ reflects the number of hydrogen atoms on a fatty acid chain.

16. Cholesterol is important in the formation of _____ hormones.

18. Cholesterol in the _____ can contribute to atherosclerosis.

Word List

AMPHIPATHIC	FATTY	PADS
BILE	GLYCEROL	PLANTS
BILAYER	HYDROGENATION	RADICAL
BLOOD	HYDROGENS	SATURATION
BRAIN	LIPIDS	SEX
CARBOHYDRATES	MEMBRANES	SOLUBILITY
FAT	NUTRIENTS	TRIGLYCERIDES

Copyright © 2008 by John Wiley & Sons, Inc.

17-2 FAT IN FOOD
Compare the Fat Content of Meats

Objectives

Students will isolate fat in food, determine the percentage of fat in food, and compare the fat content of different foods.

Teacher Notes

In this lab, students compare the fat content of lean ground beef (round or chuck) to regular, more fatty ground beef. Chicken and fish could be substituted for either of the beef samples or added for additional comparison.

Meat samples are boiled to separate the fat from the protein. Fat floats on top of the water and can be removed easily.

Samples of 100 grams are used to make calculations of fat percentage more convenient. However, any size sample can be used. The following formula helps calculate the percentage of fat:

grams of fat ÷ grams of sample × 100 = percentage of fat

Copyright © 2008 by John Wiley & Sons, Inc.

FAT IN FOOD
Compare the Fat Content of Meats

Introduction

U.S. citizens probably take in more fat than citizens of any other country, often eating 40% to 50% of their calories as lipids. Nine-tenths of this fat comes from three groups of food: fats and oils; meat, poultry, and fish; and dairy products. All meats contain fat, but some contain more than others. Leaner cuts of meat contain about 3 grams of fat per ounce, medium cuts of meat contain about 5.5 grams of fat per ounce, and high-fat meats contain about 8 grams per ounce.

Meats that are considered lean are chicken or turkey without skin, leg of lamb, and fish. Meats in the medium-fat group include ground round steak, liver, heart, and kidney. High-fat meats are ground hamburger, steak, cold cuts, and hot dogs.

Consumers may think of meat as a source of protein, but analysis of meat's content shows that it often contains more fat than protein. For example, a quarter pound of hamburger contains 28 grams of protein and 23 grams of fat. Protein provides 4 calories per gram, and fat provides 9 calories per gram, making the protein contribution of a hamburger 112 calories and the fat contribution 207 calories.

Prelab Questions

1. In your opinion, why do you think Americans eat more fat than citizens of other countries?

2. What are some lean meats? What are some fat meats?

3. How many protein calories and fat calories do you get from a quarter pound of hamburger?

Materials

100 grams lean ground chuck	Dropper
100 grams ground beef	Water
Two 600 ml beakers	Bunsen burner with ring stand, or hot plate
Beaker tongs	Balances
100 ml graduated cylinder	

Procedure

1. Label your beakers 1 and 2.

2. Weigh 100 grams of lean beef and put it in beaker 1.

3. Weigh 100 grams of ground beef and put it in beaker 2.

4. Place each sample of meat in 400 ml of water. Place both beakers of water on the hot plate and set on High for 10 minutes.

Copyright © 2008 by John Wiley & Sons, Inc.

5. Carefully remove the beakers from the hot plate using beaker tongs. Allow the beakers to cool for a few minutes.

6. Carefully pour the fat layer from beaker 1 into a 100 ml graduated cylinder. (The fat floats on top of the water.) Use a dropper to transfer the last traces of fat to the graduated cylinder. Record the volume of fat on the data table.

7. Discard the fat and wash out the graduated cylinder.

8. Repeat steps 6 and 7 for beaker 2.

9. One milliliter of fat has a mass of about 1 gram. Therefore, the volume of fat in your graduated cylinder is the approximate percentage of fat in your 100-gram sample. Record your percentage of fat for each sample in the data table.

10. Answer the postlab questions.

DATA TABLE. VOLUMES AND PERCENTAGES OF FAT IN MEAT SAMPLES

Sample Number	Type of Meat	Volume of Fat	Percentage of Fat

Postlab Questions

1. Which type of meat contains the most fat per gram?

2. What are some health problems associated with high fat intake?

3. What is the purpose of cooking the meat sample?

4. If you used 100 grams of skinless chicken in this experiment, how do you think it would compare to the beef?

Copyright © 2008 by John Wiley & Sons, Inc.

SECTION 5

Biology

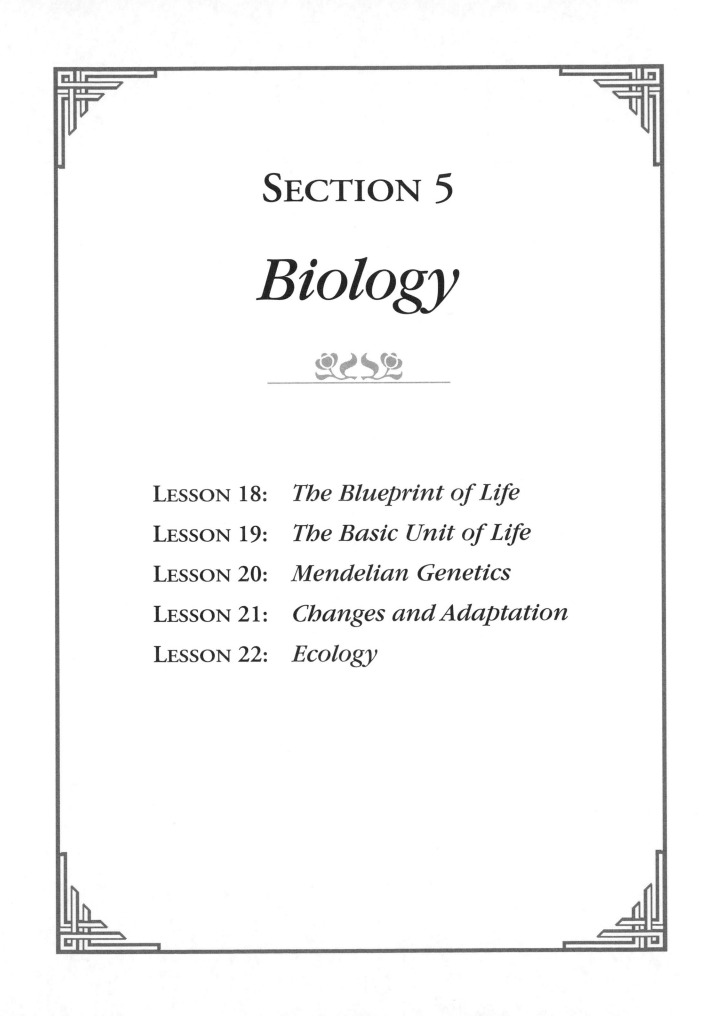

LESSON 18: THE BLUEPRINT OF LIFE

18-1 THE STRUCTURE AND FUNCTION OF DNA
Content on DNA

Why Do You Look Like That?

The hair on our head grows up to 25 inches, but the hair on our eyebrows grows only an inch or less. Why? Why do most humans have five fingers on each hand instead of six? Why are most people less than 6½ feet tall? We are not surprised that all people have two arms and two legs, but how did the developing fetus "know" to grow two arms and two legs?

The Answers Are in the Nucleus

The answers to all these questions can be found within the nuclei of our cells. Our bodies, and the bodies of all living things, are made of cells. A cell is a tiny living structure that contains a set of directions that tells the cell what to do, when to do it, and how much of it to do. All of these directions are tightly packed in the cell's nucleus, a large, dark structure in the cell. Inside the nucleus are long, thin strands of chromatin, a molecule made of deoxyribonucleic acid, or DNA. The chromatin is made up of units called nucleotides, each of which is composed of a nitrogen base, a sugar, and a phosphate group (see Figure A).

Let's take a close look at the DNA inside a cell's nucleus. If we had a super microscope, we could see that a filament of chromatin is made of two strands of DNA that are arranged in a spiral shape, or double helix (see Figure B).

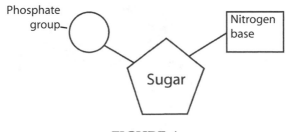

FIGURE A

Copyright © 2008 by John Wiley & Sons, Inc.

FIGURE B. DNA IS A DOUBLE HELIX.

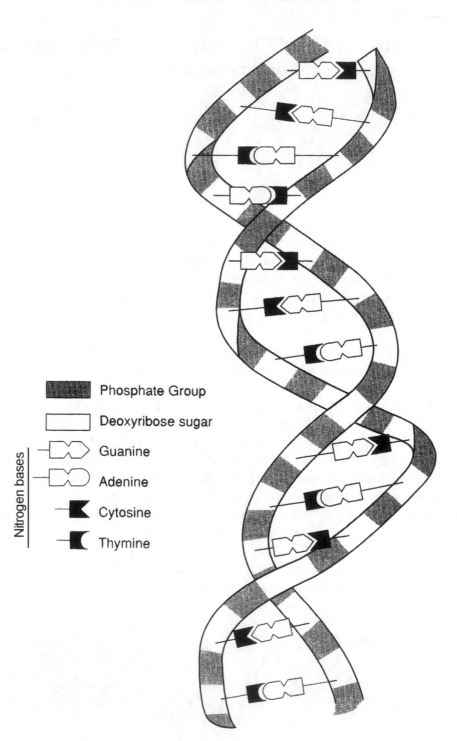

Phosphate Group

Deoxyribose sugar

Nitrogen bases
Guanine
Adenine
Cytosine
Thymine

Copyright © 2008 by John Wiley & Sons, Inc.

A Molecule That Has a Familiar Shape

If we could take a strand of chromatin and straighten it out so that the helix shape is gone, it would look something like a ladder (see Figure C). The outside parts of the ladder are made of alternating sugar (S) and phosphate (P) molecules. The sugar in a DNA molecule is deoxyribose.

FIGURE C. DNA STRAND. GUANINE, ADENINE, CYTOSINE, AND THYMINE ARE NITROGEN BASES.

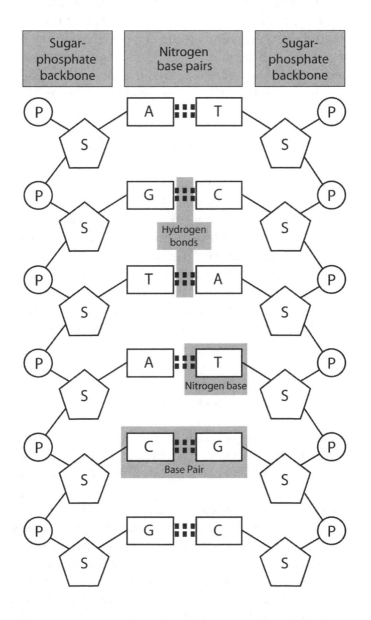

Copyright © 2008 by John Wiley & Sons, Inc.

The rungs of the DNA ladder are made of pairs of nitrogen bases. There are only four types of nitrogen bases in any DNA molecule: thymine, adenine, guanine, and cytosine. Thymine and adenine fit together like two puzzle pieces, and guanine and cytosine fit together. Because of these special fits, thymine always pairs with adenine, and guanine always pairs with cytosine in a DNA molecule. Pairs of nitrogen bases are held together by hydrogen bonds.

The DNA Code

How does DNA direct the cell and tell it exactly what to do? The sequence of the nitrogen bases in a DNA strand forms a code, very much like the sequence of letters forms a word. In a word, the code forms terms that have meaning. In DNA, the code specifies which protein will be made. Proteins are important molecules in living things. Every protein is made up of a long string of amino acids. Each amino acid is coded for by a sequence of three DNA bases, a triplet, on the DNA strand.

Protein Synthesizers

Although DNA carries the code for assembling each protein, the structures that actually assemble proteins, the ribosomes, are located in the cytoplasm. DNA cannot leave the nucleus because it is too large to squeeze through pores in the nuclear membrane. Therefore, DNA has to send a message to the ribosomes to tell them what kind of protein to assemble. The messenger that DNA makes and sends is called messenger ribonucleic acid, or mRNA. Although mRNA is very similar to DNA, it differs from DNA in three important ways: it is single stranded and can leave the nucleus by passing through the nuclear pores; the sugar in mRNA is ribose instead of deoxyribose; and mRNA contains the nitrogen base uracil instead of thymine. Like thymine, uracil can pair with adenine.

DNA's Message

To make a messenger, the DNA molecule in the cell's nucleus unwinds and separates. RNA nucleotides floating around in the nucleus line up along one side of the open DNA. They arrange themselves so that adenine pairs with uracil and guanine pairs with cytosine (see Figure D).

When the mRNA strand is complete, it separates from the DNA strand, exits the nucleus, and enters the cell's cytoplasm. In the cytoplasm, the mRNA strand attaches to a ribosome. The cytoplasm contains all the parts necessary for the construction of a new protein. Amino acids, the subunits of proteins, are floating around in the cytoplasm. The job of mRNA is to arrange these amino acids in the correct order to make a particular protein. There are 22 different amino acids, and their arrangement in a protein is of vital importance. Just one mistake in amino acid sequencing can produce a defective protein.

Copyright © 2008 by John Wiley & Sons, Inc.

FIGURE D. A STRAND OF DNA OPENS, AND RNA NUCLEOTIDES FORM AN MRNA STRAND.

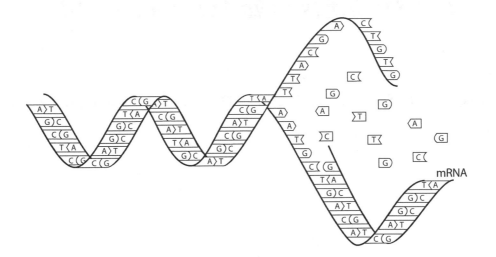

Codons and Anticodons

Three bases on the mRNA that correspond to a particular amino acid are called a codon. A strand of mRNA carries the correct sequence of codons needed to make a protein. The problem is that something has to deliver each amino acid to its position on the mRNA. This something is a special form of RNA called transfer RNA, or tRNA. There are 22 amino acids and 22 tRNAs. On a tRNA, the spot that matches the mRNA's codon is called the anticodon. A molecule of tRNA can pick up an amino acid and deliver it to the ribosome. Here several amino acids are joined to form a protein.

Copyright © 2008 by John Wiley & Sons, Inc.

Name _____ Date _____ (18-1)

DNA CONCEPT MAP—VOCABULARY ACTIVITY ON THE STRUCTURE AND FUNCTION OF DNA

Directions

After you have read *The Structure and Function of DNA,* fill in the blanks in the concept map.

Copyright © 2008 by John Wiley & Sons, Inc.

Copyright © 2008 by John Wiley & Sons, Inc.

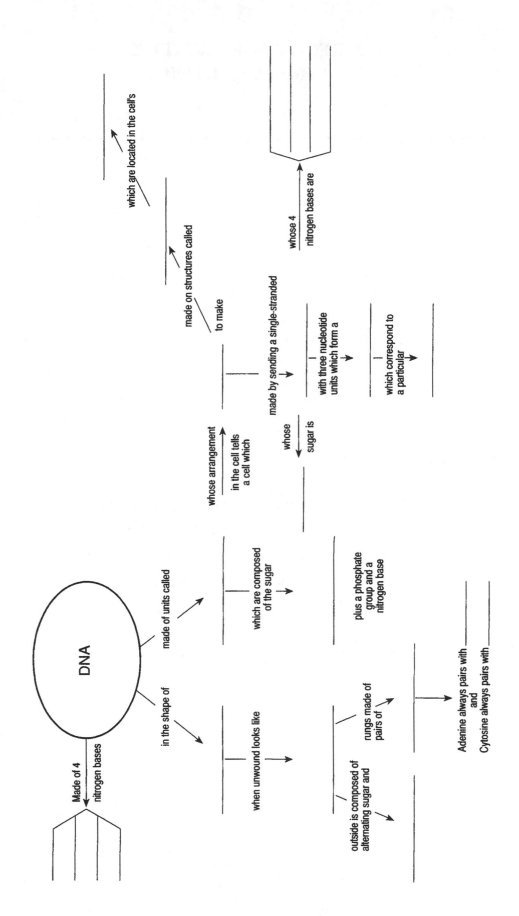

18-2 RECIPE FOR PROTEINS
DNA Modeling Activity

Objectives

Students will learn the steps of translation and transcription. They will also make a paper model of a short polypeptide.

Teacher Notes

Give each lab group a strip of paper numbered 1, 2, 3, 4, 5, or 6 that represents a strand of DNA.

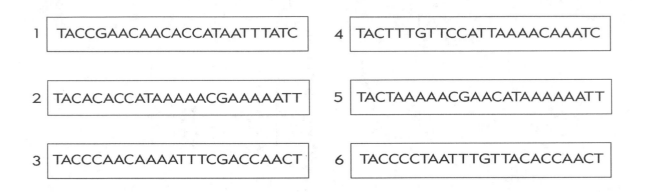

1 | TACCGAACAACACCATAATTTATC

4 | TACTTTGTTCCATTAAAACAAATC

2 | TACACACCATAAAAACGAAAAATT

5 | TACTAAAAACGAACATAAAAAATT

3 | TACCCAACAAAATTTCGACCAACT

6 | TACCCCTAATTTGTTACACCAACT

When students have completed the exercise, they will have created the following polypeptide chains:

1. Initiation-alanine-cysteine-cysteine-glycine-isoleucine-lysine-termination

2. Initiation-cysteine-glycine-isoleucine-phenylalanine-alanine-phenylalanine-termination

3. Initiation-glycine-cysteine-phenylalanine-lysine-alanine-glycine-termination

4. Initiation-lysine-glutamine-glycine-aspargine-phenylalanine-valine-termination

5. Initiation-isoleucine-phenylalanine-alanine-cysteine-isoleucine-phenylalanine-termination

6. Initiation-glycine-isoleucine-lysine-glutamine-cysteine-glycine-termination

Copyright © 2008 by John Wiley & Sons, Inc.

Copyright © 2008 by John Wiley & Sons, Inc.

Name _____ Date _____ (18-2)

Recipe for Proteins
DNA Modeling Activity

Introduction

DNA is a large, molecule made of units called nucleotides. Each nucleotide contains a molecule of the sugar deoxyribose, a phosphate group, and one of four nitrogen bases. In DNA, the bases are guanine, cytosine, adenine, and thymine. The sequence of these bases determines which protein will be made.

The DNA code is transferred to a strand of mRNA, whose nucleotides are made of a molecule of the sugar ribose, a phosphate group, and one of four nitrogen bases. DNA and mRNA do not have exactly the same bases; instead of thymine, mRNA contains uracil.

A protein is made of a string of amino acids arranged in a specific sequence. Proteins play several roles in cells. Many proteins are involved in cell structure. Others are important chemicals that regulate cell functions.

In this activity, you will make a model of DNA, mRNA, and a short protein.

Materials

Scissors	Glue
Construction paper (2 sheets)	Ruler
Two strips of green construction paper	Components Handout
One strip of yellow construction paper	Nitrogen Base Cutouts

Procedure, Part A—DNA and RNA

1. Place a large piece of construction paper on your desktop. This represents a cell. Use another sheet of construction paper to make a nucleus that is 30 cm wide and position it on the cell.

2. Use the DNA sequence your teacher gives you as a guide for making a left-hand strand of a DNA molecule. To do so,

   a. Cut out the bases indicated on your DNA sequence from the Nitrogen Base Cutouts handout.

   b. Glue the bases to a strip of green construction paper following the order of the sequence given to you by your teacher.

   c. When all the nitrogen bases have been glued to the strip of paper, place the strip in the nucleus. Do not glue the strip to the nucleus.

3. Create a complementary, right-hand strand of DNA by pairing each base on the strip of paper with an appropriate nitrogen base cutout. These cutouts represent free nucleotides

floating in the cytoplasm. Glue these complementary bases to another strip of green construction paper. Place the second strip in the nucleus alongside the left-hand strand of DNA. Arrange the two strands so that there is some space between them. These two strands represent your complete double strand of DNA.

4. Open the two strands of DNA by pushing them apart. Make a strand of messenger RNA (mRNA) that has bases that pair with the original (left-hand strand) of DNA. To do so, pair each base on the left-hand DNA strip to appropriate nitrogen base cutouts from the Nitrogen Base Cutouts handout. Remember: mRNA does not contain thymine. Glue the appropriate mRNA bases to a strip of yellow construction paper and place this strand of mRNA out in the cytoplasm.

Procedure, Part B—Make a Short Protein

1. Cut out the tRNAs, amino acids, and the ribosome from the Components Handout.

2. Underline the first three bases on your strand of mRNA on the yellow construction paper. Three bases on mRNA compose a codon. Bases on a tRNA anticodon can pair with the bases of a codon. Determine the bases that will form an anticodon to the first codon on your strand of mRNA. Cut out and glue these bases to a tRNA model.

3. Repeat step 2 to form anticodons on the other five tRNAs that pair with the remaining codons on the strand of mRNA.

4. Each tRNA can pick up one type of amino acid depending on the mRNA codon with which it pairs. Examine your strand of mRNA and read the first codon. In Table 1, find the name of the amino acid that is coded for by this codon. Write the name of this amino acid on an amino acid model. Repeat the procedure with the other codons on the mRNA strand, writing the name of each amino acid on a separate model.

5. Attach each amino acid to its appropriate tRNA, the one that has an anticodon to match the codon that codes for that amino acid.

6. Glue the ribosome in the cytoplasm of your cell.

7. Position the strip of mRNA so that the left side of the mRNA is in the ribosome and the right side is sticking out.

8. Match the first mRNA codon to the correct anticodon on one of the tRNAs.

9. Match the second mRNA codon to the correct anticodon on one of the tRNAs. Continue matching codons to anticodons until all the tRNAs are lined up.

10. Attach the amino acids together to form a short amino acid chain. Glue the amino acid chain to your construction paper cell in the cytoplasm.

11. These amino acids form a model of a short polypeptide. Long polypeptides form proteins.

12. Answer the postlab questions.

Copyright © 2008 by John Wiley & Sons, Inc.

Postlab Questions

1. What determines which protein a cell will make?

2. What is the function of a ribosome?

3. What is the function of a tRNA?

4. Why is it important that amino acids be assembled in a particular sequence?

5. DNA is in the nucleus, and ribosomes are in the cytoplasm. Explain how DNA sends a message about protein synthesis to the ribosomes.

TABLE 1. AMINO ACIDS AND CODONS

Amino Acid	RNA Codons
Alanine	GCU, GCC, GCA, GCG
Arginine	AGA, AGG, CGU, CGC, CGA, CGG
Asparagine	AAU, AAC
Aspartic Acid	GAU, GAC
Cysteine	UGU, UGC
Glutamic Acid	GAA, GAG
Glutamine	CAA, CAG
Glycine	GGU, GGC, GGA, GGG
Histidine	CAU, CAC
Isoleucine	AUU, AUC, AUA
Leucine	UUA, UUG, CUU, CUC, CUA, CUG
Lysine	AAA, AAG
Methionine (Initiation)	AUG, GUG
Phenylalanine	UUU, UCC
Proline	CCU, CCC, CCA, CCG
Serine	UCU, UCC, UCA, UCG, AGU, AGC
Threonine	ACU, ACC, ACA, ACG
Tryptophan	UGG
Tyrosine	UAU, UAC
Valine	GUU, GUC, GUA, GUG
Termination	UAA, UAG, UGA

Copyright © 2008 by John Wiley & Sons, Inc.

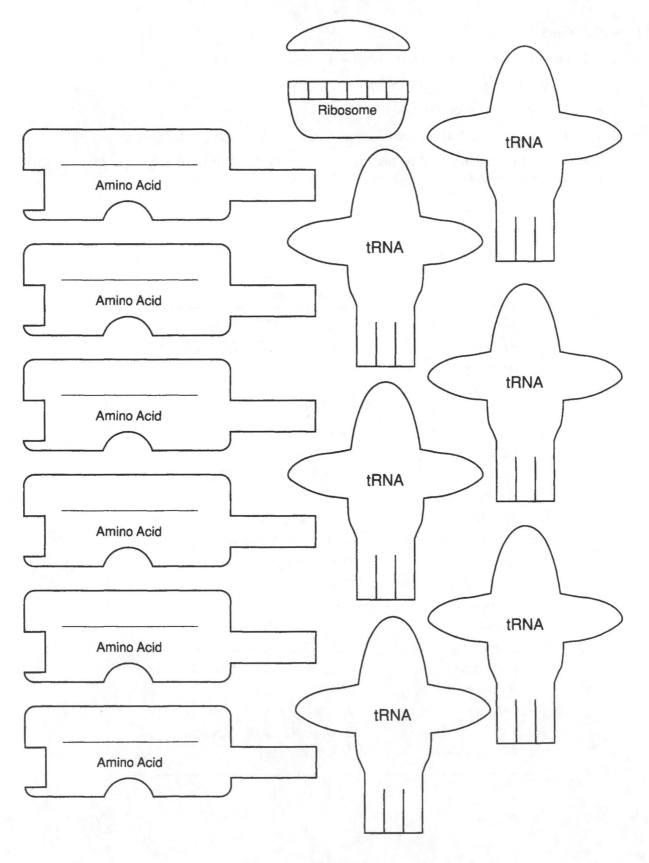

Copyright © 2008 by John Wiley & Sons, Inc.

Copyright © 2008 by John Wiley & Sons, Inc.

LESSON 19: THE BASIC UNIT OF LIFE

19-1 CELLULAR STRUCTURE AND FUNCTION
Content on Cells

A Celebration: Meeting the Cell

Everyone begins life as a single cell, a fertilized ovum. This cell divides and eventually grows into an adult composed of trillions of cells. Cells in the body are constantly dying and being replaced by cell division. Cytologists, scientists who study cells, have compiled much information about the anatomy (structure) and physiology (function) of the cell.

The English naturalist Robert Hooke named cells in 1665. He selected this term from the Latin word *cella* ("small container"). Hooke observed cork cells under the microscope and described them as resembling small honeycombs. Due to the poor quality of microscope lenses in that day, Hooke could see only the outer casing of the cell. In 1831, the scientist Robert Brown made the first exciting observations of internal cell parts. Later in the seventeenth century, the scientist Matthias Schleiden recognized that the cytoplasm and nucleus were vital parts of the cell. In this same year, an anatomist, Theodor Schwann, understood the importance of a membrane in protecting the contents of a cell. Over the next three centuries, the invention of the electron microscope and the development of improved sectioning and staining techniques led to continued expansion of knowledge about the contents of a cell.

All cells have certain basic components that enable them to carry out life processes. Even though there are hundreds of different types of cells, some structures are common to almost all: the plasma membrane, cytoplasm, and organelles (structures within the cell that have specific functions).

The Ins and Outs of the Cell

The outer membrane, called the plasma membrane or plasmalemma, is made of a double layer of phospholipids. The plasmalemma separates the cell's internal contents from the external environment, receives communication from other cells, transports substances into and out of the cell, and plays a role in immunity. This membrane contains and protects the organelles of the cell. It is selectively permeable, which means that the membrane regulates which materials can enter and exit the cell based on their composition and size.

Copyright © 2008 by John Wiley & Sons, Inc.

Copyright © 2008 by John Wiley & Sons, Inc.

Some very small molecules, such as oxygen and carbon dioxide, can enter and exit the cell by the process of diffusion, the movement of molecules from a place of greater concentration to a place of lesser concentration. Diffusion requires no expenditure of energy by the cell and is a form of passive transport. Larger particles, such as glucose, require energy to make their way across the cell membrane, so their passage is a form of active transport. Endocytosis and pinocytosis are two more mechanisms that allow materials to be transported into the cell. During endocytosis, large particles are taken into the cell and stored in vacuoles. There they are digested and passed out of the cell in a process of exocytosis. Pinocytosis involves the ingestion of fluid by inward movement of part of the membrane.

The cytoplasm is the jellylike material inside the cell membrane. It is made up of proteins, water, and minerals, and it contains organelles and inclusions. An organelle is a structure that is vital to the life of the cell. Inclusions are nonliving accumulations of cell products, such as fat and wastes. Also within the cell membrane is the cytoskeleton, a network of protein filaments that acts like flexible scaffolding to maintain the cellular shape and provide the cell with the ability to move.

Cilia and flagella are moveable cell parts that protrude from the cell. Cilia look like small hairs on the surface of a cell. In the respiratory tract, cilia propel mucus upward to keep the lungs clear. Flagella are whiplike extensions of the cell that enable it to swim. The flagella of sperm enable these motile cells to travel toward the egg for fertilization.

Cellular Organelles

The nucleus of the cell is the largest of the cell structures. It governs all the activities of the cell because it dictates protein synthesis.

The nucleus contains nucleoplasm and is bounded by a double-layered nuclear envelope that is similar in structure to the cell membrane. Within the nucleus, genetic material in the form of DNA molecules is wrapped around histone proteins to form chromosomes. The nucleus also contains a nucleolus, a structure that controls the synthesis of some of the cell's RNA (ribonucleic acid). Some of the RNA is used to make ribosomes, which function in protein synthesis.

Ribosomes are small organelles that carry out protein synthesis. A cell may have thousands of ribosomes, some attached to the endoplasmic reticulum and some scattered throughout the cytoplasm. Ribosomes are the "protein factories" of the cell and contain RNA and enzymes to perform this function.

A series of canals in a cell forms intricate connecting links between the plasma membrane and the nuclear membrane. These canals, called the endoplasmic reticulum (ER), transport proteins and other materials. There are two types of ER: rough and smooth. The rough ER is so called because it has ribosomes that line the outer surface. The ribosomes on the rough ER synthesize proteins and secrete them into the canals of the ER. From there, the proteins are transported to the Golgi apparatus. Cells such as lymphocytes contain large quantities of rough ER because of their roles in antibody formation and the production of protein for export. Smooth ER does not contain ribosomes and is involved in the synthesis of lipids and carbohydrates. Much smooth ER is found in cells that specialize in making lipids, such as steroid hormones. The male testes and the female corpus luteum, a structure on the ovary, have abundant smooth ER.

The Golgi apparatus is made up of stacks of membranes. This structure makes large carbohydrate molecules and then combines them with proteins to form glycoproteins, which are secreted from the cell. Two types of cells that are rich in Golgi apparatuses are liver cells, which secrete several types of glycoproteins, and plasma cells, which make and release antibodies.

Cells rely on mitochondria to carry out cellular respiration, a process that generates energy from glucose. Each tiny powerhouse has a double membrane, with the inner membrane folded into extensions called cristae. Mitochondria synthesize adenosine triphosphate (ATP) to provide the energy for the cell. The number of mitochondria varies depending on the metabolic activity of the cell. Cells with high metabolic rates, such as those in muscle and liver tissue, contain more mitochondria than most other cell types.

Digestive enzymes in cells are stored in lysosomes. These enzymes are used to dispose of bacteria or other foreign material that enters a cell. Because of the strength of these enzymes, lysosomes have such nicknames as "suicide sacs," "digestive bags," and "cellular garbage disposals." White blood cells contain a large number of lysosomes because they function as scavengers that engulf and destroy bacteria.

Near the nucleus are small centrosomes, organelles that play a role in cell division. Centrosomes contain a pair of centrioles that look like two cylinders located at right angles to each other. Centrioles become prominent during cell division.

The storage chambers of the cell are called vacuoles. Because they contain mostly water, they are often referred to as the "water bubbles" of the cell. There are fewer vacuoles in animal cells than in plant cells. In plant cells, they take up most of the space in cells.

Special Cells

Cells have evolved in numerous ways to fulfill specific tasks within organisms. An enormous degree of variability exists in cell structure. In simple animals, such as paramecia, a cell must be able to carry out a wide range of functions to be self-sufficient. In complex animals, such as humans, cells have become specialized to carry out one type of function only.

Human cells can be classified in a variety of ways based on function and appearance. One of the most common means of classification groups cells into four principal tissue types. Tissues are groups of cells with a common function. The four tissues are epithelial, connective, muscular, and nervous. (See Figure A for a diagram of some human cells.)

Specialized Cell and Tissue Types

Epithelial tissue consists of cells that cover body surfaces, line organs, and compose the secretory cells of glands. Epithelial cells are avascular, meaning that they lack

Copyright © 2008 by John Wiley & Sons, Inc.

Copyright © 2008 by John Wiley & Sons, Inc.

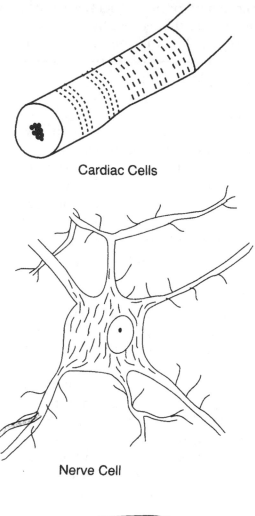

Cardiac Cells

Nerve Cell

Smooth Muscle

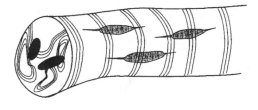

Striated Muscle

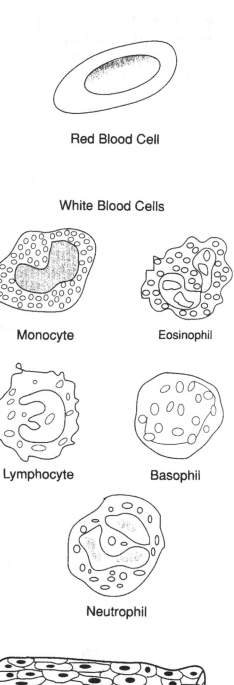

Red Blood Cell

White Blood Cells

Monocyte   Eosinophil

Lymphocyte   Basophil

Neutrophil

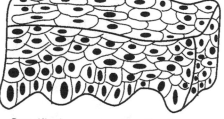

Stratified squamous epithelium
in mouth lining

FIGURE A

blood vessels, and some have cilia. Because they cover and protect other tissues, ep-ithelial cells are subject to wear and tear and must replace themselves by mitosis at a high rate. Epithelial cells compose the surface of the skin and the lining of the mouth, esophagus, and vagina. Glandular epithelial tissue is also found in sweat glands, salivary glands, the pituitary gland, and the thyroid gland.

Connective tissue, the most widespread and abundant tissue in the body, is highly variable. Some examples of connective tissue are bone, cartilage, blood, and adipose (fat). Connective tissue is made of cells that provide support, flexibility, transport, and defense. Red blood cells, or erythrocytes, are a component of con-nective tissue that functions solely to carry oxygen and carbon dioxide around the body to where it can be used or exhaled. In its immature state, each red blood cell possesses a nucleus and all the other major organelles, but it pushes out its nucleus and disintegrates its organelles as it ages. At maturity, a red blood cell has only a cell membrane, hemoglobin (pigment for carrying oxygen), and a few enzymes. White blood cells, called leucocytes, serve as the body's defense against microorganisms. They possess a nucleus and a large number of lysosomes.

Muscle cells are specialized for contraction to produce movement of the body. They possess such specialized structures as a sarcolemma (plasma membrane), endoplas-mic reticulum (ER), large numbers of mitochondria, and sarcoplasm (cytoplasm).

Muscle is supported by bone tissue. Bone may seem to be dry and lifeless, but it is made up of living cells within a strong matrix. Young bone cells, osteoblasts, help build bone tissue. Osteoblasts mature into osteocytes, which help regulate the use of calcium in bones. When the body needs to remove calcium from bone for other uses, specialized bone cells called osteoclasts break down bone tissue. Bones are constantly being remodeled by these three types of cells.

Adipose cells (fat cells) are among the largest connective tissue cells in the body. They have a nucleus and a thin area of cytoplasm containing the organelles. The re-mainder of the cellular space is composed of a large fat droplet that makes up 95 percent of the cell.

Nerve tissue is adapted to collecting information and transmitting it as electri-cal impulses. Nerve cells (neurons) vary in size and function. A neuron has a cell body (soma) that contains a nucleus. Extensions called dendrites carry impulses to the soma, and an axon conducts impulses away from the soma. Some nerve cells are more than three feet long, so they can carry messages from the spinal cord down to the extremities of the body. The human brain contains about 100 billion neu-rons, which is approximately the same number as that of stars in our galaxy.

Groups of tissues make up the organs of the body. Organs of common function make up organ systems. Groups of organ systems make up the organism. Underly-ing this organizational structure of an organism is the basic unit of structure we call the cell.

Copyright © 2008 by John Wiley & Sons, Inc.

TRI-ING CELL PUZZLE—VOCABULARY ACTIVITY ON
CELLULAR STRUCTURE AND FUNCTION

Directions

After reading *Cellular Structure and Function,* read puzzle clues 1 through 15. Find the vocabulary word that matches the clue. The letter next to the correct answer will correspond to the letter on the triangle. Place the number of the clue above this letter on the triangle. The first one is done for you. Repeat until all 15 blocks are filled with numbers.

    You can check to see if you have the correct answers by adding up the numbers on the FOCUS side of the triangle and entering that number in the box above this word. Do the same for the numbers on the BREAK side of the triangle and for the numbers on the LIGHT side. If all your choices are correct and you have added correctly, the three boxes will contain the same number.

Clues

1. __*Tissues*__ are groups of cells with a common function.

2. _____ are cells that transport oxygen throughout the body.

3. The _____ contains chromosomes and is the director of the cell.

4. _____ are found on rough endoplasmic reticulum.

5. _____ have cell bodies, dendrites, and an axon.

6. The higher the metabolic requirements of the cell, the more _____ you will find in that cell to provide energy.

7. _____ are the cellular garbage disposal units.

8. _____ are organelles that play a major role in cell division.

9. _____ are canals that connect the plasma and nuclear membrane.

10. _____ are protrusions from the epithelial cells that can propel particles or instigate movement of the cell itself.

11. _____ is a type of tissue that lines organs and other body surfaces and acts in a protective function.

12. _____ are related to the secretory activity of the cell. They also synthesize glycoproteins.

13. Osteoclasts and osteoblasts are examples of _____.

14. _____ are specialized for contraction and for production of body movements.

15. _____ make up adipose tissue.

Copyright © 2008 by John Wiley & Sons, Inc.

Vocabulary Words

A. Lysosomes

B. Cilia

C. Nucleus

E. Ribosomes

F. Centrosomes

G. Endoplasmic reticula

H. Golgi apparatus

I. Mitochondria

K. Nerve cells

L. Erythrocytes

O. Fat cells

R. Muscle cells

S. Tissues

T. Epithelium

U. Bone cells

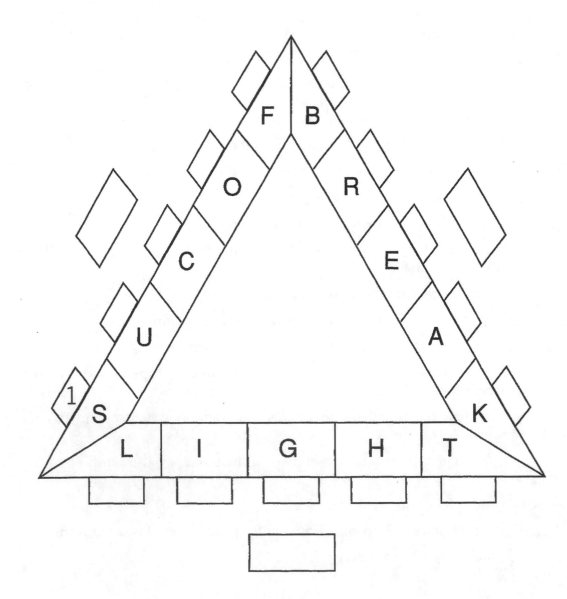

Copyright © 2008 by John Wiley & Sons, Inc.

19-2 CELL TREK
Review Board Game on the Cell

Objectives

Students will learn the organelles and their functions in an animal cell.

Teacher Notes

Before beginning the game, make copies of the Student Cell Worksheet so each participant in the game has a copy. The Cell Trek game boards should be duplicated so that one of each is available for every four students. Several copies of the Cell Part Worksheet should be made for each group. Each cell part on the worksheets should be cut out with scissors and placed in a white envelope labeled Cell Organelles.

Questions 1 through 66 should be duplicated (one set for each group) and cut apart into 66 separate cards. Questions 55 through 66 are complex questions that require higher-level thinking skills; their inclusion is optional. Place the questions in an envelope or manila folder marked Cell Trek Questions.

To protect the game board, glue it on cardboard and have it laminated. Multiple boards and worksheets can be made so that every group of students has a board and a Cell Part Worksheet.

A die is needed to determine the number of times a person moves on the board, and any object can serve as the marker each player moves. Two to four students can play this game. Assign a student to ask the questions and give out the organelles.

If your class only wants to review cell organelles (and not tissues), omit questions 1, 5, 8, 11, 12, 13, 20, 32, 40, 41, and 42. As an incentive, you may want to award extra test points to the winner of each group.

Copyright © 2008 by John Wiley & Sons, Inc.

CELL TREK
Review Board Game on the Cell

Directions

Cell Trek can be played by two to four people. One person must ask the questions and distribute the organelles.

Materials

One die

Cell Trek Game Board (one board per group of two to four players)

A "man" or game piece of any type for each player (such as a coin, paper clip, or small piece of clay)

One Student Cell Worksheet for each player

The student who will ask the questions should gather these materials:

Envelope of organelles cut out from the Cell Part Worksheet

Envelope of question cards

Purpose of the Game

Each player will try to collect cutout organelles to place on his or her cell worksheet. Organelles are earned as players land on them on the game board and correctly answer a question. Each time a player receives an organelle, the player must place it in the proper location on the worksheet. When someone lands on an organelle that he or she has already collected, the turn goes on to the next player. The game is over when a player has collected all the organelles.

To Begin the Game

One student is appointed to ask questions. Other players should place his or her game pieces anywhere on the game board. The players roll the die, and the person who rolls the highest number goes first.

To begin the game, the first player rolls the die again. He or she moves the marker the appropriate number of spaces. If the player lands on an organelle, he or she can get that organelle by correctly answering a question. The student chosen to ask the questions draws a question from the envelope and reads it aloud. If the player answers this question correctly, he or she will receive that organelle from the organelle envelope from the student who asked the question. The player will place this organelle in the proper location on the Student Cell Worksheet. (*Note:* Answers are provided in parentheses at the bottom of each card.)

Copyright © 2008 by John Wiley & Sons, Inc.

The game continues in this manner. If a student fails to answer a question correctly, he or she does not receive an organelle but is not penalized. The game board has some spaces that cause players to lose organelles or gain other players' organelles.

End of the Game

Once a player has completed the Student Cell Worksheet, the game is over and that player is declared the winner.

Play the game again, switching the role of question-asker with one of the players.

Copyright © 2008 by John Wiley & Sons, Inc.

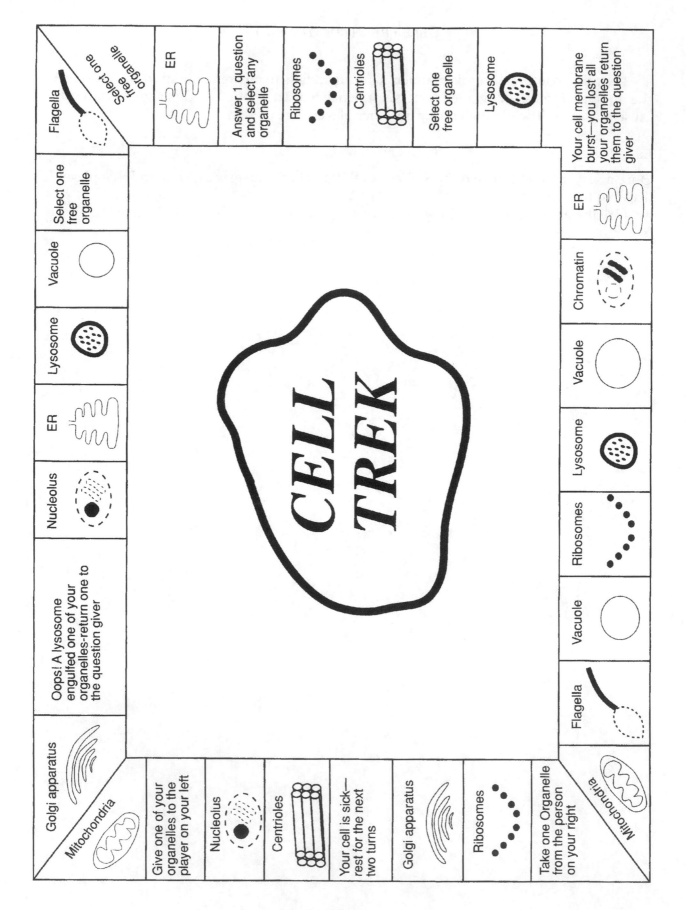

272

Copyright © 2008 by John Wiley & Sons, Inc.

STUDENT CELL WORKSHEET

Copyright © 2008 by John Wiley & Sons, Inc.

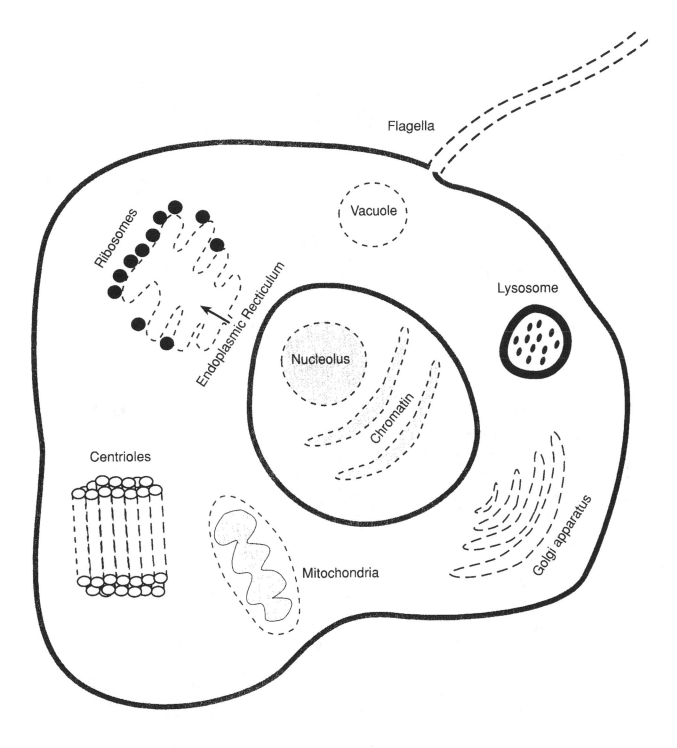

CELL PART WORKSHEET

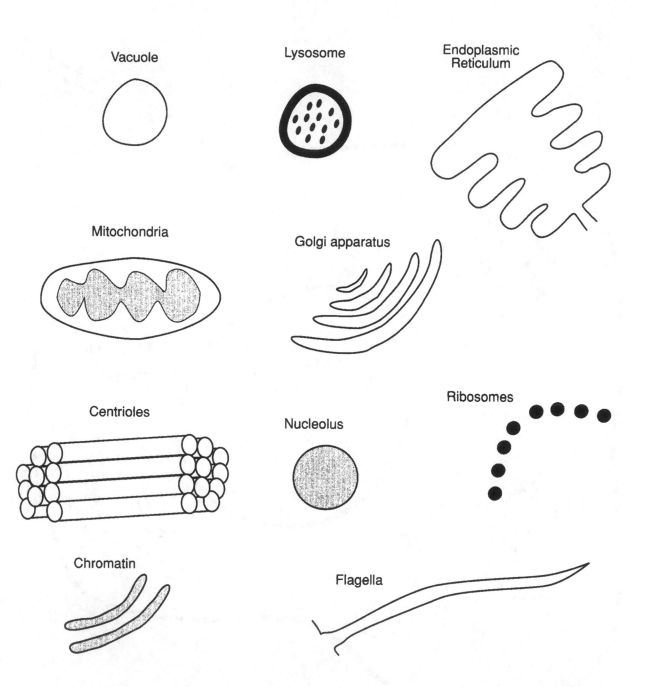

Vacuole

Lysosome

Endoplasmic Reticulum

Mitochondria

Golgi apparatus

Centrioles

Nucleolus

Ribosomes

Chromatin

Flagella

Copyright © 2008 by John Wiley & Sons, Inc.

Copyright © 2008 by John Wiley & Sons, Inc.

1

Leucocytes are also called _____ blood cells.

(white)

2

_____ is the organelle that transports, packages, and releases secretory material.

(Golgi apparatus)

3

A(n) _____ is a motile projection on a sperm cell.

(flagellum)

4

The nucleus is bounded by a double-layered _____.

(nuclear envelope or membrane)

5

A(n) _____ is a group of cells with a common function.

(tissue)

6

Name the scientist who discovered the importance of the cell membrane.

a. Hooke
b. Schleiden
c. Schwann
d. Brown

(Schwann)

7

DNA is the molecule in the nucleus that holds _____ information.

(genetic)

8

Avascular means that the tissue does not have _____.

(blood vessels)

9

Which organelle is known as the cellular garbage disposal?

(lysosome)

10

What structure in the nucleus makes RNA?

(nucleolus)

11

A red blood cell is also called a(n) _____.

(erythrocyte)

12

Adipose cells are commonly called _____ cells.

(fat)

13

_____ tissues are specially adapted to collect and transmit information.

(Nerve)

14

A cell's DNA is located within the ____.

(nucleus)

15

The plasma membrane is made of a double layer of _____.

(phospholipids)

16

Who was the scientist who named cells?

a. Schleiden
b. Schwann
c. Golgi
d. Hooke

(Hooke)

17

Cells that make a lot of protein for export contain a large amount of which organelle?

(rough ER)

18

A _____ is made up of a network of protein filaments that maintain the shape of a cell.

(cytoskeleton)

Copyright © 2008 by John Wiley & Sons, Inc.

Copyright © 2008 by John Wiley & Sons, Inc.

19

_____ are made of groups of tissues with a common function.

(Organs)

20

The cells of this basic tissue type undergo rapid mitosis and replace themselves frequently.

(epithelium)

21

Nonliving accumulations of cell products like fat and waste in a cell are called _____.

(inclusions)

22

The plasmalemma is also called the _____.

(plasma membrane)

23

What projections on the respiratory tract help move mucus away from the lungs?

(cilia)

24

The basic unit of structure of an organism is the _____.

(cell)

25

Which organelle is abundant in muscle cells and other cells that have high energy requirements?

(mitochondria)

26

The _____ is an organelle that acts as the powerhouse of the cell.

(mitochondrion)

27

_____ are organelles that are also called "protein factories."

(Ribosomes)

28

Which tissue type has cells that line and protect the surface of organs?

(epithelial)

29

Oxygen and carbon dioxide are small molecules. They travel through the cell membrane by the process of _____.

(diffusion)

30

Small, hairlike, motile projections on the cell are called _____.

(cilia)

31

What do ribosomes synthesize?

(protein)

32

What type of tissue is bone and cartilage?

(connective)

33

Which organelle is responsible for cellular respiration?

(mitochondria)

34

The inner membrane of mitochondria is folded into extensions called _____.

(cristae)

35

What does smooth ER synthesize?

(lipids and carbohydrates)

36

ATP is a molecule in the cell that provides the cell with _____.

(energy)

Copyright © 2008 by John Wiley & Sons, Inc.

Copyright © 2008 by John Wiley & Sons, Inc.

37

A system of tiny tubes in a cell is called the _____.

(endoplasmic reticulum)

38

_____ is the ingestion of liquid into the cell with the help of the cell membrane.

(Pinocytosis)

39

Glands that produce steroids and other hormones will have a large amount of _____.

a. rough ER
b. smooth ER
c. centrioles
d. lysosomes

(smooth ER)

40

_____ cells compose the lining of the mouth, esophagus, and skin.

(Epithelial)

41

_____ tissue provides support, flexibility, transport, and defense for an organism.

(Connective)

42

Sarcolemma is the plasma membrane of a _____ cell.

(muscle)

43

_____ is the process in which solids are removed from a cell.

(Exocytosis)

44

_____ are living, permanent structures with specialized functions vital to the cell.

(Organelles)

45

_____ transport across the plasma membrane requires no energy expenditure.

(Passive)

46

The invention of this piece of equipment permitted viewing of cellular organelles.

(electron microscope)

47

During _____, bacteria and foreign bodies are taken into a cell and stored in a vacuole.

(Endocytosis)

48

_____ means that a membrane can select which substances enter and leave the cell.

(Selectively permeable)

49

These organelles can be seen during mitosis.

(centrosomes [centrioles])

50

_____ are scientists who study cells.

(Cytologists)

51

This cellular structure separates the contents of a cell from the external environment.

(cell membrane)

52

_____ is the jellylike material inside the cell.

(Cytoplasm)

53

95% of adipose tissue is composed of _____.

(fat globules)

54

What cell part is responsible for changing carbohydrates into ATP?

a. Golgi apparatus
b. Ribosomes
c. Nucleus
d. Mitochondria

(mitochondria)

Copyright © 2008 by John Wiley & Sons, Inc.

Copyright © 2008 by John Wiley & Sons, Inc.

55

Which organelles are called "suicide sacs"?

(lysosomes)

56

What makes the ER rough?

(ribosomes)

57

_____ is the movement of molecules from a place of greater to lesser concentration.

(Diffusion)

58

When blood flows through the kidneys, small molecules move out of the blood and into the kidney tubules. This type of transport is called

a. diffusion
b. osmosis
c. endocytosis
d. exocytosis

(diffusion)

59

The job of the nuclear membrane is similar to the job of the cell membrane, which controls the things that enter and leave the cell. Which type of material would most likely make up the nuclear membrane?

a. DNA
b. carbohydrates
c. phospholipids
d. amino acids

(phospholipids)

60

White blood cells have a large number of these organelles because they take in and destroy microbes and dead cell parts.

a. plasma membranes
b. centrioles
c. lysosomes
d. vacuoles

(lysosomes)

61

During development, some cells must be destroyed to make structures such as fingers and toes. Organelles called _____ release enzymes that break down unwanted cellular material.

a. lysosomes
b. plasma membranes
c. centrioles
d. ribosomes

(lysosomes)

62

Nerve cells do not divide. Therefore, it is not surprising that nerve cells lack _____.

a. Golgi apparatuses
b. mitochondria
c. lysosomes
d. centrioles

(centrioles)

63

Researchers have discovered a toxin that interferes with a cell's ability to release stored energy. Cells exposed to this toxin cannot carry out many of their normal processes. Which of these cell organelles are most directly affected by this toxin?

a. ribosomes
b. chloroplasts
c. mitochondria
d. vacuoles

(mitochondria)

64

Heart muscle beats 24 hours a day, 7 days a week. Cells in heart muscle have an unusually large number of ___.

a. ribosomes
b. lysosomes
c. mitochondria
d. centrioles

(mitochondria)

65

A two-year-old child is always tired. His doctor finds that this child has a rare birth defect that causes an abnormally low production of one type of cellular organelle. This organelle is most likely the ___.

a. Golgi apparatus
b. nucleus
c. nucleolus
d. mitochondria

(mitochondria)

66

You examine a cell under the microscope and find that it has an extremely large water vacuole. This cell most likely came from a(n) ___.

a. cat
b. plant
c. child
d. adult

(plant)

Copyright © 2008 by John Wiley & Sons, Inc.

19-3 CELLS ARE WITHIN YOUR GRASP
Performance Assessment on Cells

Objectives

Students will conduct a presentation that demonstrates their understanding of the structure and function of a cell.

Teacher Notes

This project should be done near the conclusion of the study of cell structure and function. You can place students in groups or allow them to select their own group. In your role as facilitator, provide the materials and resources students will need to do their research and produce their visual aid. Give out the grading rubric at the beginning of the project so that students are aware of the point totals assigned each task.

Copyright © 2008 by John Wiley & Sons, Inc.

CELLS ARE WITHIN YOUR GRASP
Performance Assessment on Cells

Introduction

GRASP is an acronym that stands for *goal*, *role*, *audience*, *situation*, and *product*. To demonstrate your understanding of the structure and function of cells, you will complete each component of the GRASP performance assessment activity as outlined below. A grading rubric is provided so that you know how you will be graded on each part of this performance assessment.

The following are the components of the GRASP activity on cells:

GOAL: Perform a presentation, complete with visual aid, that answers questions linking the main concepts of cell function and structure.

ROLE: Your group plays the role of an educational consultant team employed by a major science textbook publisher.

AUDIENCE: You will address your presentation to middle school life science teachers in a school system that is considering adoption of the textbook you are marketing.

SITUATION: You and your group are a team of educational consultants who helped develop a middle school life science textbook. The Fairfield County School District is considering your textbook and has requested that your company send a team of consultants to describe and explain why your textbook is of higher quality than those marketed by competing publishers.

The Fairfield County middle school science teachers would like your team to describe some special features about the first unit in the book, The Cell. Because Fairfield schools place high emphasis on critical thinking skills and conceptual understandings, the life science teachers have sent you seven questions they would like for you to cover in your presentation.

When you present to the teachers of Fairfield County, you need to emphasize how your book will grab the attention of the reader. The teachers will be especially interested in hearing about real-life examples, thoroughness, and accuracy.

PRODUCT: A presentation that includes a team-constructed visual aid will be presented to the Fairfield science teachers. The visual aid should include colorful graphics, pictures, or diagrams that are included in your textbook, and these visuals should be used to help sell your book to the audience. Each team member should orally participate in the presentation, and each person should be well versed in the material so that he or she can respond to questions at the conclusion of the presentation. Note cards are permissible, but presenters are encouraged only to refer to the notes rather than read them word for word. Some examples of products include PowerPoints, trifold boards, posters, and cartoons.

A grading rubric is attached. You will be graded by the teacher (science supervisor) and your peers (the middle school life science teachers).

Copyright © 2008 by John Wiley & Sons, Inc.

Questions from Fairfield Science Teachers
That Need to Be Addressed During Presentation

1. What are the characteristics of all cells? Describe some examples of cells.

2. Why is energy important to a cell, and how does a cell produce this energy?

3. How do cells obtain nutrients, and why is it important that they do so?

4. What organelles are common to both plant and animal cells, and what is the function of each organelle?

5. What are the differences in plant and animal cells?

6. Differentiate between the terms *unicellular* and *multicellular*. Why aren't all organisms unicellular?

7. Why do multicellular organisms have specialized cells? Name and describe at least three cells in humans that have specialized functions.

8. What is homeostasis, and how do cells attempt to maintain this condition? Give some examples.

Copyright © 2008 by John Wiley & Sons, Inc.

RUBRIC FOR ANSWERS TO QUESTIONS

	Exemplary— 4	*Well Done— 3*	*Satisfactory but Needs Some Work— 2*	*Below Par— 1*	*Evaluation Score*
Question 1	Thorough, correct answer with real-life examples	Correct, but answer is not thorough, or no examples are given	Correct, but lacking a thorough explanation and examples	Incorrect answer or not thoroughly covered or explained	
Question 2	Thorough, correct answer with real-life examples	Correct, but answer is not thorough, or no examples are given	Correct, but lacking a thorough explanation and examples	Incorrect answer or not thoroughly covered or explained	
Question 3	Thorough, correct answer with real-life examples	Correct, but answer is not thorough, or no examples are given	Correct, but lacking a thorough explanation and examples	Incorrect answer or not thoroughly covered or explained	
Question 4	Thorough, correct answer with real-life examples	Correct, but answer is not thorough, or no examples are given	Correct, but lacking a thorough explanation and examples	Incorrect answer or not thoroughly covered or explained	
Question 5	Thorough, correct answer with real-life examples	Correct, but answer is not thorough, or no examples are given	Correct, but lacking in thorough explanation and examples	Incorrect answer or not thoroughly covered or explained	
Question 6	Thorough, correct answer with real-life examples	Correct, but answer is not thorough, or no examples are given	Correct, but lacking in thorough explanation and examples	Incorrect answer or not thoroughly covered or explained	
Question 7	Thorough, correct answer with real-life examples	Correct, but answer is not thorough, or no examples are given	Correct, but lacking in thorough explanation and examples	Incorrect answer or not thoroughly covered orf explained	
Question 8	Thorough, correct answer with real-life examples	Correct, but answer is not thorough, or no examples are given	Correct, but lacking a thorough explanation and examples	Incorrect answer or not thoroughly covered or explained	

Comments: _____

_____

Points possible: 32

Points earned: _____

Copyright © 2008 by John Wiley & Sons, Inc.

RUBRIC FOR VISUAL AID, PRESENTATION, AND WORK ETHIC

Copyright © 2008 by John Wiley & Sons, Inc.

Elements and Criteria	Exemplary— 4	Well Done— 3	Satisfactory but Needs Some Work— 2	Below Par— 1	Evaluation Score
Visual aid used during presentation	Colorful graphics/ pictures were used to help explain the concepts. All terms were spelled correctly.	Colorful graphics/ pictures were used to help explain the concepts. At least one word was misspelled.	Had a minimal number of colorful graphics or diagrams, or several words were misspelled.	Very few graphics or diagrams were included, or those that were included did not explain the topic. Several words were misspelled.	
Presentation: • Made good eye contact • Spoke in a clear voice • Had a good understanding of material • Spoke without reading word for word	Demonstrated 4 of 4 criteria.	Demonstrated 3 of 4 criteria.	Demonstrated 2 of 4 criteria.	Demonstrated 1 or none of the 4 criteria.	
Group skills: • Organization and advance planning evident • Convincing presentation • Group worked well together to convince the audience • Smooth transitions during the presentation	All 4 criteria were met.	3 of 4 criteria were met.	2 of 4 criteria were met.	None or 1 of 4 criteria was met.	

Points possible: 36

Points earned: _____

LESSON 20: MENDELIAN GENETICS

20-1 MENDEL'S IDEAS ON INHERITANCE OF TRAITS
Content on Mendelian Genetics

Father of Genetics

Why do you look like you do? For centuries, people knew that the offspring of plants and animals, including humans, had many of the traits of their parents, but they had no idea why. Gregor Mendel (1822–1884), an Austrian monk, was the first person to conduct research on, and propose a scientific explanation for, the process by which traits are passed from parent to offspring. Mendel discovered the basic principles of inheritance, and for his work he is remembered as the Father of Genetics.

When preparing for his research, Mendel first had to select an organism with which to study inheritance. Mendel selected plants rather than animals because plants reproduce quickly and are much easier to manage in experiments. He wanted a type of plant that had several distinctive, easy-to-identify characteristics. In addition, he needed a plant that could self-fertilize. He settled on a common organism, the garden pea, *Pisum sativum*.

Pea Plant Pollination

Garden peas were ideal for Mendel's work for several reasons. The reproductive structures of peas and most other plants are the flowers. The female part of the flower is the pistil (see Figure A). Egg cells are produced in the ovary at the base of the pistil. The male parts of a flower are the stamens, which supply pollen. A pollen grain contains a sperm cell and a pollen tube cell. During the process of pollination, pollen grains are transferred from the stamen to the top of the pistil, a region known as the stigma. The pollen tube cell generates a channel through which the sperm cell travels to the egg-laden ovary. Within the ovary, fertilization occurs when the sperm combines with one egg cell.

Once fertilized, the ovary develops into a fruit. Fruits take on a variety of sizes and shapes. In the case of the pea, the fruit is a pea pod. The peas inside a pea pod are the seeds for the next generation of young plants. Seeds germinate and grow into plants similar to their parents.

Most flowers are capable of cross-pollinating, a process in which the sperm produced by the anther of one flower fertilizes the eggs in the ovary of another flower.

Copyright © 2008 by John Wiley & Sons, Inc.

Copyright © 2008 by John Wiley & Sons, Inc.

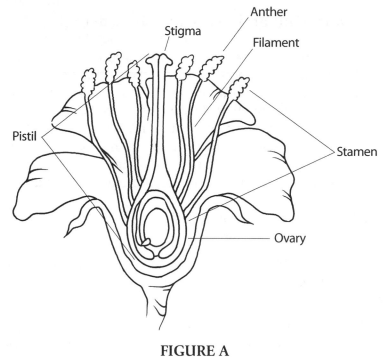

FIGURE A

Cross-pollination makes it difficult to conduct genetic studies because the source of pollen is not easy to trace. This is one reason why Mendel chose self-pollinating pea plants for his experiments. When Mendel's research called for cross-pollination in the peas, he transferred pollen from the anther of one plant to the stigma of a different plant.

Pea plants have 34 clearly distinguishable characteristics, each of which has two distinct forms. For example, the characteristic of height may be expressed in the form of tall or short. The texture of a pea seed is a characteristic; it may be smooth or wrinkled. Flower color in pea plants can be purple or white, and seed color can be yellow or green.

Mendel's Methods

Mendel studied one trait at a time, beginning with seed texture. Mendel raised hundreds of two types of pea plants: those that produce only smooth seeds and those that yield only wrinkled seeds. He called these pure-breeding plants the parental (P) generation.

When Mendel cross-pollinated these two types of pure-breeding plants, the offspring were all smooth seeded. He designated the offspring of the parental generation the first filial (F_1) generation. Mendel planted the F_1 seeds and let them mature into plants. When these F_1 plants produced flowers, he allowed them to self-pollinate. He called the offspring of the F_1 generation the second filial (F_2) generation. Examination of the F_2 seeds revealed that most were smooth seeded, but a few had wrinkled seeds. In statistical analysis, Mendel found that the ratio of smooth to wrinkled seeds in this F_2 generation was 3:1.

Dominant and Recessive Characteristics

Mendel designated the characteristic that appeared in the F_1 generation as the *dominant* factor. In this study, smooth texture was the characteristic seen in all F_1 plants, and it was found to be a dominant factor over wrinkled texture. Mendel described the wrinkled trait, the one that showed up in the F_2 generation, as *recessive*.

According to Mendel, factors were inherited in pairs. In each generation, a pea plant has a pair of factors for each characteristic. This means that F_1 plants had two factors that coded for their smooth texture. In the same way, F_2 plants had two factors that could be coded for smooth texture in some individuals and wrinkled texture in others.

Mendel conducted thousands of genetic crosses in pea plants. From these crosses, he drew some fascinating conclusions:

1. In the F_1 generation, only one of the two factors inherited from the parents can be seen. For example, in the case of seed texture, the F_1 generation showed smooth coats.

2. The parental factor that did not appear in the F_1 generation appears in the F_2 generation. In the seed texture study, if the F_1 seeds were all smooth, the trait for wrinkles would show up in the F_2 seeds.

3. Factors are passed from the parents to the offspring. In the process, they do not change.

4. Each parent plant donates the same amount of inheritable information to the offspring.

Principle of Segregation

The outward appearance of a trait, such as smooth or wrinkled texture of seed coat, is called the phenotype. The term *genotype* refers to the genetic makeup, the factors that cause the appearance of the organism. Uppercase letters indicate the dominant trait, and lowercase the recessive trait. Two factors for smooth texture are written as *SS*, whereas *ss* shows two factors for wrinkled texture. If both factors are present, the genotype is written as *Ss*.

Mendel suggested that during the formation of a gamete, an egg or sperm, the paired factors separate. For example, if a cell in a pure-breeding smooth-seeded (SS) plant forms two sperm, one sperm receives one of the paired factors (S), and the other sperm receives the other paired factor (S). In the same way, if a cell in a pure-breeding wrinkled-seeded (ss) plant forms two eggs, one egg gets one of the paired factors (s), and the other egg receives the other one (s). When an F_1 plant (Ss) produces gametes, one receives a dominant factor (S) and the other a recessive factor (s). This concept of separating factors is known as the principle of segregation.

Copyright © 2008 by John Wiley & Sons, Inc.

Principle of Independent Assortment

In reality, a pea plant or any other type of organism does not have just one trait. Organisms have many traits, each of which has two different types of factors. Mendel's first experiments examined only one trait; this type of genetic cross is referred to as a monohybrid cross. Mendel expanded his pea plant experiments to include dihybrid crosses in which he studied two different traits: seed texture (wrinkled [s] or smooth [S]) and seed color (green [y] or yellow [Y]). He analyzed each of the inherited traits as if the other trait were not even present.

In the F_2 generation of dihybrid crosses, Mendel could still see the 3:1 ratio that he found in monohybrid crosses. He concluded that when gametes form, the segregation of S and s factors takes place independently of the separation of Y and y factors. For example, the S factor is not always paired with the Y factor. The chance that any gamete will inherit an S is 1:2. The chance that any gamete will inherit a Y is 1:2. So the chance that any gamete will inherit both of these factors (Y and S) is 1:4. These results helped Mendel form the principle of independent assortment, which states that during gamete formation, different traits assort independently of each other.

Since Mendel

Mendel spent eight years raising peas and analyzing their characteristics. His careful work and strict devotion to the scientific method laid the foundation for modern-day genetics. Nearly all the genetic discoveries that followed Mendel have been based on his work. Geneticists now know that Mendel's inheritable factors are actually genes. Research has shown that genes are made up of segments of deoxyribonucleic acid, or DNA, which is located within the nuclei of cells.

Since Mendel's day, it has become clear that his discoveries about inheritance in peas do not apply to all traits. In some cases, the principle of independent assortment does not apply because some traits are linked; inheriting one increases the chance of inheriting the other. In addition, it is now known that sometimes traits blend instead of being inherited in the original forms and that dominance and recessiveness can be expressed in degrees. In addition, there are "factors" that Mendel never suspected, such as modifier genes that affect the expression of other genes.

Copyright © 2008 by John Wiley & Sons, Inc.

ACROSTIC—VOCABULARY ACTIVITY ON
MENDEL'S IDEAS ON INHERITANCE OF TRAITS

Directions

After reading *Mendel's Ideas on Inheritance of Traits,* read each clue and write your answer in the corresponding vertical blanks. Numbers 1 and 2 are done for you as examples. When you complete the puzzle, there will be a message in the horizontal boxes.

Clues

1. The male part of a flower is the _____.

2. During _____-pollination, pollen is transferred from the stamen to the pistil of the same flower.

3. A(n) _____ cross examines only one set of inheritable factors.

4. A fruit contains one or more _____.

5. The _____ trait does not appear until the F_2 generation.

6. The transfer of pollen from the anther of one flower to the pistil of another flower is _____.

7. The _____ is the female part of a flower.

8. The common garden pea is *Pisum* _____.

9. Mendel theorized that there are _____ forms of each inheritable factor.

10. The flowers of garden peas may be _____ or purple.

11. The fusion of egg and sperm is _____.

12. The offspring of the parental generation produce the first _____ generation.

13. Gregor Mendel lived in _____.

14. An organism's _____ is its particular combination of inheritable factors.

15. An organism's _____ is the way it looks.

16. According to the principle of _____, pairs of heritable factors separate when gametes form.

17. Eggs are produced in the _____.

18. In plants, grains of _____ contain sperm.

19. Mendel called inheritable traits _____.

20. Eggs and sperm are _____.

21. The P, or _____, generation is usually made up of pure-breeding organisms.

Copyright © 2008 by John Wiley & Sons, Inc.

22. Genetic information is carried on _____, a molecule within the nuclei of cells.

23. Segments of DNA that code for traits make up _____.

24. When a pollen grain lands on the top of the pistil, the grain generates a _____ through which sperm can travel to the ovary.

25. Mendel used the _____ method to learn more about inheritance.

26. During _____-pollination, the pollen of one plant pollinates the flower of a different plant.

27. According to the principle of independent _____, different traits sort independently during gamete production.

Copyright © 2008 by John Wiley & Sons, Inc.

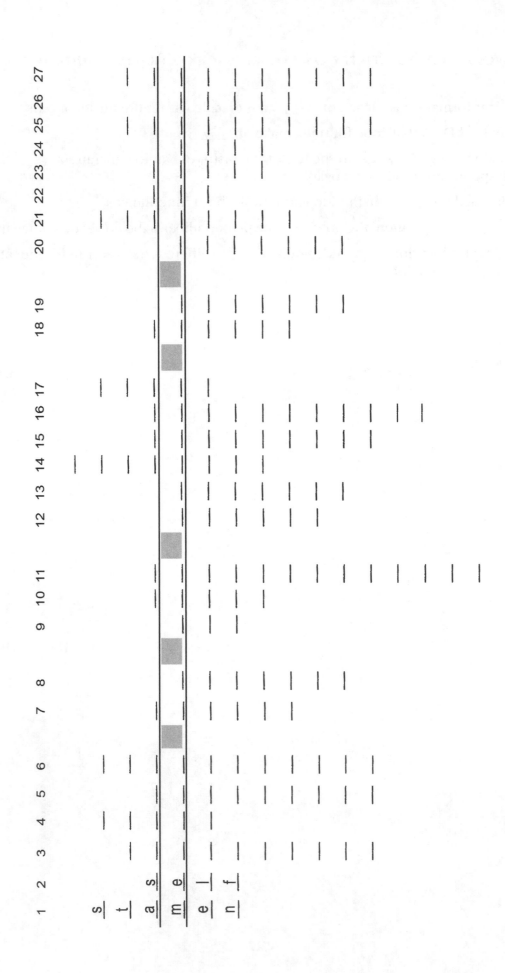

Copyright © 2008 by John Wiley & Sons, Inc.

20-2 MENDELIAN GENETICS
Lab on Inheritance of Traits in Pea Plants

Objective

Students will simulate Mendel's work on the inheritance of seed coat texture in pea plants.

Teacher Notes

Prepare ten pea pods for each lab group: five F_1 pods and five F_2 pods. Make pods out of small squares of green plastic wrap. To construct each F_1 pod, place four smooth peas (dried peas from the grocery store) in each pod. The F_2 pods should contain three smooth peas and one wrinkled pea. If smooth and wrinkled peas are not available, use peas of two different colors.

Make a copy of the answer sheet for each lab group.

Copyright © 2008 by John Wiley & Sons, Inc.

MENDELIAN GENETICS
Lab on Inheritance of Traits in Pea Plants

Introduction

Mendel believed that the inheritance of traits was determined by factors that passed unchanged from parent to offspring. Mendel was able to use his ideas of hereditary factors to predict characteristics in peas. In his experiments with pea plants, Mendel strictly adhered to the steps of the scientific method. After he formed a hypothesis, he set up experiments in which he carefully controlled variables. During and after the experiment, Mendel collected and recorded data, then analyzed it before drawing any conclusions.

Although Mendel chose plants as his test subjects, the contributions he made were universal because they applied the basic principles of heredity. Mendel's work paved the way for future discoveries, including the understanding of dominant and recessive traits and the analysis of the influence of genes on health, sex, and appearance.

In this experiment, you will play the role of Gregor Mendel. You have been given ten pea pods: five are F_1 pods, and five are F_2 pods. The F_1 pods are the offspring of the parental generation, and they were produced by cross-pollinating a parental pea plant that produces smooth peas with a parental pea plant that produces wrinkled peas. These two parental pea organisms were both pure-breeding pea plants.

Materials

   5 F_1 pea pods
   5 F_2 pea pods

Prelab Questions

   1. What organisms did Mendel use in his experiments on the mechanisms of inheritance?

   2. Name two essential elements of the scientific method.

   3. Explain the difference between the F_1 and F_2 generations.

   4. Why were Mendel's experiments important?

Procedure, Part A

   1. Place the 5 F_1 pods on your desktop. Each pod contains four peas. Each pea will be either smooth or wrinkled.

   2. Predict the number of smooth peas and the number of wrinkled peas you expect to find in each pod. Remember, the peas in these pods are the offspring of a cross between a parental pea plant that produces smooth peas and a parental pea plant that produces wrinkled peas. Record your prediction on the answer sheet.

   3. Open each of the F_1 pea pods. Count the number of smooth and wrinkled seeds in each pod. Record the numbers of each in the F_1 data table on your answer sheet.

Copyright © 2008 by John Wiley & Sons, Inc.

4. Calculate the total number of smooth peas and the total number of wrinkled peas in these five pea pods. Record these totals on the F_1 data table.

5. Determine the percentage of smooth peas in the four pods. To do so,

   a. Divide the total number of smooth seeds by the total number of all the seeds in the pods.

   b. Move your decimal two places to the right to express the percentage.

   Record the percentage on the data table.

6. Use the same procedure to determine the percentage of wrinkled peas in the four pods. Record the percentage on the data table. (Hint: The total percentages of smooth and wrinkled peas should equal 100.)

7. Compare your findings to your predictions in step 1. If your predictions do not agree with your findings, explain why not in the space provided on the answer sheet. If your predictions do agree with your findings, explain the rationale behind your original predictions.

Procedure, Part B

1. Set aside the F_1 generation pea pods.

2. Place the five F_2 pea pods on your desktop. Remember, these pods are the result of self-pollination of the F_1 plants.

3. Repeat steps 2 through 7 in Part A, entering your data in the F_2 data table.

4. Answer the postlab questions.

Postlab Questions

1. In this experiment, what was the dominant trait, smooth or wrinkled? How do you know?

2. In the F_1 generation, what percentage of peas expressed the dominant gene?

3. In the F_2 generation, what percentage of peas expressed the recessive gene?

4. Imagine that you are repeating Gregor Mendel's experiment. You will use the same lab procedure that you used in this experiment, but this time you will study the trait of flower color. In peas, flowers may be purple or white. You know that purple flowers are more prevalent in your garden. When you cross the two parental generations, you get 80 flowers. Now you allow the 80 F_1 plants to self-pollinate. You get 80 F_2 plants.

   a. How many of the 80 F_1 plants do you expect to have purple flowers?

   b. How many of the 80 F_2 plants do you expect to have white flowers?

5. Summarize what your learned in class in a 3-2-1 reflection by

   a. Describing three ways that Mendel's work changed the way scientists thought about genetics.

   b. Explaining two ways that Mendel demonstrated the characteristics of an exemplary scientist.

   c. Stating one thing about today's lab that you don't completely understand and would like to have clarified.

Copyright © 2008 by John Wiley & Sons, Inc.

LAB ON INHERITANCE OF TRAITS IN PEA PLANTS
Student Answer Sheet

Prelab Questions

1. _____

2. _____

3. _____

   _____

4. _____

   _____

Procedure, Part 1

Prediction for the first filial seeds: _____

_____

F_1 DATA TABLE

	Pod 1	Pod 2	Pod 3	Pod 4	Pod 5	Total	Percentage
Smooth							
Wrinkled							

Explanation for the F_1 seeds: _____

_____

Procedure, Part 2

Prediction for the second filial seeds: _____

_____

298

Copyright © 2008 by John Wiley & Sons, Inc.

F$_2$ DATA TABLE

	Pod 1	Pod 2	Pod 3	Pod 4	Pod 5	Total	Percentage
Smooth							
Wrinkled							

Explanation for the F$_2$ seeds: _____

_____

Postlab Questions

1. _____

_____

2. _____

_____

3. _____

_____

4a. _____

_____

4b. _____

_____

5a. _____

_____

5b. _____

_____

5c. _____

_____

Copyright © 2008 by John Wiley & Sons, Inc.

LESSON 21: CHANGES AND ADAPTATIONS

21-1 CHANGING WITH THE TIMES
Content on Adaptations

Adaptations—Changes for the Better

Why do ducks have webbed feet while horses have hooves? Why do roses have thorns while trees have thick bark? Why do birds fly south for the winter while humans shiver when they are cold? These kinds of questions plagued scientists throughout history. In 1809, the French naturalist Jean Lamarck attempted to answer them. Lamarck stated that organisms recognize the need to acquire a trait that helps them adapt to a changing environment. According to his line of thinking, ducks developed webbed feet because they needed them to paddle in water. Once a duck acquired webbed feet, it could pass them on to its offspring. Lamarck gave the name *acquired characteristics* to these traits.

In 1859, Charles Darwin challenged Lamarck's theory. In his book *The Origin of Species,* Darwin proposed a different idea. He pointed out that organisms produce more offspring than survive. Some of them die from lack of resources, and others because they cannot compete with stronger organisms for food or space. He also noted that no two individuals in a population are exactly alike; some have traits that are advantageous in some way. Darwin said that organisms with advantageous traits are more likely to survive and pass those traits on to their offspring. According to Darwin, the environment selects which organisms survive and which ones die. Organisms best adapted to live in an environment are the ones that succeed and pass on their genes.

Fit to Survive

Variations are traits that make one organism different from another individual of the same species. These traits are controlled by genes. Organisms without useful traits rarely live long enough to reproduce. Only the fittest organisms, or those that possess the traits that help them overcome challenges in the environment, survive.

Darwin had no knowledge of modern genetics when he first proposed his theory of the survival of the fittest. He could not explain how variations appear in a population of organisms. But he understood that variations exist. Today we know that variations result from mutations within organisms. A mutation is any change

Copyright © 2008 by John Wiley & Sons, Inc.

300

Copyright © 2008 by John Wiley & Sons, Inc.

in the DNA code of an organism that produces a trait that is different than expected. Mutations are random changes that cannot be predicted. Useful traits that are produced by mutations are described as adaptations. However, not all mutations are helpful. Some have no effect on an organism; others are harmful. If the trait increases the probability of survival, it is passed on to future offspring and therefore retained in the population.

Manchester Moths

The concept of natural selection was illustrated in Manchester, England, in the nineteenth century. Until 1850, the populations of peppered moths in Manchester were primarily light colored. By 1895, almost all the moths were dark in coloration. What caused the change from light to dark coloration in moths? The Industrial Revolution helps explain this reversal of moth color. Before the Industrial Revolution, the bark on most trees was light colored. When light-colored moths landed on the bark, they were naturally camouflaged from birds and other predators. The few dark-colored members of their population usually died young because they were easy prey.

The Industrial Revolution produced a lot of smoke and soot. Within a few years, soot from factories covered rocks and trees in the countryside. When the light-colored moths landed on these newly darkened surfaces, they were visible to predators. This increased visibility made it possible for predators to consume more and more of the light moths. The relatively small number of dark moths that existed in Manchester at that time blended in with the dark bark and survived long enough to reproduce. The offspring of dark moths were dark like their parents. This resulted in a dominance of dark moths as the twentieth century approached.

To understand natural selection, notice that genetic variation existed in the population of peppered moths when the Industrial Revolution began changing the environment. Because dark moths were already present in small numbers in 1850, natural selection could proceed. The amount of time required for a complete change in a population depends on the reproductive capabilities of an organism. Moths accomplished this reversal in less than 50 years, whereas such organisms as bacteria can do so in hours or days. The fast reproductive rates of bacteria help explain why some types become resistant to particular antibiotics so quickly. Humans require hundreds or thousands of years to undergo an evolution of comparable magnitude.

FRAYER DIAGRAMS—VOCABULARY ACTIVITY ON
CHANGING WITH THE TIMES

Directions

After reading *Changing with the Times,* draw a box like the one below for each term or phrase. Write the term or phrase in the top left-hand section of the box. Complete the three other quadrants of the box. Be sure that the definitions, sentences, and examples you use relate to this topic.

Term or phrase	Use this term in a sentence.
Define the term in your own words.	Draw a picture of something that reminds you of this term.

Copyright © 2008 by John Wiley & Sons, Inc.

For example, a Frayer diagram for *gene* might look like this:

GENE	Light color and dark color in peppered moths are due to variations in their genes.
A gene is part of the DNA of an organism that codes for a trait.	

Copyright © 2008 by John Wiley & Sons, Inc.

Terms and Phrases

1. Acquired characteristic
2. Adaptation
3. Darwin
4. Lamarck
5. Mutation

6. Natural selection
7. *The Origin of Species*
8. Peppered moths
9. Survival of the fittest
10. Variation

21-2 PLANT PRODUCTION
Project on Plant Adaptations

Objective

Students will design and create a fictitious plant that has adaptations enabling it to survive in a designated set of environmental conditions.

Teacher Notes

Cut 10 slips of paper and write a number from 1 through 10 on each slip. Place the numbers in a paper bag. The numbers in the bag correspond to the numbers found on Chart 1.

Possible Evaluation Scale

Correctness of information on poster	20 points
Design and creativity of poster	20 points
Neatness and colorfulness of poster	15 points
Amount of research done	10 points
Information presented on Student Answer Sheet	20 points
Oral presentation and ability to explain the design of the plant	15 points
Total	100 points

Copyright © 2008 by John Wiley & Sons, Inc.

PLANT PRODUCTION
Project on Plant Adaptations

Introduction

You may be familiar with some adaptations that help animals survive. The white fur of polar bears camouflages them in their snowy habitats. The wings of birds enable them to live in treetops and find food in places that are not accessible to other organisms. However, you may not be as familiar with the special adaptations of plants. Plants are also well equipped with survival traits. Plant adaptations enable them to take in adequate sunlight, conserve water, acquire nutrients, attract pollinators, and avoid predators.

There are millions of species of plant-eating animals in the world, so plants need plenty of defenses. Running away is not an option for them. To fend off hungry herbivores, plants have developed an arsenal of weapons. Sharp points are very effective deterrents. Thorns (sharply pointed woody branches) and prickles (pointed outgrowths of stems) on shrubs and bushes protect these plants from being consumed by herbivores. Cacti have specialized leaves called spines to discourage grazing animals from dining on these fluid-filled delicacies in the dry desert environment.

Plants also wage chemical warfare against their enemies. Nettles are a group of plants that have tips on their stems and leaves that break off when touched. These tips release a hypodermic-size injection of fluid that causes stinging and swelling. Poison ivy is another plant that discourages predators by causing irritation upon contact. Milkweed takes a different approach; instead of poisoning its attackers, it revolts them. The sap of milkweed has such a terrible taste that most animals avoid eating it.

Most plants get the water and minerals they need from the soil. However, not all environments supply all the nutrients required by plants. Epiphytes, such as bromeliads and orchids, are adapted for life in the dark, well-shaded rain forest. They live on the upper branches of tall trees where sunlight is available. However, at these heights, their roots cannot reach the soil. Epiphytes have developed specialized roots that take in water and nutrients from the air. You have probably heard of insect-eating plants, such as the pitcher plant and Venus fly trap. These organisms often live in bogs and swamps, a relatively safe environment but one that may be lacking in essential nutrients. To make sure they get enough nutrients, these plants trap and digest insects.

In this activity, you will be thinking about the special adaptations that plants have to help them survive in their environments. You will design a plant that can survive in one particular environment.

Materials

Poster board

Markers and crayons

Reference books on plants and adaptations

Reference books on biomes or access to the Internet

Copyright © 2008 by John Wiley & Sons, Inc.

Procedure

1. Work with a partner.

2. Draw a number from the paper bag that the teacher provides. This number will correspond to the plant in Chart 1 you will be designing.

3. Read the information in the chart about your plant's environment. Use the reference material provided and the Internet to find information about the adaptations a plant might develop to survive under the conditions listed. Your plant should be able to protect itself from predators and disease, get adequate sunlight, adjust to temperature extremes, gather nutrients, and obtain water.

4. The project will be completed by thoroughly filling in the answer sheet. After completing the answer sheet, draw, color, and name your special plant on a piece of poster board. You and your partner will show this poster to the class and explain it at a later date.

Copyright © 2008 by John Wiley & Sons, Inc.

PLANT PRODUCTION (*continued*)

CHART 1

Plant	Predators	Exposure to Sunlight	Soil Nutrients (good/fair/poor)	Temperature (degrees F)	Rainfall (inches)	Other Information on the Environment
1	Insects	Open field with tall grasses	Good	70–100	25	Fires occur annually.
2	Fungi	Full	Epiphyte (soil not required)	70–95	300	Air pollution is a problem.
3	Deer	Moderate	Poor	10–90	60	Soil erosion is common.
4	Bison	Extreme	Poor	40–70	10	Droughts occur annually.
5	Grazing animals	Great	Poor	–30–110	3	Droughts and fire can occur on alternating cycles.
6	Root parasites	Poor	Poor; little nitrogen	50–85	50	The area is boggy and nutrient-poor.
7	Fungi and fish	Poor	Poor	40–90	N/A	The area is flooded in water.
8	Birds	Great	Fair	50–80	15	Wind erosion occurs frequently.
9	Vines that strangle trees	Moderate	Fair	–20–30	10	Freezing occurs throughout the winter.
10	Caterpillars	Full	Good	30–80	60	Toxic waste is dumped nearby.

Copyright © 2008 by John Wiley & Sons, Inc.

PROJECT ON PLANT ADAPTATIONS
Student Answer Sheet

Your name _____ Date: _____

Plant no.: _____ Predators: _____

Sunlight exposure: _____ Soil nutrients: _____

Temperature range: _____ Rainfall range: _____

Other special conditions listed:

Name you gave your plant and the reason: _____

_____

Describe the following adaptations the plant you designed would possess to help it survive in the conditions you listed above:

Features of the stem: _____

_____

_____

Features of the leaves: _____

_____

_____

Features of the roots: _____

_____

_____

Average height of the plant as an adult: _____

Describe what will be the most difficult problem your plant will encounter for survival:

_____

_____

_____

Copyright © 2008 by John Wiley & Sons, Inc.

What biome would be the most likely candidate to house one of the plants you designed?

_____

Explain your reason: _____

_____

Write a scenario that describes how the special features (From the other special conditions listed) would be accommodated in the environment:

Copyright © 2008 by John Wiley & Sons, Inc.

21-3 MONSTROUS MUTATIONS
Lab on the Effect of Random Mutations

Objectives

Students will evaluate the effect of random mutations on the ability of a species to survive.

Teacher Notes

You may wish to make up your own mutations if the ones suggested in this activity are not compatible with the materials available in your school. You may also wish to vary the layout of the classroom or conduct this activity outdoors. In preparation for the activity, write the letters A through H on slips of paper (one letter per slip) and place them in a paper bag. These letters will correspond to the letters in Chart 1 in the Procedure section.

Figure A (in the Introduction section) shows a suggested configuration for preparing the classroom for this activity. Place a blanket in the center of the room. Put three peanuts for each student on the blanket. Place plastic bowls with lids or tennis ball cans with lids in different locations around the room. These bowls or cans represent the storage locations for different groups. Assign each group a home location, as in Figure A.

Check with your students to find out if anyone is allergic to peanuts. You may prefer to substitute individually wrapped pieces of candy.

Copyright © 2008 by John Wiley & Sons, Inc.

Copyright © 2008 by John Wiley & Sons, Inc.

MONSTROUS MUTATIONS
Lab on the Effect of Random Mutations

Introduction

The process of evolution involves changes in the genetic makeup of a population over a period of time. Mutations, or alterations in DNA, produce new genetic material that can yield novel traits. Mutations do not appear because of the needs of a group of organisms; they occur merely by chance.

Because of mutations, some individuals in a population may possess characteristics that enable them to flourish in the current environmental conditions. These organisms have a better chance of surviving, producing offspring, and passing on their genes than others in the population.

Not all mutations are helpful. Some alterations of DNA result in characteristics that have no effect, and others actually reduce the individual's chance of survival. For example, if a lizard were born with a mutation that caused it to have white skin, it probably would not survive long enough to reproduce because of its inability to hide from predators. Such a harmful mutation does not remain in the population long enough to be passed on to offspring.

The useful characteristics that are retained and passed on to offspring are called adaptations. Adaptations can be structural, physiological, or behavioral. Some structural adaptations found in animals provide defense mechanisms for the organism. Antlers on deer, quills on porcupines, and venomous glands in rattlesnakes are a few examples of structural adaptations. Behavioral adaptations refer to certain things organisms do that help them survive. A cat arching its back and an owl ruffling its feathers are examples of behavioral adaptations that make animals appear bigger than they actually are to their enemies. A physiological adaptation is one that affects the way an organism's body works. Diving animals, such as seals and whales, have physiological adaptations that let them stay underwater for long periods of time. These changes are beneficial because they help the animals survive.

At the start of this activity, your teacher will have the room arranged as shown in Figure A, with a blanket in the center of the room and three peanuts on the blanket for each student. Peanuts represent the food supply of a population of animals. Plastic bowls with lids represent places where the animals store their food. The teacher will have the home location for each group marked as shown in Figure A.

Prelab Questions

1. What is a mutation?

2. Explain the role of mutations in the ability of organisms to survive.

3. An opossum's ability to play dead when approached by a predator is an example of a _____ adaptation.

4. A bird's ability to fly south when winter weather approaches is an example of a _____ adaptation.

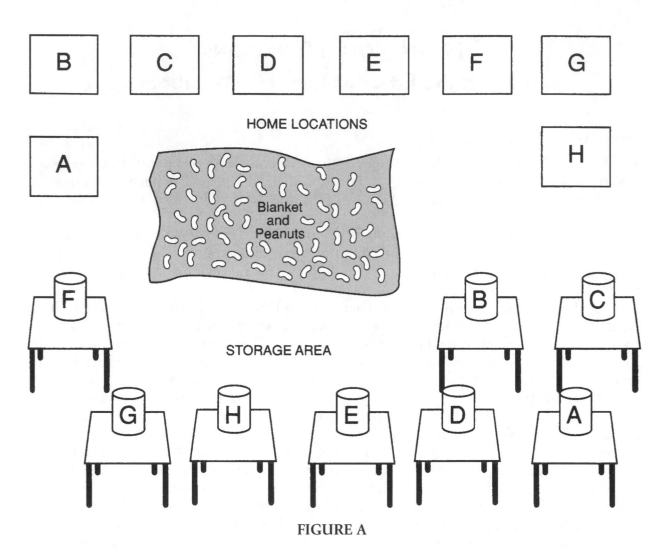

FIGURE A

5. The growth of a heavy coat of hair by an organism in response to cold temperatures is an example of a _____ adaptation.

6. On the back of this sheet, name five adaptations not mentioned in the Introduction section.

Materials

Nine dry peanuts in shells (per group of three students)	Cotton
Table or desk	Three pairs of socks
One can or plastic container with snap-on lid (per group of three students)	Stopwatch or clock with a second hand
15 plastic knives	Six pairs of goggles
Several rolls of duct tape	

Copyright © 2008 by John Wiley & Sons, Inc.

Procedure

1. Work with two other students. Each student represents an animal that can digest only peanuts as its food source. The entire class represents a population of these organisms.

2. Random mutations have produced some unusual characteristics in recent offspring. Each lab group will find out what mutation they possess by selecting a letter from the paper bag your teacher has provided.

3. The letter drawn will correspond to a characteristic listed in Chart 1. This letter will also represent the letter of your group's home location and storage container. Figure A will help you locate these areas.

CHART 1

Letter Drawn by Groups	Characteristic Produced by Mutation
A	Long fingernails (produced by taping plastic knives to fingers with duct tape)
B	No fingers (produced by placing a sock over each hand and taping the hand closed)
C	Lack of peripheral vision (produced by putting on goggles and stuffing cotton in the sides)
D	Hands fused together in front of the body (produced by placing the hands together in front of the body and taping them together)
E	Feet and ankles fused together (produced by taping the ankles tightly together with duct tape)
F	No arms (produced by taping the arms down to the side of the body with duct tape)
G	Arms fused together behind the back at the wrists (produced by placing arms behind the back and taping them tightly at the wrists)
H	Blind (produced by using goggles taped over securely with duct tape)

4. Outfit each member of the group to represent the appropriate mutation. (See Figure B for an illustration of the mutations.)

Copyright © 2008 by John Wiley & Sons, Inc.

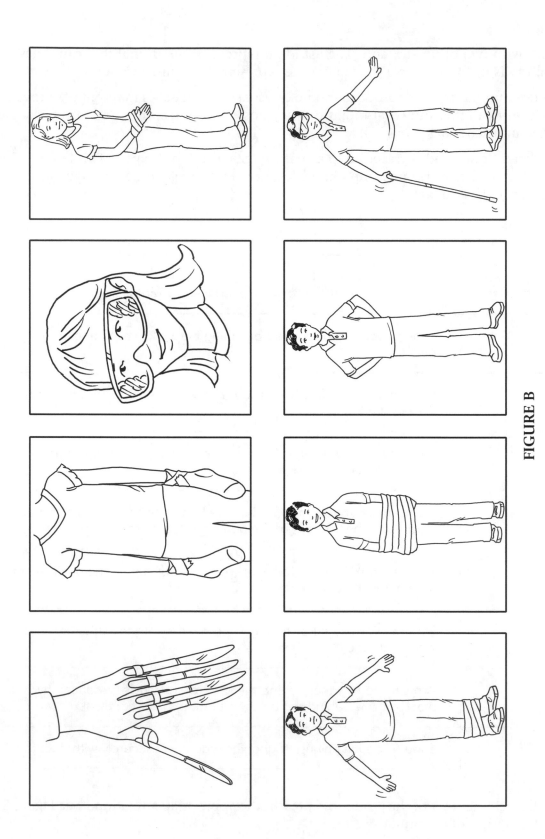

FIGURE B

Copyright © 2008 by John Wiley & Sons, Inc.

5. To begin the activity, each group positions itself at its specified home location. When the teacher starts the stopwatch, all members of the group proceed to the blanket to help collect nine peanuts. These group members take the nine peanuts to their storage container in the storage area, place the peanuts in the container, secure the lid, then return to their home location (leaving the storage container in its original location). Next the group returns to the container to retrieve its food. Once the group has removed all nine peanuts, it takes the food to the home location. The group opens the peanut shells and removes the contents. Each group member consumes three peanuts. When the last peanut has been eaten, record the amount of time that has passed since the activity began.

6. The activity ends when all groups have eaten their peanuts and recorded their times.

7. The teacher writes the times for each group on the chalkboard.

8. Groups answer the postlab questions.

Postlab Questions

1. Which mutation appeared to be the most detrimental to the survival of the species? Explain your answer.

2. Which mutation appeared to have the least detrimental effect on the organism's ability to survive? Explain your answer.

3. What activity in nature is represented by placing peanuts in the plastic bowl?

4. Select an animal in nature and describe how it gathers, stores, retrieves, and processes its food.

5. Make up an adaptation that might result from a mutation that would enable the organism to achieve these goals.

6. Make up an adaptation that might result from a mutation that would prevent the organism from achieving these goals.

Copyright © 2008 by John Wiley & Sons, Inc.

LESSON 22: ECOLOGY

22-1 RELATIONSHIPS IN LIFE
Content on Ecology

Populations and Communities

Nothing exists in isolation on this earth. Every living thing is part of a community of organisms that interact with each other and with their surroundings. Ecologists are scientists who study these relationships between organisms and environment. The term *relationship* refers to interactions with the physical world as well as interactions with other organisms.

A group of the same organisms composes a population, and several populations living in an area form a community. An example of a community is a pond, which might contain populations of bluegills, bass, turtles, snakes, water striders, algae, and cattails. Tumbleweeds, cacti, rattlesnakes, kangaroo mice, skinks, and hawks are populations that might be members of a desert community.

Types of Relationships

The relationships among organisms in a community are complex and varied. Some species develop symbiotic relationships with other species. There are several forms of symbiosis. If symbiots help each other, the relationship between them is called mutualism. The clown fish and sea anemone have a mutualistic living arrangement. The sea anemone is a marine invertebrate that is attached to rock or coral. Its poisonous tentacles wave through the water in search of small fish as prey. The tiny orange-and-white-striped clown fish swims freely into the dangerous anemone tentacles to rest or hide, and it is never stung (see Figure A). The anemone provides protection for the clown fish, and the clown fish often brings food particles to the anemone.

If two symbiots live together and one is helped but the other is neither helped nor harmed, the relationship between them is referred to as commensalism. The orchid plant is a commensal of trees in the rain forest. The orchid is an epiphyte, a plant that does not grow roots into the

FIGURE A

316

Copyright © 2008 by John Wiley & Sons, Inc.

Copyright © 2008 by John Wiley & Sons, Inc.

ground but gets all its nutrients from the air. The host tree is not benefited by the epiphyte, but the epiphyte is helped because the top of the tree provides more light than the forest floor.

In most communities, resources such as food and space are available in limited supplies. Many organisms compete with each other for access to these resources. One form of competition is predation, in which one organism (the predator) kills and eats another organism (the prey). Lions are predators that eat any animal they can catch. Another form of competition is parasitism, in which one organism (the parasite) feeds on another organism (the host). Tapeworms are very specialized parasites that live in the digestive tracts of many organisms. Parasites rarely kill their host, but may weaken it. Parasitoidism is a form of competition in which the larvae of one animal develop inside another animal, consuming the host as they grow. Many wasps lay their eggs inside the bodies of caterpillars. The eggs hatch and begin eating the caterpillar from the inside out.

The Sun's Energy

All living things require energy to maintain life, move, eat, digest, reproduce, and perform a host of other activities. The energy that keeps organisms alive comes from the sun. A very small fraction of the sun's energy shines on Earth, but that little bit is enough to sustain life on this planet. Green plants, or autotrophs, have the ability to absorb the sun's energy and change it to chemical energy in the process of photosynthesis. They can do this because they contain the green pigment chlorophyll, which captures the sun's energy and uses it to change carbon dioxide and water vapor into glucose and oxygen. In this reaction, the sun's energy becomes tied up in the bonds of the glucose molecules. Plants convert glucose to energy in the process of cellular respiration.

Energy Moves Through a Community

Organisms that lack chlorophyll, such as fungi and animals, cannot capture the sun's energy and make glucose. These types of organisms are called heterotrophs. Heterotrophs get the sun's energy by eating glucose-rich green plants. In the process of cellular respiration, heterotrophs break down glucose into carbon dioxide, water vapor, and energy. Like plants, heterotrophs need energy for maintenance, growth, movement, and other life activities.

Energy is transferred from one organism to another along a food chain. When a grasshopper eats a blade of grass, the grasshopper is the first, or primary, consumer in a food chain. If a frog eats the grasshopper, the frog is the secondary consumer. The frog does not get as much energy from the grasshopper as the grasshopper got from the grass, so the frog must eat several grasshoppers to maintain life. A food chain is a small part of a much larger system called a food web. In reality frogs are not the only organisms that eat grasshoppers. Birds also eat grasshoppers and are therefore secondary consumers also. Birds themselves may be eaten, or they may eat

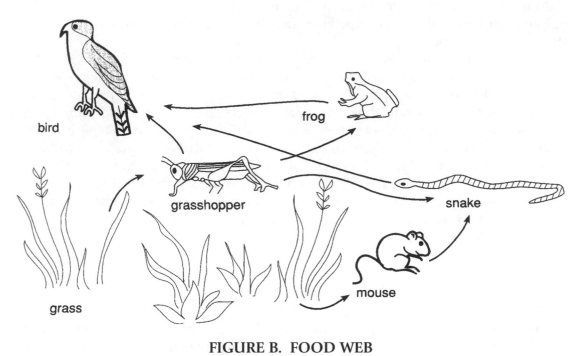

FIGURE B. FOOD WEB

small frogs. This set of interrelationships between organisms creates a food web (see Figure B).

It is easy to visualize grazing food webs, those above ground. We can generally see all the organisms involved and have often witnessed their relationships. A tremendous amount of energy falls to the ground in the form of dead vegetation, however, this vegetation supports the detrital food web. Detritus is dead or decaying matter. Organisms in this food web are extremely small, and we are often unaware of their existence.

Detritivores

The detrital food web can be found in all ecosystems (communities of living things and their nonliving environment). Of the total amount of energy captured by trees, 50 percent is used by the tree for respiration and maintenance, 13 percent for growth, and 2 percent by plant eaters (herbivores). The remaining energy, 35 percent, falls to the ground and enters the detrital food web. The forest floor supports a detrital food web that includes such herbivores as mites, millipedes, springtails, cave crickets, and snails. Earthworms live in the soil and eat bits of decaying organic matter. Predatory mites and spiders feed on these and other organisms. Saprophages, organisms such as fungi and bacteria that live on dead and decaying matter, aid in the decomposition of leaves and other organic matter. Some organic material is changed into animal, plant, fungal, and microbial tissue during decomposition. Other material is broken down into simple compounds and returned to

Copyright © 2008 by John Wiley & Sons, Inc.

Copyright © 2008 by John Wiley & Sons, Inc.

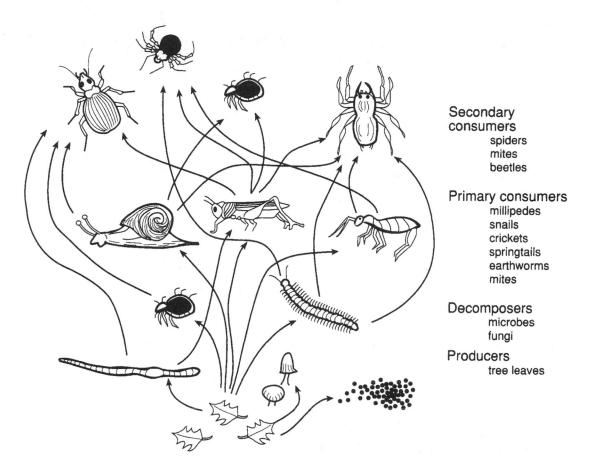

FIGURE C. ORGANISMS IN A DETRITAL FOOD WEB

the soil. These compounds can then be used in different food chains (see Figure C). The rate of decomposition is influenced by moisture, temperature, exposure, and other variables. Warm temperatures and plenty of water greatly increase microbial activity.

Restoring Natural Cycles

Many people are learning that the decomposition of organic material is an important natural cycle. When matter is removed from this cycle, there may not be enough nutrients available to sustain other food chains. Most Americans send their garbage to landfills, where it is entombed in layers of plastic and covered with soil. No decomposition occurs in sanitary landfills because water and sunlight never reach the garbage. Composting—the biological decomposition of organic waste generated by people, such as food scraps, grass clippings, and leaves—is one way that we can help keep nutrients and organic matter in the soil and reduce the amount of garbage that we send to landfills.

ECOLOGICALLY SPEAKING—VOCABULARY ACTIVITY ON *RELATIONSHIPS IN LIFE*

Directions

After reading *Relationships in Life,* use the clues to fill in the following blanks. When you have completed the puzzle, a message will appear in the vertical box.

Clues

1. _____ consumers eat primary consumers.

2. _____ is the study of relationships between organisms and their environment.

3. When resources are limited, there is _____ between organisms.

4. A(n) _____ kills and eats its prey.

5. An orchid is a(n) _____ that lives in a tree but does not help or harm the tree.

6. _____ are organisms that can make their own food.

7. _____ is dead or decaying matter.

8. An organism that eats plants is a(n) _____.

9. A community of living and nonliving things forms a(n) _____.

10. The green plant pigment that can capture the sun's energy is _____.

11. _____ are organisms that cannot make glucose from carbon dioxide and water.

12. _____ is organic matter from kitchens and yards that decomposes.

13. _____ are ground-dwelling invertebrates that eat decaying organic matter.

14. In _____ , both organisms are helped.

15. In _____ , one organism is helped and the other is neither helped nor harmed.

16. _____ is transferred along a food chain.

Copyright © 2008 by John Wiley & Sons, Inc.

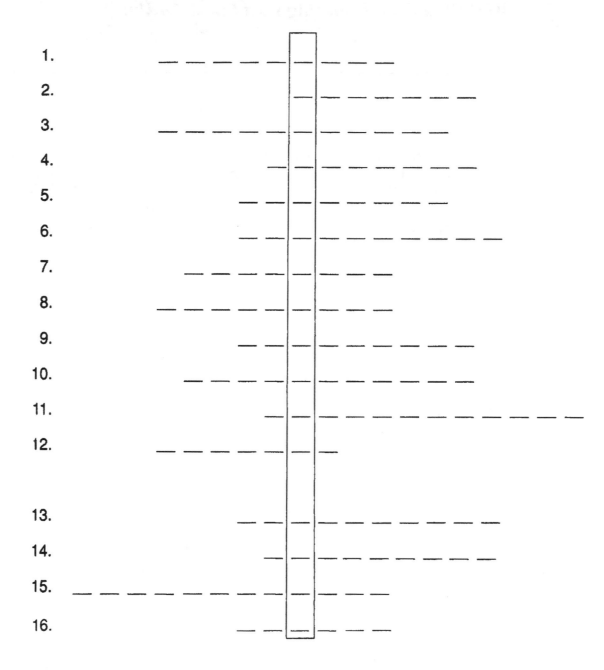

1.

2.

3.

4.

5.

6.

7.

8.

9.

10.

11.

12.

13.

14.

15.

16.

Copyright © 2008 by John Wiley & Sons, Inc.

22-2 WHO LIVES IN OUR TRASH?
Activity on Composting and Food Chains

Objectives

Students will practice deductive reasoning, learn the roles of organisms in food chains, and create a compost pile.

Teacher Notes

This lab is designed to teach students how to compost and is generally an outdoor activity. Because many teachers do not have access to an outdoor area, an indoor version of composting is presented in Part A, followed by an outdoor version in Part B. In Part A, students should put the same amounts of food and paper scraps in each soda bottle so that comparisons at the end of the activity will be valid. Do not use potting soil; it has been sterilized and will not work.

Copyright © 2008 by John Wiley & Sons, Inc.

Copyright © 2008 by John Wiley & Sons, Inc.

WHO LIVES IN OUR TRASH?
Activity on Composting and Food Chains

Introduction

Composting has regained popularity in the United States in recent years. Before the days of landfills and garbage haulers, everyone threw their food scraps and yard wastes into vacant fields and forests. The material decomposed, and nutrients in the material were released to return to the soil.

Today we live in apartments and houses that are closely arranged. Because organic matter thrown into the yard is unsightly and undesirable, we package our trash and send it to the landfill. Contemporary landfills are not just holes in the ground. Our new sanitary landfills have layers of clay and plastic on the bottom to prevent contamination of water supplies. After garbage is deposited in a landfill, it is covered with soil and more plastic. Engineers design landfills to keep water and sunlight out. Unfortunately, garbage cannot decompose under these cool, dry conditions. "Garbologists" have found readable 40-year-old newspapers and pink, edible-looking hot dogs in sanitary landfills.

Organic matter should be returned to the earth so that minerals and nutrients tied up in that material can be reused. We can help nature's recycling process by composting our own organic wastes. Food scraps, leaves, and grass clippings are ideal candidates for the compost pile. Organisms that are members of the detrital food web will move into the decaying matter and speed up the decomposition process.

Part A: Indoor Composting

Materials

Three soda bottles with caps	Packet of yeast mixed with warm water
Three sheets of dark construction paper	Nine thin slices of apple, all the same size
Masking, electrical, or packaging tape	Nine cubes of bread, all the same size
Plastic wrap	Newspaper, torn into tiny strips
Soil from outdoors	Three thermometers
Four or five worms	Graph paper

Procedure

1. Soak the three soda bottles in hot water to remove labels. Discard the labels.

2. Punch holes in the caps and in the sides of the bottles.

3. Cut off approximately a third of each bottle. The cutoff bottoms will serve as bases.

4. Label the bases 1, 2, and 3.

5. Put the caps on the bottles, and invert them into the bases (see Figure A).

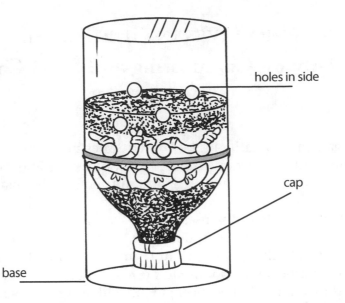

FIGURE A. INVERTED SODA BOTTLE COMPOST CONTAINER

Copyright © 2008 by John Wiley & Sons, Inc.

6. Fill the bottles as follows:

Bottle 1: Layer of dirt

Layer of food (two apple slices and two bread cubes) and paper scraps

Layer of dirt

Bottle 2: Layer of dirt

Layer of food (two apple slices and two bread cubes) and paper scraps

Tablespoon of yeast and water mixture

Layer of dirt

Bottle 3: Layer of dirt

Layer of food (two apple slices and two bread cubes) and paper scraps

Four or five worms

Layer of dirt

6. Insert thermometers into each bottle. Record the temperature in each bottle in the temperature data table.

7. Loosely cover the open end of each bottle with plastic. Wrap each bottle in dark construction paper.

8. Put the bottles in a warm place.

9. Every other day, remove the plastic wrap and check the soil to see if it is dry to the touch. If so, sprinkle the soil with water. Be sure to add the same amount of water to each bottle. Replace the plastic wrap.

10. Check the temperature in each bottle weekly. Record temperatures in the temperature data table.

11. After 6 to 9 weeks, pour out the contents of all three bottles and compare the amount of decomposition that occurred in each. To do so, examine the pieces of bread and apple to see how much they have changed.

Postlab Questions

1. Record temperatures in the temperature data table.

TEMPERATURE DATA TABLE

	Bottle 1	Bottle 2	Bottle 3
Week 0			
Week 1			
Week 2			
Week 3			
Week 4			
Week 5			
Week 6			

2. On graph paper, create a line graph that shows the temperature changes in each bottle over the experimental period. Draw bottle 1 in red, bottle 2 in blue, and bottle 3 in green on the graph.

3. In which bottle did the most decomposition occur? Why?

4. Which bottle got the warmest during composting? Why?

5. Yeast is a fungus. Why was it added to bottle 2?

Copyright © 2008 by John Wiley & Sons, Inc.

6. What did the yeast in bottle 2 consume?

7. What other organisms are in these bottles? Where did these other organisms come from?

Part B: Create a Compost Pile Outdoors

Materials

Rake	Gallon milk jug with cap, rinsed
Pitchfork	Scissors
Leaves, grass clippings, wood chips, food scraps	Petri dish or saucer
Soil (not potting soil)	Alcohol or Bioperm™
Thermometer	Lamp
Wire fencing and four posts (optional)	Graph paper

Procedure

1. In an area about 4 feet by 4 feet, clear the soil of weeds and grass. Build a short wooden fence around this area if desired.

2. Cover the area with leaves and loose soil. Add a layer of food scraps, then leaves, grass clippings, wood chips, and more soil. Continue layering to a height of 3 feet. (Layers can be added all at once or over a period of weeks.)

3. Wet the compost pile until slightly moist.

4. Push the thermometer deep into the compost pile. Record the temperature in the temperature data table.

5. Once a week, check and record the temperature of the compost pile.

6. Once a week, use a pitchfork to turn the compost pile to circulate air. This speeds up the process of decomposition. Sprinkle with water as needed.

7. After 6 to 9 weeks, spread out the compost pile and examine the contents.

8. Create a Soil Critter Catcher for collecting soil organisms. To do so, cut the gallon milk jug in half. Punch holes in the cap and replace it on the top half. Invert the top half of the milk jug into the bottom half. Put a shovel full of compost soil and scraps in the inverted milk jug.

9. Put a lamp directly over the soil and a petri dish or saucer of alcohol or Bioperm under the cap (see Figure B).

10. Leave the soil in this position for 24 hours.

11. Remove the petri dish and place under a dissecting microscope.

12. Count and sketch the different kinds of organisms that you see.

Copyright © 2008 by John Wiley & Sons, Inc.

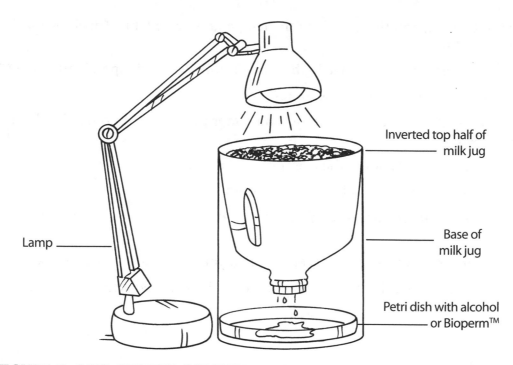

FIGURE B. SOIL CRITTER CATCHER MADE FROM AN INVERTED MILK JUG

Postlab Questions

1. Record temperatures in the temperature data table.

TEMPERATURE DATA TABLE

	Temperature
Week 0	
Week 1	
Week 2	
Week 3	
Week 4	
Week 5	
Week 6	

Copyright © 2008 by John Wiley & Sons, Inc.

2. On graph paper, graph the data from the temperature data table. Label the y-axis "Temperature" and the x-axis "Weeks."

3. How did the temperature change in the compost pile over the experimental period?

4. What caused this change in temperature?

5. When you examined the condition of food scraps placed in the compost pile, how had they changed?

6. What caused these changes in the composted material?

7. What organisms did you find living in the compost pile?

8. These organisms are members of the detrital food web. Where did these organisms come from?

9. What organisms do you suspect are present that you cannot see in the detrital food web?

10. What would life on Earth be like if there were no detrital food web?

Copyright © 2008 by John Wiley & Sons, Inc.

22-3 WEB OF LIFE
Activity on Food Chains and Food Webs

Objectives

Students will play the roles of various living things in an ecosystem to determine their relationships.

Teacher Notes

You can use these cards or develop some that are tailored to your geographical region. Students need to be generally familiar with the kinds of organisms on the cards so that they can discuss them. If time permits, have students color each set of cards—autotrophs, primary consumers, secondary consumers, tertiary consumers, and decomposers—a different color. To truly represent the quantities of organisms in the food chain, you may want to make duplicates or triplicates of each autotroph. There are three bacteria cards (decomposers) to indicate the large numbers of bacteria in the ecosystem.

Copyright © 2008 by John Wiley & Sons, Inc.

Autotroph	Autotroph	Autotroph	Autotroph	Autotroph
Grass	Seeds	Green leaves	Dead leaves	Stems

Autotroph	Autotroph	Autotroph	Autotroph	Autotroph
Nectar	Plant juices	Roots	Berries	Bark and wood

Primary Consumer	Primary Consumer	Primary Consumer	Primary Consumer	Primary Consumer
Gray squirrel (eats cones, fruit, fungi, seeds)	Deer (eats shoots and leaves)	Cardinal (eats seeds, fruits)	Caterpillar (eats green leaves)	Grasshopper (eats leaves)

Primary Consumer	Primary Consumer	Primary Consumer	Primary Consumer	Primary Consumer
Aphid (drinks plant)	Bee (drinks nectar)	Vole (eats grasses and seeds)	Worm (eats dead plant matter)	Insect larva (eats plant parts)

Secondary Consumer	Secondary Consumer	Secondary Consumer	Secondary Consumer	Secondary Consumer
Robin (eats worms and other invertebrates)	Spider (eats other small invertebrates)	Mole (eats worms and insects)	Snake (eats mice, voles, frogs)	Lizard (eats insects, small herbivorous vertebrates)

	Tertiary Consumer	Tertiary Consumer	Tertiary Consumer	
	Owl (eats mice, shrews, small birds)	Coyote (eats insects, small mammals, reptiles, amphibians)	Woodpecker (eats insects)	

Decomposer	Decomposer	Decomposers	Decomposers	Decomposers
Mushroom	Mildew	Bacteria	Bacteria	Bacteria

Copyright © 2008 by John Wiley & Sons, Inc.

WEB OF LIFE
Activity on Food Chains and Food Webs

Introduction

In an ecosystem, all living things are interdependent. Some organisms, called autotrophs, capture the sun's energy and change it into glucose in the process of photosynthesis. These autotrophs are the basis for most of the food chains on Earth. Autotrophs are consumed by primary consumers, heterotrophs that eat plant parts. Primary consumers provide food for secondary consumers, heterotrophs that eat meat. In some food chains, there are also tertiary consumers. Figure A shows a food chain that starts with plants. Mice, the primary consumers, eat plants. Mice are consumed by secondary consumers, such as snakes, which are preyed on by tertiary consumers, eagles.

FIGURE A

As one organism consumes another, it takes in energy. In Figure A, energy is indicated by arrows between organisms. Primary consumers get 10% of the energy that autotrophs captured from the sun. Secondary consumers get 10% of the energy that autotrophs possess. With each step up the food chain, only 10% is passed along to the next organism; 90% is lost to the ecosystem in each step. Each level of the food chain contains fewer organisms than the step before it because there is less and less energy available to support those organisms.

When organisms die, their bodies still contain energy. All food chains include decomposers, organisms that break down the tissue of dead organisms. Decomposers are small and

Copyright © 2008 by John Wiley & Sons, Inc.

difficult to see, but exist in large numbers. Mushrooms, underground fungi, slime molds, bracket fungi, mildews, and hundreds of different species of bacteria make up the tremendous community of decomposers.

Prelab Questions

1. What is the difference between an autotroph and a heterotroph? Give examples of each.

2. Falcons eat small, seed-eating birds and rodents. Are falcons autotrophs, primary consumers, secondary consumers, or tertiary consumers?

3. An ecosystem contains more primary consumers than secondary or tertiary consumers. Why do you think this is so?

Materials

Cards

Tape

Yarn (20 to 30 pieces, each 3 or 4 yards long)

Procedure

1. The teacher will tape a card on your back. Cards contain the names of members of an ecosystem.

2. Once your card is in place, ask another student to look at it. Ask that student one question that will help you determine what is written on your card. If you can identify the organism on your card, move the card from your back to your chest, then go to the front of the room and wait for other students to guess what is on their cards. If you do not guess correctly, go to another student and ask him or her one question.

3. When everyone has guessed what is on his or her card, pick up two or three pieces of yarn.

4. Work as a group to arrange yourselves in a four-level food web with all the autotrophs on one level, primary consumers on a second level, secondary consumers on a third level, and tertiary consumers on a fourth level. Create a fifth level for decomposers.

5. Have everyone who might be in the same food chain hold on to the same piece of yarn. In other words, connect yourself to an organism that you consume and an organism that can consume you.

6. Show how the food web changes if one organism (a caterpillar, for example) is killed by a farmer's insecticide. To do so, have that organism (student) drop all of his or her strings and sit down.

7. Answer the postlab questions.

Copyright © 2008 by John Wiley & Sons, Inc.

Postlab Questions

1. What kinds of organisms do decomposers consume?

   _____

   _____

2. What happened to the food web when one organism was removed?

   _____

   _____

3. How would the food web change if all the autotrophs disappeared?

   _____

   _____

4. When decomposers consume dead organisms, they release the minerals in those organisms back into the soil. What do you think happens to those minerals?

   _____

   _____

5. Explain the following statement: Energy travels straight through an ecosystem, but minerals are recycled.

   _____

   _____

Copyright © 2008 by John Wiley & Sons, Inc.

Answer Keys

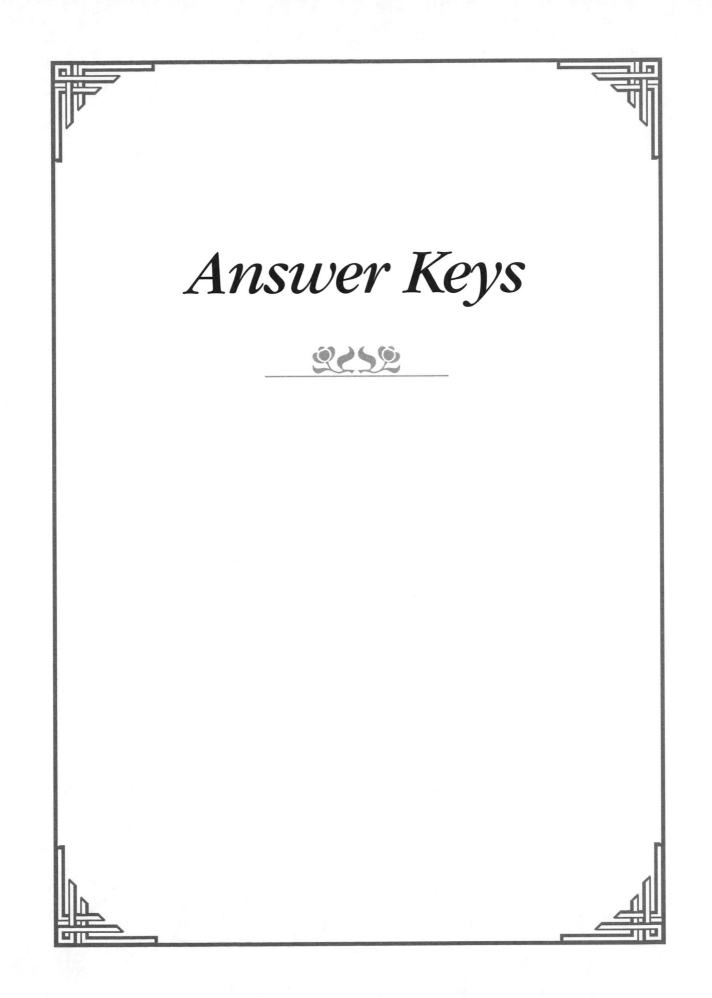

KEY 1-1
Acrostic—As the Earth Moves

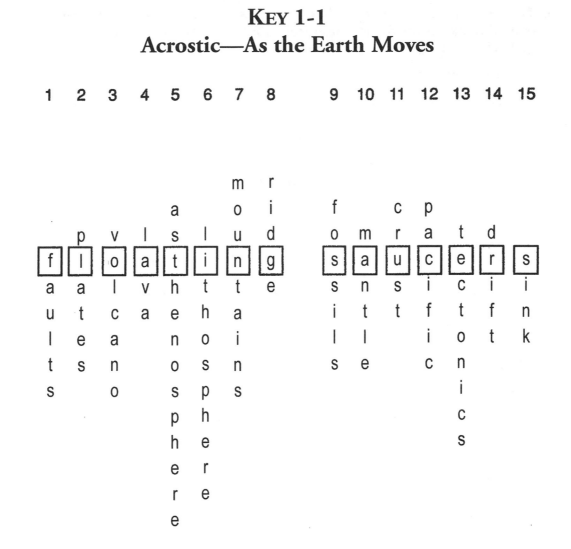

KEY 1-2
Rockin' and Rollin' in the U.S.A.

Prelab Questions

1. A seismologist studies earthquakes.

2. Scientists compute the arrival time of shock waves at three or more stations around the world to locate the epicenter.

3. A P wave would travel 500 km in 82 seconds (16.4 × 5); an S wave would require 122 seconds (24.4 × 5).

4. The greater the difference in arrival times, the farther the station is from the earthquake epicenter.

Copyright © 2008 by John Wiley & Sons, Inc.

5. The place where stress energy changes to wave energy, or the point of origin of an earthquake, is the focus. The epicenter is the point on the earth's surface directly above the focus.

6. Stored energy.

7. Scientists measure the energy given off by the earthquake on the Richter scale.

DATA TABLE

City	Difference in P and S Wave Arrival Times (seconds)	Distance (km)
New York	57	712.5
Louisville	40	500
Pittsburgh	32	400

Postlab Questions

1. Pittsburgh; New York.

2. Either North Carolina or Virginia would be acceptable answers.

3. Before. It would be closer to the epicenter than New York.

4. 89.6 sec.

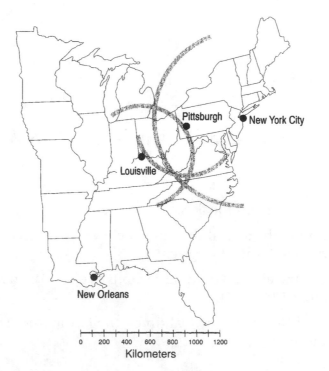

KEY 1-2. Rockin' and Rollin' in the U.S.A.

Copyright © 2008 by John Wiley & Sons, Inc.

Copyright © 2008 by John Wiley & Sons, Inc.

KEY 1-3
Quakes and Plates

Prelab Questions

1. A tectonic plate is a section of the earth's crust.

2. Tectonic plates move because they float atop the mantle, which moves by convection currents.

3. Tectonic plates produce seismic waves because they collide along their borders, releasing energy.

Postlab Questions

1. Earthquakes are most common along the edges of plates.

2. Answers will vary based on student research.

3. At their edges, plates collide and release energy.

4. Answers will vary. Few earthquakes occur in the center of Africa because that area is not located on the edge of a plate.

5. Yes. By knowing the direction and frequency of plate movements, seismologists can predict some earthquakes.

KEY 2-1
Word Trace—The Scoop on Soil

1. Weathering
2. Roots
3. Bedrock
4. Humus
5. Topsoil
6. Glacier
7. Abrasion
8. Gravity
9. Ventifacts
10. Windbreak
11. Sand
12. Dunes
13. Stream load
14. Vegetation
15. Conservation
16. Contour
17. Terracing
18. Mature
19. Oxidation
20. Carbonization
21. Rust
22. Iron oxide

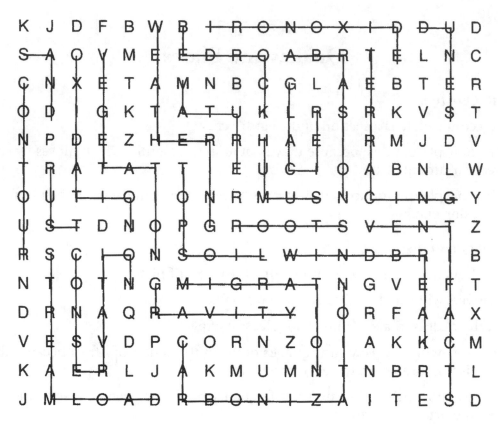

KEY 2-2
Breaking Up Is Easy to Do

Prelab Questions

1. Physical weathering does not alter the composition of rock, only the size. Chemical weathering creates new substances.

2. Ice wedging is the movement of water into the cracks and pores of rocks. The water expands as it freezes and causes rock to crack or break apart.

3. Carbonization is the action of carbonic acid on rock. Carbonic acid can dissolve certain minerals, such as calcium carbonate in limestone, to create openings like those found in limestone caves.

4. Sandstone is more porous than granite.

5. Limestone contains calcium carbonate, which can be dissolved by acid; granite does not contain this compound.

6. Type of rock, type and hardness of minerals in rock, and climate.

Copyright © 2008 by John Wiley & Sons, Inc.

Copyright © 2008 by John Wiley & Sons, Inc.

Results on the Data Table

Answers will vary, but the following should be noted:

In water, sandstone will be the only rock to gain mass. The measurement of other rocks will stay fairly constant. In vinegar, sandstone and granite will remain unchanged, but both marble and limestone will decrease in mass.

Postlab Questions

1. Sandstone. It is more porous and absorbs more water.

2. Limestone or marble. They can be dissolved by weak acids.

3. Granite.

4. Yes. Climatic factors and materials in the air can cause rocks to weather more quickly.

5. Water represents rain and water flowing over rocks on earth.

Key 2-3
Shaking Sugar

Prelab Questions

1. Forces that change the size, shape, and position of earth's rocks.

2. Physical—wind, glaciers, and water. Chemical—water and atmospheric gases.

3. The erosion of rocks.

Results on the Data Table

Answers will vary, but the mass of sugar grains should increase as the number of shakes increases.

Postlab Questions

1. The mass of the sugar grains increases as the number of shakes increases.

2. Physical weathering.

3. Rocks.

4. Small and rounded.

5. Smaller and more rounded.

6. Answers will vary. Physical weathering is the mechanical breakdown of rocks.

KEY 3-1
Weather Crossword—The Weather Report

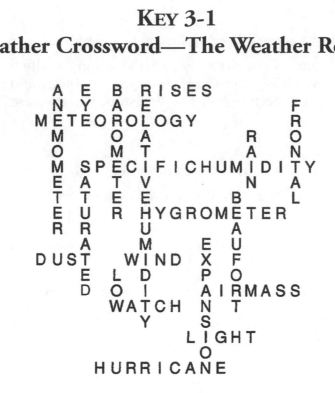

KEY 3-2
Hygrometer Lab

Prelab Questions

1. Relative humidity is a comparison between the actual amount of water vapor in the air and the maximum amount of water vapor the air can hold at that temperature.

2. At 75% relative humidity, the air can assume only 25% more moisture before it is saturated.

3. A jogger is probably more comfortable at a higher temperature and lower humidity. Jogging in high humidity will make it seem hot because sweat cannot evaporate from the body and cool it.

4. A saturated atmosphere is completely full of water vapor at that temperature. At this point, the relative humidity is 100%.

5. The hot, sticky feeling you get in humid weather results from the accumulation of sweat on the skin. The failure of this sweat to evaporate prevents the body from cooling adequately.

Copyright © 2008 by John Wiley & Sons, Inc.

Copyright © 2008 by John Wiley & Sons, Inc.

Postlab Questions

1. Dry bulb. Answers will vary, but students may explain that the wet bulb has moisture that, as it evaporates from the bulb, cools the bulb.

2. Decrease. When the temperature is very similar on the dry and wet bulbs, the air is already so full of moisture that it is not accepting much water vapor by evaporation.

3. When there is no difference in the two temperatures, the air is completely saturated with water vapor.

4. Decrease. This would indicate that the air temperature is cool and dry.

5. Answers will vary.

6. Answers will vary.

KEY 3-3
Weather Tracking

Prelab Questions

1. A meteorologist studies the weather.

2. Barometer.

3. Anemometer and wind vane.

4. Answers will vary, but students might explain that knowing the weather helps people plan their daily lives and protects them from dangerous weather conditions.

Postlab Questions

1. Answers will vary.

2. Answers will vary.

3. Answers will vary, but students might see wind during periods of changing air pressure.

4. Answers will vary, but students, might be able to identify short-term trends, such as afternoon showers.

5. Answers will vary. Students might suggest that by understanding weather patterns over long periods of time, a person would be better able to predict future weather conditions.

KEY 4-1
Water Puzzle—The Water Planet

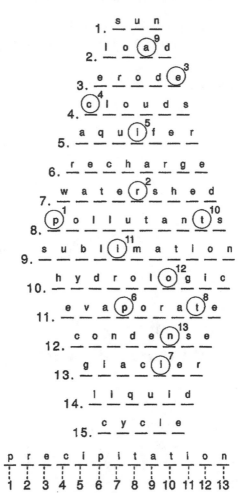

1. s u n
2. l o a d
3. e r o d e
4. c l o u d s
5. a q u i f e r
6. r e c h a r g e
7. w a t e r s h e d
8. p o l l u t a n t s
9. s u b l i m a t i o n
10. h y d r o l o g i c
11. e v a p o r a t e
12. c o n d e n s e
13. g l a c i e r
14. l i q u i d
15. c y c l e

p r e c i p i t a t i o n
1 2 3 4 5 6 7 8 9 10 11 12 13

KEY 4-2
Bearly Raining

Postlab Questions

1. DATA TABLE

Rain on Little Dipper High School Campus					
Annual Rain Volume	Monthly Rain Volume	Weight of Annual Rain in Pounds	Weight of Annual Rain in Kilograms	Weight of Monthly Rain in Pounds	Weight of Monthly Rain in Kilograms
8,406,048	703,363	525,378,000	238,521,610	43,960,200	19,957,931

Copyright © 2008 by John Wiley & Sons, Inc.

Copyright © 2008 by John Wiley & Sons, Inc.

2. 1250 feet.

3. Answers will vary. Additions that include concrete or blacktop increase the volume of runoff because rain cannot percolate into the soil. Farms, feedlots, lawns, golf courses, and nurseries increase the amount of pesticides and fertilizers in the runoff. Industries and businesses have varying effects on runoff, depending on the nature of the business.

4. Answers will vary.

5. Removing ground cover and vegetation increases the amount of erosion that occurs. Roots, dead leaves, and other plant matter slow the impact of rain and prevent soil from being carried away by runoff.

Key 4-3
Aquifer Project

Prelab Questions

1. Aquifers are underground regions made up of porous materials, such as small rocks, sand, gravel, and sandstone, that contain water.

2. Water seeps into aquifers from the soil above.

3. Water can be extracted by humans, it may be discharged into a lake or river, or it may rise to the surface through a spring.

Postlab Questions

1. When it rains, an aquifer fills with water. During a drought, water levels in an aquifer remain the same or diminish.

2. Answers will vary. In some cases, land over an aquifer sinks.

3. No. The rock and soil are not porous.

4. Answers will vary. Pollutants poured onto the soil can seep into aquifers. Pollutants can be picked up and carried to the soil over aquifers from a variety of sources.

KEY 5-1
Ride the Wave—Wave On

1. Frequency
2. Transverse
3. Rarefaction
4. Dogs
5. Wave
6. Longitudinal
7. Crest
8. Doppler
9. Ultrasonic
10. Medium
11. Hertz
12. Compression
13. Sound
14. Decibels
15. Amplitude
16. Trough
17. Intensity
18. Ultrasonic
19. Hertz
20. Decibels

KEY 5-2
Telephone Waves

Prelab Questions

1. Answers will vary. To vibrate is to move rapidly back and forth.

2. Sound is a vibration that strikes the eardrums.

3. Sound waves produced by a speaker cause the air molecules to vibrate. Vibrations of air molecules strike the listener's eardrums, causing them to vibrate.

Postlab Questions

1. Sound waves strike the bottom of the can and cause the string to vibrate. The vibrating string causes the bottom of the second can to vibrate. These vibrations are transmitted to the ear of the listener.

2. Answers will vary. Students will find that the string must be kept taut to transmit the waves.

3. Answers will vary. As the length of the string increases, the quality of sound transmission decreases.

4. Answers will vary. Students might have used paper or plastic cups, or they might have changed the material that makes the string.

5. Answers will vary. Students might suggest using two paper cups and a fine wire to make the talking cans device.

Copyright © 2008 by John Wiley & Sons, Inc.

Key 5-3
Assessing the Vibrations of Music

Prelab Questions

1. A sound is produced when something vibrates.

2. Sound is classified as music if the sound is pleasing and has an identifiable pitch and repeated rhythm.

3. A musician changes the pitch in a string by placing a finger on the string to shorten it.

4. A thick string vibrates at a lower frequency than a thin one.

Postlab Questions

1. Answers to both questions will vary.

2. a. The string with the highest pitch is the tightest string.

   b. The string with the lowest pitch is the thickest string.

3. The length at the string is shortened.

4. Low-pitched sounds are produced by thick strings. Thick strings vibrate more slowly than thin ones.

Key 6-1
Atomic Crossword—Doing the Atomic Shake

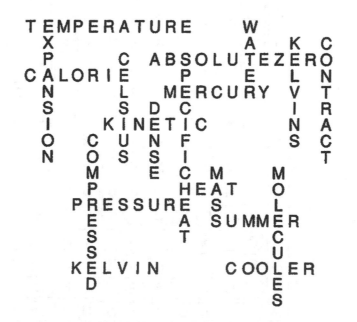

Copyright © 2008 by John Wiley & Sons, Inc.

KEY 6-2
Up, Up, and Away

Prelab Questions

1. Hot air is less dense than cold air.

2. As cold air moves underneath warm air, the warm air rises and creates a current.

3. Air and hair spray inside the bottle expand and may destroy the bottle.

4. Answers will vary. The balloon over the bottle of hot water expands because the hot air in the mouth of the bottle is moving rapidly and has a lot of kinetic energy.

Postlab Questions

1. Answers will vary depending on individual designs and group results.

2. Answers will vary. Winning balloons most likely were very good at holding warm air.

3. Answers will vary.

4. Answers will vary. Students may state that because air pressure below a region of warmed air is greater than the pressure above this region, warm air rises.

KEY 7-1
Word Find—Let's Get Movin'

1. Speed
2. Odometer
3. Average
4. Inertia
5. Force
6. Inversely
7. Frame of reference
8. Displacement
9. Vector
10. Acceleration
11. Instantaneous
12. Gravity
13. Reaction
14. Deceleration
15. Friction
16. Scalar
17. Rest
18. Second
19. Sun
20. Mass

Copyright © 2008 by John Wiley & Sons, Inc.

KEY 7-2
Solving Your Problems in Motion

1. A. S = d/t = 25/15 = 1.67 miles/min

   B. 1.67 × 60 = 100 miles/hr

2. A. S = 25/20 = 1.25 miles/min

   B. 1.25 × 60 = 75 miles/hr

3. V = displacement/time = 100 miles/hr west

4. V = 75 miles/hr east

5. A. a = final velocity − initial velocity/time = 60 miles/hr − 0 miles/hr/2.5 sec

   a = 60 miles/hr/0.0007 hr = 85,714 miles/hr^2

   (*Note:* 2.5 seconds must be converted to hours by dividing by 3600 in this problem.)

   B. First change 60 miles/hr to miles/sec by dividing by 3600. This will give you 0.017 miles/sec.

   a = 0.017 miles/sec/2.5 sec = 0.007 miles/sec^2

6. a = 0 − 120 miles/hr/4 sec = −120 miles/hr/0.0011 hr = −109,091 miles/hr/hr

7. 10 miles

8. 3 miles (displacement from the house to Max's)

9. S = 10 miles/2 hr = 5 miles/hr

10. V = 3 miles/2 hr = 1.5 miles/hr south

11. Final velocity = initial velocity + (acceleration)(time)

    V = 0 + (10)(2.5) = 25 m/sec

12. d = S × t = 250 miles/hr × 1.5 hr = 375 miles

13. t = d/S = 20 miles/60 miles/hr = 0.33 hr × 60 min = 20 min

KEY 7-3
The Ball Drop

Prelab Questions

1. ½ (10)(8)(8) = 320 m.

2. Air resistance will prevent it from falling at 10 m/sec^2.

3. Change in velocity over time.

4. The pull of gravity is different.

Copyright © 2008 by John Wiley & Sons, Inc.

5. Timing will not be exact; object must be placed in a vacuum to get an exact value.

6. Answers will vary.

Postlab Questions

1. Answers will vary.

2. Answers will vary.

3. Tall. Answers will vary, but could include the idea that a long fall provides more opportunity for measurement of time.

4. ½ (10)(4)(4) = 80 m

KEY 8-1
Energy Unscramble—Full of Energy

1. Power

2. Newton

3. Kinetic

4. Pitch

5. Friction

6. Watts

7. Joules

8. Energy

9. Horses

10. Height

11. Velocity

12. Machines

13. Levers

14. Knife

15. Horsepower

16. Direction

17. Seesaw

18. Work

19. Kilograms

20. Final velocity

KEY 8-2
Golf Balls and Their Potential

Prelab Questions

1. a. PE = m × g × h = (2 kg)(10 m/sec/sec)(20 m) = 400 J

   b. On top of the fence.

   c. At the bottom; speed increases as objects fall.

2. Answers will vary.

Postlab Questions

1. Increased. Increased distance from the cup, so d is greater in the W = F × d formula.

2. KE = ½mv². As the ball assumes motion, it obtains kinetic energy.

3. Inclined plane.

4. Velocity would have increased, resulting in greater kinetic energy.

Copyright © 2008 by John Wiley & Sons, Inc.

KEY 8-3
Problems with Energy

1. W = F × d = 20 N × 80 m = 1600 J

2. P = W/t = 1600 J/6 sec = 266.7 W

3. KE = ½ mv^2 = ½ (10 kg)(2 m/sec)^2
     = (5 kg)(4 m^2/sec^2) = 20 J

4. KE = ½ (70 kg + 2 kg)(1.2 m/sec)(1.2 m/sec) = (36)(1.44) = 51.8 J

5. You cannot compute this because acceleration due to gravity is not 10 m/sec^2 in this situation, due to the effect of air resistance on the parachute.

6. a. W = F × d = 80 kg × 70 m = 800 N × 70 m = 56,000 J

   b. P = W/t = 56,000 J/3.5 sec = 16,000 W

7. a. PE = m × *g* × h = 6 × 10 × 22 = 1320 J

   b. PE = m × *g* × h = (25)(10)(10) = 2500 J

   c. PE = m × *g* × h = (50)(10)(30) = 15,000 J

8. Efficiency = output ÷ input = 100 J ÷ 500 J = 0.20 = 20%

   This is low efficiency because you only get one-fifth of the work you put into this equipment.

KEY 9-1
AC-DC—Dancing Electrons

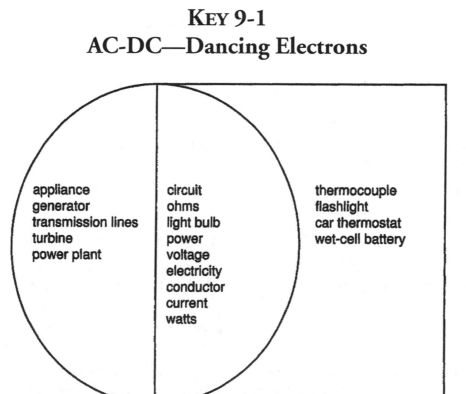

Copyright © 2008 by John Wiley & Sons, Inc.

KEY 9-2
Paying the Bills

1. $259.59

2. $63.64

3. $297.09

4. Summer; yes.

5. Answers will vary. One way to conserve is to increase the temperature at which you set your thermostat in the summer.

6. Discourage. Rates are higher in summer.

KEY 9-3
Shocking Solutions

1. 4 amps
2. 0.005 amps
3. 1200 W
4. 17 ohms

5. 19 amps

6. Washing machine, 0.9 kWh; dryer, 4 kWh. Total cost: $0.294.

KEY 9-4
Wired for Action

Postlab Questions

1. Answers will vary. An electrical circuit is a path through which electricity flows.

2. Batteries; wires and light bulbs.

3. Answers will vary. In a series circuit, if one light is missing, current cannot flow through the circuit.

4. When you remove one light bulb, the others go out because the circuit is interrupted.

5. Lights went out; string does not conduct an electrical current.

6. Answers will vary. A conductor carries an electrical current. An insulator does not carry an electrical current.

7. Answers will vary. In a parallel circuit, electrical current can follow more than one path.

8. The other lights remained burning. The others remained burning because the current could take alternative routes.

9. Answers will vary. Students will most likely select parallel circuits because they would still have electrical services if one bulb or appliance went out.

Copyright © 2008 by John Wiley & Sons, Inc.

KEY 10-1
Planet Unscramble—Planetary Family

1. Terrestrial	5. Saturn	9. Winds
2. Uranus	6. Nitrogen	10. Comets
3. Mercury	7. Venus	
4. Pluto	8. Craters	

KEY 10-2
Bringing the Solar System Down to Earth

CHART 1

Object	Diameter (km)	Number of Times Smaller Than the Sun	Scaled-Down Diameter (mm)
Sun	1,380,000	—	1000
Mercury	4989	277	3.6
Venus	12,392	111.36	8.98
Earth	12,757	108.17	9.24
Mars	6959	204.16	4.898
Jupiter	142,749	9.67	103.4
Saturn	120,862	11.42	87.58
Uranus	51,499	26.797	37.32
Neptune	44,579	30.956	32.3
Pluto	2414	571.66	1.75

Copyright © 2008 by John Wiley & Sons, Inc.

CHART 2

Object	Distance from the Sun (in millions of miles)	AU Equivalent (astronomical unit)	Scaled-Down Distance (mm)
Mercury	36	.39	390
Venus	67.27	0.7	700
Earth	93	1	1000
Mars	141.7	1.52	1520
Jupiter	483.9	5.2	5200
Saturn	887.1	9.54	9540
Uranus	1783.98	19.18	19,180
Neptune	2795.5	30.06	30,060
Pluto	3675.3	39.52	39,520

Copyright © 2008 by John Wiley & Sons, Inc.

Postlab Questions

1. A scale model shows the relative sizes of objects and their relative distances apart.

2. One AU, or astronomical unit, is the distance of Earth from the sun.

3. The solar system is too large to view or visualize easily. A scale model helps us see the relationships between different components of the solar system.

4. The two planets that are closest together are Venus and Earth.

5.   **CHART 3**

Object	Scaled-Down Diameter (mm)	Size Reduced by a Factor of 10 (mm)	Size Reduced by a Factor of 100 (mm)
Sun	1000	100	10
Mercury	3.6	0.36	0.036
Venus	8.98	0.89	0.089
Earth	9.24	0.92	0.092
Mars	4.89	0.49	0.049
Jupiter	103.4	10.34	1.03
Saturn	87.58	8.76	0.88
Uranus	37.32	3.73	0.37
Neptune	32.3	3.23	0.32
Pluto	1.75	0.18	0.018

6. Answers will vary.

Copyright © 2008 by John Wiley & Sons, Inc.

KEY 11-1
Star Puzzle—Star Light, Star Bright

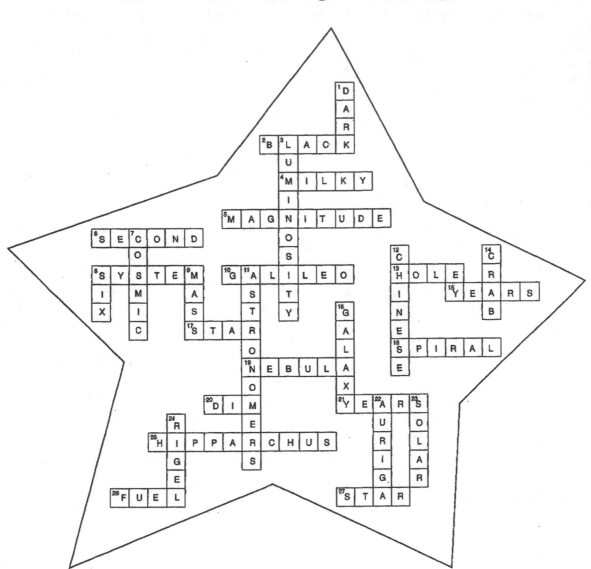

KEY 11-2
Star Chamber Activity

Postlab Questions

1. Polaris is the North Star, which indicates the position of celestial north. Someone who is lost might be able to use the North Star as a reference point.

2. We study constellations because they are one way to learn about stars and other heavenly bodies.

Copyright © 2008 by John Wiley & Sons, Inc.

3. Answers will vary.

4. 1. b
2. c
3. a
4. b
5. b
6. d
7. f
8. b
9. c
10. g

Copyright © 2008 by John Wiley & Sons, Inc.

KEY 12-1
Lunar Message—The Man in the Moon

1. **s** e a
2. k i n **e** t i c
3. **l** u n a r s
4. t h i e **f**
5. s e r **e** n i t a t i s
6. **m** o o n i t e s
7. a n **g** l e
8. m a **r** i a
9. **l** a v a
10. **p** e a k
11. **h** e a t
12. r a **y** s

13. r **i** m
14. d u **s** t

15. v o **l** c a n o e s
16. l **u** n a t i c
17. C o p e r **n** i c u s
18. g r **a** v i t y
19. v a p o **r** i z i n g

KEY 12-2
Moon Madness

Postlab Questions

1. Answers will vary.

2. Peas and beans thrown from a squatting position have the lowest angle of impact. Angle of impact affects the shape of the crater. When the angle is less than 10°, the crater takes on a distinct oblique appearance.

3. Answers will vary.

4. One student is appointed as the one who throws the peas and beans to reduce variation between trials.

5. The oldest crater has rays that are partially covered by the rays from younger craters.

6. The moon's craters were probably formed by an explosion of meteor material. The crater was created when rock and soil in the area of impact were thrown out in a circular pattern.

7. Yes. Rays are made of ejecta blanket, or material that is thrown out of the crater.

KEY 12-3
Dear Moon

Prelab Questions

1. The moon reflects light from the sun.

2. About one month.

3. The moon's phases are due to the relative positions of the moon and sun.

4. The moon is between Earth and the sun.

Postlab Questions

1. Half of the moon is always facing the sun, and therefore is always lit. However, we are viewing the moon from the side. The amount of lighted surface that we can see depends on the relative positions of Earth, the sun, and the moon.

2. The new moon is between Earth and the sun, so we cannot see its lighted surface. You can see the entire side of the moon when it is a full moon.

3. Answers will vary.

4. Answers will vary.

Copyright © 2008 by John Wiley & Sons, Inc.

KEY 13-1
Landing Spacecraft—The Space Shuttle

1. Byrd

2. Sputnik

3. Adapter module

4. Friendship

5. Only used when near the sun

6. Open trays

7. Highly trained astronauts

8. Gasoline

9. Shower stalls

10. Laundry

11. Loss of memory

12. Visit planets

KEY 14-1
Periodic Crossword—Periodic Properties

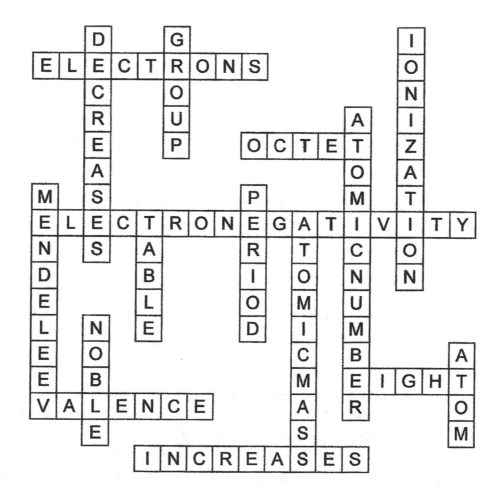

Copyright © 2008 by John Wiley & Sons, Inc.

KEY 14-2
Trend Setters

Prelab Questions

1. A period is a horizontal row; it indicates the number of energy shells each element possesses. A family is a vertical column. Members of a family have similar properties. The family indicates the number of valence electrons.

2. The periodic table shows you the atomic number, atomic mass, number of valence electrons, reactivity, electronegativity, and relative atomic size. It also indicates whether an element is metal, nonmetal, or metalloid, and whether it is a solid, liquid, or gas.

3. Two. Families 1, 2, and 13 through 18 have 1, 2, 3, 4, 5, 6, 7, or 8 outer electrons respectively.

4. It is possible to predict the properties of elements based on their location on the periodic table.

5. Answers will vary. Students may predict an increase in density.

Postlab Questions

1. Answers will vary.

2. Lead.

3. g/ml.

4. Answers will vary. The bars on the graph will increase in size as atomic number increases.

5. Increases.

6. Answers will vary, but should be based on the bar graph.

7. Answers will vary.

8. Answers will vary, but should include human error.

9. Answers will vary.

KEY 14-3
Berth of a Periodic Table

Prelab Questions

1. Mendeleev devised a periodic table to organize the known elements.

2. Mendeleev arranged the elements in order of increasing atomic weight. They are now arranged in order of increasing atomic number.

3. He felt that gaps represented elements that were yet undiscovered.

4. He felt that some of the information on elements (such as their atomic weight) was incorrect.

5. Answers will vary, but could include number of protons, number of neutrons, number of electrons, relative size, and electronegativity.

Copyright © 2008 by John Wiley & Sons, Inc.

Copyright © 2008 by John Wiley & Sons, Inc.

Balloonium (Bl)

Atomic #: _1_

Atomic mass: _4.003_

Series: _1_

Group: _18_

State: _Gas_

Fact: Lightest noble gas on planet

Gasite (Gt)

Atomic #: _9_

Atomic mass: _18.998_

Series: _2_

Group: _17_

State: Gas

Fact: Most chemically active of all nonmetals

Use: _Etching glass; added to water supply to prevent tooth decay_

Rockite (R)

Atomic #: _5_

Atomic mass: _10.811_

Series: 2

Group: _13_

State: _Solid_

Fact: This element is classified as a metalloid.

Use: _In semiconductors_

Sandide (Sd)

Atomic #: _14_

Atomic mass: _28.086_

Series: _3_

Group: _14_

State: _Solid_

Fact: This metalloid is a common component of the metallic oxide, sand.

Use: _In semiconductors_

Medicon (M)

Atomic #: _12_

Atomic mass: _24.305_

Series: 3

Group: _2_

State: _Solid_

Use: Metal used to make Epsom salts

Atmospherium (A)

Atomic #: _8_

Atomic mass: _15.999_

Series: 2

Group: _16_

State: _Gas_

Fact: During electrical storms, this element can form ozone.

Universium (U)

Atomic #: _36_

Atomic mass: _83.80_

Series: _4_

Group: _18_

State: _Gas_

Fact: Heaviest noble gas on planet

Toxigas (Tg)

Atomic #: _37_

Atomic mass: _35.453_

Series: 3

Group: _17_

State: _Gas_

Fact: In its diatomic form, this element becomes a toxic green gas.

Use: _Oxidizing and bleaching agent_

Malleabium (Ma)

Atomic #: _13_

Atomic mass: _26.982_

Series: 3

Group: 13

State: _Solid_

Fact: _Second most malleable metal_

Use: _To make kitchen utensils and in building materials_

Nocorrodium (Nc)

Atomic #: _4_

Atomic mass: _9.012_

Series: _2_

Group: 2

State: _Solid_

Fact: Weight per weight, this metal is stronger than steel.

Floatium (Ft)

Atomic #: _1_

Atomic mass: _1.008_

Series: 1

Group: _1_

State: _Gas_

Fact: This element has 1 proton.

Use: _Potential fuel in the future_

Coatide (Ci)

Atomic #: _50_

Atomic mass: _118.71_

Series: _5_

Group: _14_

State: _Solid_

Fact: This element has 50 electrons.

Use: _Constituent of solder_

Explosium (Ex)

Atomic #: _19_

Atomic mass: _39.098_

Series: _4_

Group: _1_

State: _Solid_

Use: When combined with nitrate, this alkali metal is used for explosives.

Bonine (Bn)

Atomic #: _20_

Atomic mass: _40.078_

Series: _4_

Group: 2

State: _Solid_

Use: Most abundant mineral in the human body

Saltium (Sa)

Atomic #: _11_

Atomic mass: _22.990_

Series: _3_

Group: _1_

State: _Solid_

Use: Alkali metal found in table salt

Lightemupium (Lp)

Atomic #: _18_

Atomic mass: _39.948_

Series: _3_

Group: _18_

State: _Gas_

Use: Noble gas used in electric light bulbs

Ammonite (Ae)

Atomic #: _7_

Atomic mass: _14.007_

Series: _2_

Group: _15_

State: _Gas_

Fact: This element composes 79% of the Earth's atmosphere.

Use: _Fertilizers_

Reactium (R)

Atomic #: _37_

Atomic mass: _85.468_

Series: _5_

Group: 1

State: _Solid_

Fact: _Potential future use in ion engines_

Pyrotechnium (Py)

Atomic #: _38_

Atomic mass: _87.62_

Series: _5_

Group: _2_

State: _Solid_

Fact: Heaviest of the alkaline earth metals

Use: Commonly used in pyrotechnics

Glowium (G)

Atomic #: _10_

Atomic mass: _20.180_

Series: _2_

Group: _18_

State: _Gas_

Use: Noble gas commonly used in glowing signs

Hotium (Ho)

Atomic #: _49_

Atomic mass: _114.818_

Series: 5

Group: _13_

State: _Solid_

Fact: Has properties very similar to Changium but has almost twice its atomic mass

---

Covalentite (Cv)

Atomic #: _33_

Atomic mass: _74.922_

Series: _4_

Group: 15

State: _Solid_

Fact: Metalloid

Use: _Pesticides, herbicides_

Organican (Or)

Atomic #: _6_

Atomic mass: _12.011_

Series: _2_

Group: _14_

State: _Solid_

Fact: Has four electrons in its outer energy shell. It has the lowest atomic mass in its family.

Use: _Hydrocarbons_

Liquidite (Ld)

Atomic #: _35_

Atomic mass: _79.904_

Series: _4_

Group: _17_

State: _Liquid_

Fact: The only nonmetal that is liquid at room temperature

Use: _Disinfectant_

Semicondite (Sm)

Atomic #: _32_

Atomic mass: _72.64_

Series: _4_

Group: _14_

State: Solid

Fact: Mendeleev predicted the discovery of this element, which he called ekasilicon.

Use: _Communication industry; filling teeth_

Painteon (Pa)

Atomic #: _16_

Atomic mass: _32.065_

Series: 3

Group: _16_

State: _Solid_

Fact: This element needs two more electrons in its outer shell to reach an octet.

Use: _Gunpowder, matches_

Redpowderite (Rd)

Atomic #: _34_

Atomic mass: _78.96_

Series: _4_

Group: 16

State: _Solid_

Fact: The heaviest of the elements in this family

Use: _Manufacture of glass_

Matchium (Mc)

Atomic #: _15_

Atomic mass: _30.174_

Series: _3_

Group: _15_

State: _Solid_

Fact: This element has properties similar to Ammonite.

Use: This element is used to make the head of matches.

Sparkese (Sp)

Atomic #: _3_

Atomic mass: _6.941_

Series: 2

Group: _1_

State: _Solid_

Fact: Very reactive metal with only two energy shells

Changium (Cg)

Atomic #: _31_

Atomic mass: _69.723_

Series: _4_

Group: 13

State: _Solid_

Fact: Solid at room temperature but becomes liquid when heated slightly

Copyright © 2008 by John Wiley & Sons, Inc.

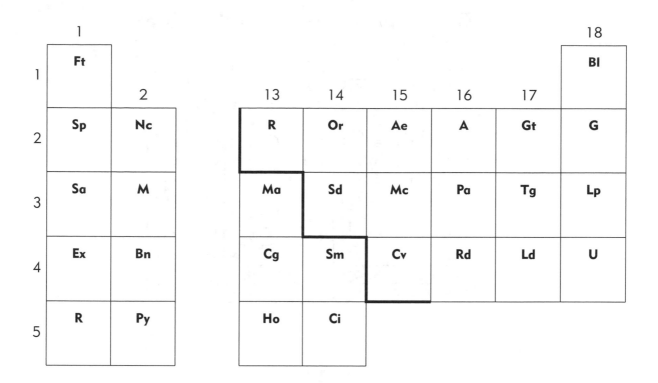

Postlab Questions

1. A series is a row of elements; moving from left to right, the number of electrons increases. A row is a column of elements. In a row, the number of valence electrons remains the same, although the total number of electrons increases.

2. SaTg

3. Ft_2A

4. SdA_2

5. Sp, Sa, Ex, and R. These elements are very reactive because they only have one electron in the outer energy shell.

6. Answers will vary. Students may find the elements with the least amount of information given as the most difficult ones to classify.

Copyright © 2008 by John Wiley & Sons, Inc.

KEY 15-1
Word Find—Walking on the Water

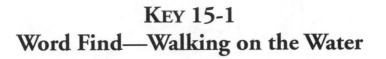

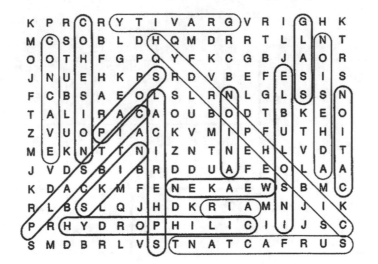

KEY 15-2
Surface Tension

Prelab Questions

1. Surface tension is the skin-like texture that forms on the surface of water. It is due to the cohesion of water molecules.

2. Temperature—increases the forces of attraction between water and air vapor molecules. Surfactants—reduce the cohesion of water molecules.

3. Water striders have a hairlike covering on their feet that keeps them dry and helps them walk on the surface of water.

4. Cohesion is the attraction of water molecules to each other.

5. Substances such as soap and detergent that reduce surface tension are called surfactants. These substances increase the spreading and wetting property of water, enabling water to remove oily dirt.

Chart 1 Results

Answers will vary. The room-temperature tap water will hold the most gem clips. The heated tap water will hold the second most, followed by the room-temperature detergent water. The fewest clips will be held by the heated detergent water.

Copyright © 2008 by John Wiley & Sons, Inc.

Postlab Questions, Part 1

1. Cup D. Its surface tension was lowered by both heat and surfactant.

2. Cup A. It had nothing added to lower its surface tension.

3. Heat lowers surface tension.

4. Detergent lowers surface tension.

5. The dome formed due to cohesion, which held the water molecules together at the surface.

Postlab Questions, Part 2

1. Student designs will vary.

2. It prevents the feet from getting wet.

3. The insect would sink.

4. The insect sank.

5. The surface tension had been lowered, and the skin on the surface of water broke.

6. They would not walk as easily on the water's surface.

Copyright © 2008 by John Wiley & Sons, Inc.

KEY 16-1
A Tri-ing and Hairy Experience—Hair Care Chemistry

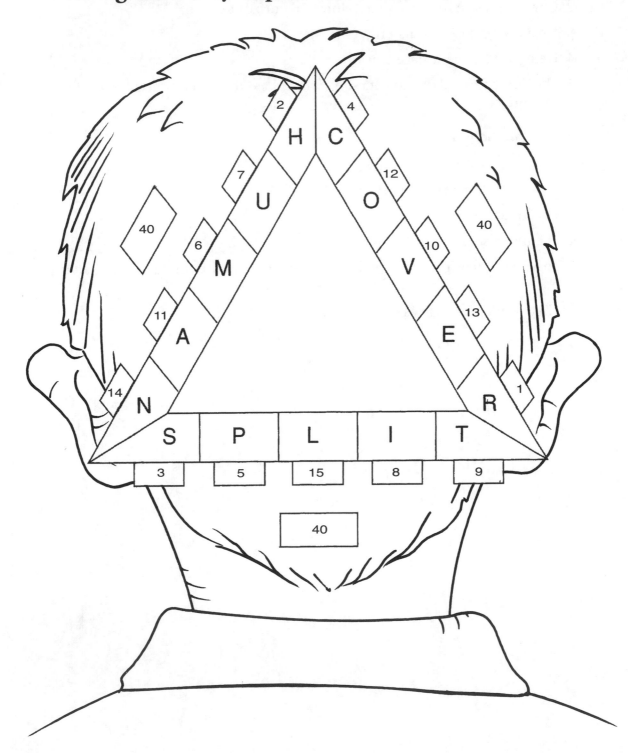

Copyright © 2008 by John Wiley & Sons, Inc.

Copyright © 2008 by John Wiley & Sons, Inc.

KEY 16-2
Homemade Perms

Postlab Questions

1–4. Sketches will vary.

5. NaOH is a strong base that causes the hair cuticle to swell and open. The hair is then more porous, and the NaOH molecules can enter the cortex, where they disrupt the sulfur bonds between cysteine molecules.

6. The vinegar neutralizes NaOH.

7. Answers will vary.

KEY 17-1
Fat Crossword—Fats

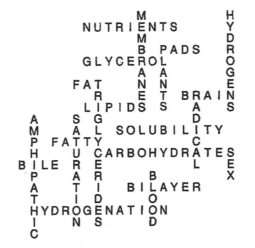

KEY 17-2
Fat in Food

Prelab Questions

1. Answers will vary. Students might suggest that fast food diets contain a lot of fat.

2. Skinless chicken and turkey, leg of lamb, and fish are very lean meats. Ground beef, steaks, hot dogs, and specialty meats are high in fat.

3. From a quarter pound of hamburger, you get 112 calories of protein and 207 calories of fat.

Postlab Questions

1. Answers will vary with student results. Ground beef contains more fat than ground chuck.

2. Atherosclerosis and obesity are two health problems associated with high fat intake.

3. Cooking causes the fat in meat to separate. Because fat is lighter than water, it floats to the surface.

4. Skinless chicken would have less fat than ground beef or ground chuck.

KEY 18-1
DNA Concept Map—The Structure and Function of DNA

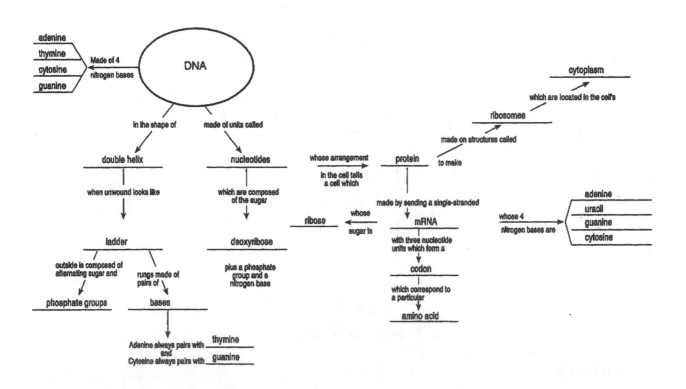

Copyright © 2008 by John Wiley & Sons, Inc.

KEY 18-2
Recipe for Proteins

Postlab Questions

1. The sequence of bases in DNA determines which proteins a cell will make.

2. The ribosomes hold an mRNA strand so that amino acids can be properly lined up by tRNAs.

3. tRNAs carry appropriate amino acids to the mRNA strand.

4. If amino acids are not assembled in the proper order, the resulting protein may be defective.

5. DNA sends its message for protein synthesis to the ribosomes by making a copy of itself in the form of mRNA.

KEY 19-1
Tri-ing Cell Puzzle—Cellular Structure and Function

1. Tissues
2. Erythrocytes
3. Nucleus
4. Ribosomes
5. Nerve cells

6. Mitochondria
7. Lysosomes
8. Centrosomes
9. Endoplasmic reticula
10. Cilia

11. Epithelium
12. Golgi apparatuses
13. Bone cells
14. Muscle cells
15. Fat cells

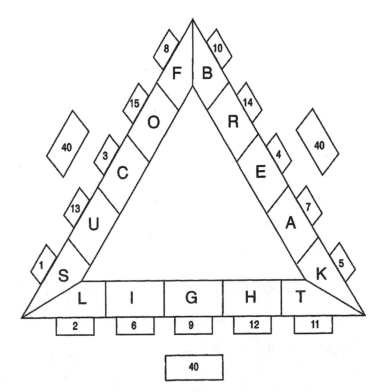

Copyright © 2008 by John Wiley & Sons, Inc.

KEY 20-1
Acrostic—Mendel's Ideas on Inheritance of Traits

	1	2	3	4	5	6	7	8	9	10	11	12	13	14	15	16	17	18	19	20	21	22	23	24	25	26	27
	s	l		s	e	s	p		w	f			g			e	o				p		s	a		s	a
	t	m	o	e	r	p	I	s	a	t	i	u	y	e	g	y	v	l	a	a	n	a	n	u	e	r	o
	a	s	h	r	c	o	s	a	w	i	r	s	p	n	r	l	a	c	m	t	e	b	n	o	t	s	t
	M	**E**	y	s	a	n	i	t	o	t	t	i	t	e	o	e	e	i	e	s	e	a	i	s	s	m	
	e	l	b	s	s	a	I	i	e	e	e	t	e	o	e	t	g	t	n	t	t	l	i	t	t		
	n	f	r	i	s	t		v				a	r	a					o	n	o	y	a	g			
			i	v	i	i		u				a		t													
			d	e	v	o		m																			
					e	n																					

Message (reading across numbers 1–27): **MENDEL IS THE FATHER OF GENETICS**

Copyright © 2008 by John Wiley & Sons, Inc.

KEY 20-2
Mendelian Genetics

Prelab Questions

1. Pea plants.

2. Answers will vary, but could include any two of the following: question, hypothesis, experiment, analysis, or conclusions.

3. The F_1 generation are the children of the parental generation; the F_2 generation are grandchildren of the parental generation.

4. Mendel demonstrated that an inheritable factor is passed from parents to offspring.

F_1 Data Table Results

All of the peas are smooth.

F_2 Data Table Results

75% of the peas are smooth; 25% are wrinkled.

Postlab Questions

1. Smooth is dominant over wrinkled. Smooth peas appeared in the F_1 generation.

2. 100%

3. 25%

4. a. 80; b. 20

5. a. Answers will vary, but could include (1) Mendel showed that inheritance could be explained using the scientific method; (2) Mendel showed that some inheritable traits are dominant over others; (3) Mendel showed that traits are passed from one generation to the next.

   b. Answers will vary, but could include (1) Mendel used a large population of organisms; (2) Mendel kept accurate data and analyzed his results.

   c. Answers will vary.

Copyright © 2008 by John Wiley & Sons, Inc.

KEY 21-1
Frayer Diagrams—Changing with the Times

Individual Frayer diagrams will vary.

Definitions for terms and phrases used in Frayer diagrams:

1. *Acquired characteristic:* according to Lamarck, acquired characteristics are traits that organisms take on because they need them.

2. *Adaptation:* a characteristic that helps an organism survive.

3. *Darwin:* the scientist who proposed the theory of natural selection.

4. *Lamarck:* the scientist who proposed the theory that organisms have acquired characteristics.

5. *Mutation:* a change in DNA.

6. *Natural selection:* the process in which a change in the environment selects the organisms that are most capable of surviving.

7. *The Origin of Species:* a book by Darwin that explains the theory of natural selection.

8. *Peppered moths:* a group of moths whose population experienced a shift in color from light to dark during the Industrial Revolution.

9. *Survival of the fittest:* the idea that those organisms best adapted to the environment are most likely to survive and reproduce.

10. *Variation:* the differences in individuals of a population.

KEY 21-3
Monstrous Mutations

Prelab Questions

1. An alteration in DNA.

2. Mutations are changes in DNA that occur by chance. Some mutations provide useful traits that help organisms survive. These traits may be passed on to off-spring.

3. Behavioral.

4. Behavioral.

5. Structural.

6. Answers will vary, but could include deer antlers, porcupine quills, rattlesnake venom, a duck's webbed feet, a beaver's flat tail, and a lion's retractable claws.

Copyright © 2008 by John Wiley & Sons, Inc.

Postlab Questions

  1. Answers will vary.

  2. Answers will vary.

  3. Storing or burying food.

4–6. Answers will vary.

KEY 22-1
Ecologically Speaking—Relationships in Life

 1. S E C O N D A R Y
 2.   E C O L O G Y
 3. C O M P E T I T I O N
 4.   P R E D A T O R
 5.   E P I P H Y T E
 6.   A U T O T R O P H S
 7. D E T R I T U S
 8. H E R B I V O R E
 9.   E C O S Y S T E M
10. C H L O R O P H Y L L
11.   H E T E R O T R O P H S
12. C O M P O S T
13.   E A R T H W O R M S
14.   M U T U A L I S M
15. C O M M E N S A L I S M
16.   E N E R G Y

KEY 22-2
Who Lives in Our Trash?

Postlab Questions, Part A

1–4. Answers will vary depending on experimental results.

5. Yeast, like many fungi, feed on dead and decaying matter. It was added to bottle 2 to increase the rate of decomposition.

6. The yeast in bottle 2 feeds on food scraps.

7. Answers will vary. Organisms that were living in the soil outdoors helped break down the food scraps.

Postlab Questions, Part B

1–3. Answers will vary. The temperature probably increased 10°F to 20°F over the experimental period.

4. The increase in temperature was caused by microbes digesting the food scraps.

5. Answers will vary. Materials may have been partially decomposed.

6. Changes in composted food are caused by organisms in the detrital food web, such as microbes, fungi, worms, and mites.

7. Answers will vary.

8. These organisms moved into the compost pile from the surrounding soil.

9. Single-cell organisms (protists and bacteria) and fungi are probably present.

10. Without the detritivores, dead things would not decompose and return their valuable minerals to the soil.

Copyright © 2008 by John Wiley & Sons, Inc.

KEY 22-3
Web of Life

Prelab Questions

1. Autotrophs make their own food; heterotrophs eat other organisms. An example of an autotroph is grass; an example of a heterotroph is a deer.

2. Primary consumers.

3. Energy is lost as it moves up the food chain. As a result, each trophic level contains less energy than the one before it and therefore cannot support as many individuals.

Postlab Questions

1. All kinds of organisms.

2. The food web changed because many organisms no longer had a food supply.

3. Everything in the food web would die.

4. Answers will vary. Minerals are taken up by plants.

5. Energy moves through an ecosystem (up a food chain) and is either used by organisms or lost as heat. Minerals stay in a food chain. After they are released by decomposers, they are taken up and used by plants.

Copyright © 2008 by John Wiley & Sons, Inc.

Standards

Lesson	Middle School Standards	High School Standards
1	**Structure of the Earth System**	**Interactions of Energy and Matter**
	The solid earth is layered with a lithosphere; hot, convecting mantle; and dense, metallic core.	Waves, including sound and seismic waves, waves on water, and light waves, have energy.
	Lithospheric plates on the scales of continents and oceans constantly move at rates of centimeters per year in response to movements in the mantle. Major geological events, such as earthquakes, volcanic eruptions, and mountain building, result from these plate motions.	
2	**Structure of the Earth System**	NA
	Land forms are the result of a combination of constructive and destructive forces. Constructive forces include crustal deformation, volcanic eruption, and deposition of sediment, while destructive forces include weathering and erosion.	
	Some changes in the solid earth can be described as the "rock cycle." Old rocks at the earth's surface weather, forming sediments that are buried, then compacted, heated, and often recrystallized into new rock. Eventually, those new rocks may be brought to the surface by the forces that drive plate motions, and the rock cycle continues.	
	Soil consists of weathered rocks and decomposed organic material from dead plants, animals, and bacteria. Soils are often found in layers, with each having a different chemical composition and texture.	

Lesson	*Middle School Standards*	*High School Standards*

3 **Structure of the Earth System**

NA

The atmosphere is a mixture of nitrogen, oxygen, and trace gases that include water vapor. The atmosphere has different properties at different elevations.

Clouds, formed by the condensation of water vapor, affect weather and climate.

Global patterns of atmospheric movement influence local weather. Oceans have a major effect on climate, because water in the oceans holds a large amount of heat.

4 **Structure of the Earth System**   **The Interdependence of Organisms**

Water, which covers the majority of the earth's surface, circulates through the crust, oceans, and atmosphere in what is known as the "water cycle." Water evaporates from the earth's surface; rises and cools as it moves to higher elevations; condenses as rain or snow; and falls to the surface, where it collects in lakes, oceans, soil, and in rocks underground.

Human beings live within the world's ecosystems. Increasingly, humans modify ecosystems as a result of population growth, technology, and consumption. Human destruction of habitats through direct harvesting, pollution, atmospheric changes, and other factors is threatening current global stability, and if not addressed, ecosystems will be adversely affected.

Water is a solvent. As it passes through the water cycle, it dissolves minerals and gases and carries them to the oceans.

5 **Transfer of Energy**   **Conservation of Energy and the Increase in Disorder**

Energy is a property of many substances and is associated with heat, light, electricity, mechanical motion, sound, nuclei, and the nature of a chemical. Energy is transferred in many ways.

The total energy of the universe is constant. Energy can be transferred by collisions in chemical and nuclear reactions, by light waves and other radiations, and in many other ways. However, it can never be destroyed. As these transfers occur, the matter involved becomes steadily less ordered.

Interactions of Energy and Matter

Waves, including sound and seismic waves, waves on water, and light waves, have energy and can transfer energy when they interact with matter.

Lesson	*Middle School Standards*	*High School Standards*

Electromagnetic waves result when a charged object is accelerated or decelerated. Electromagnetic waves include radio waves (the longest wavelength), microwaves, infrared radiation (radiant heat), visible light, ultraviolet radiation, x-rays, and gamma rays. The energy of electromagnetic waves is carried in packets whose magnitude is inversely proportional to the wavelength.

6   Transfer of Energy

Heat moves in predictable ways, flowing from warmer objects to cooler ones, until both reach the same temperature.

Conservation of Energy and the Increase in Disorder

The total energy of the universe is constant. Energy can be transferred by collisions in chemical and nuclear reactions, by light waves and other radiations, and in many other ways. However, it can never be destroyed. As these transfers occur, the matter involved becomes steadily less ordered.

Heat consists of random motion and the vibrations of atoms, molecules, and ions. The higher the temperature, the greater the atomic or molecular motion.

7   Motions and Forces

The motion of an object can be described by its position, direction of motion, and speed. That motion can be measured and represented on a graph.

An object that is not being subjected to a force will continue to move at a constant speed and in a straight line.

If more than one force acts on an object along a straight line, then the forces will reinforce or cancel one another, depending on their direction and magnitude. Unbalanced forces will cause changes in the speed or direction of an object's motion.

Conservation of Energy and the Increase in Disorder

All energy can be considered to be either kinetic energy, which is the energy of motion; potential energy, which depends on relative position; or energy contained by a field, such as electromagnetic waves.

Motions and Forces

Objects change their motion only when a net force is applied. Laws of motion are used to calculate precisely the effects of forces on the motion of objects. The magnitude of the change in motion can be calculated using the relationship $F = ma$, which is independent of the nature of the force. Whenever

Lesson	*Middle School Standards*	*High School Standards*

one object exerts force on another, a force equal in magnitude and opposite in direction is exerted on the first object.

Gravitation is a universal force that each mass exerts on any other mass. The strength of the gravitational attractive force between two masses is proportional to the masses and inversely proportional to the square of the distance between them.

8 NA

Interactions of Energy and Matter

All energy can be considered to be either kinetic energy, which is the energy of motion; potential energy, which depends on relative position; or energy contained by a field, such as electromagnetic waves.

9 **Transfer of Energy**

Electrical circuits provide a means of transferring electrical energy when heat, light, sound, and chemical changes are produced.

Motions and Forces

The electric force is a universal force that exists between any two charged objects. Opposite charges attract, while like charges repel. The strength of the force is proportional to the charges, and, as with gravitation, inversely proportional to the square of the distance between them.

Between any two charged particles, electric force is vastly greater than the gravitational force. Most observable forces, such as those exerted by a coiled spring or friction, may be traced to electric forces acting between atoms and molecules.

Electricity and magnetism are two aspects of a single electromagnetic force. Moving electric charges produce magnetic forces, and moving magnets produce electric forces. These effects help students understand electric motors and generators.

Lesson	Middle School Standards	High School Standards
10	**Earth in the Solar System**	NA

Earth is the third planet from the sun in a system that includes the moon; the sun; eight other planets and their moons; and smaller objects, such as asteroids and comets. The sun, an average star, is the central and largest body in the solar system.

Most objects in the solar system are in regular and predictable motion. Those motions explain such phenomena as the day, the year, phases of the moon, and eclipses.

Gravity is the force that keeps planets in orbit around the sun and governs the rest of the motion in the solar system. Gravity alone holds us to the earth's surface and explains the phenomena of the tides.

The sun is the major source of energy for phenomena on the earth's surface, such as growth of plants, winds, ocean currents, and the water cycle. Seasons result from variations in the amount of the sun's energy hitting the surface, due to the tilt of the earth's rotation on its axis and the length of the day.

Lesson	Middle School Standards	High School Standards
11	**Earth in the Solar System**	NA

Earth is the third planet from the sun in a system that includes the moon; the sun; eight other planets and their moons; and smaller objects, such as asteroids and comets. The sun, an average star, is the central and largest body in the solar system.

Most objects in the solar system are in regular and predictable motion. Those motions explain such phenomena as the day, the year, phases of the moon, and eclipses.

Lesson	Middle School Standards	High School Standards
12	Same as Lesson 10	NA
13	Same as Lesson 11	NA

| Lesson | Middle School Standards | High School Standards |

14   Properties and Changes of Properties in Matter

A substance has characteristic properties, such as density, a boiling point, and solubility, all of which are independent of the amount of the sample. A mixture of substances often can be separated into the original substances using one or more of the characteristic properties.

There are more than 100 known elements that combine in a multitude of ways to produce compounds, which account for the living and nonliving substances that we encounter.

Structure of Atoms

Matter is made of minute particles called atoms, and atoms are composed of even smaller components. These components have measurable properties, such as mass and electrical charge. Each atom has a positively charged nucleus surrounded by negatively charged electrons. The electric force between the nucleus and electrons holds the atom together.

The atom's nucleus is composed of protons and neutrons, which are much more massive than electrons. When an element has atoms that differ in the number of neutrons, these atoms are called different isotopes of the element.

Radioactive isotopes are unstable and undergo spontaneous nuclear reactions, emitting particles and/or wave-like radiation. The decay of any one nucleus cannot be predicted, but a large group of identical nuclei decay at a predictable rate. This predictability can be used to estimate the age of materials that contain radioactive isotopes.

Structure and Properties of Matter

Atoms interact with one another by transferring or sharing electrons that are furthest from the nucleus. These outer electrons govern the chemical properties of the element.

An element is composed of a single type of atom. When elements are listed in order according to the number of protons (called the atomic number), repeating patterns of physical and chemical properties identify families of elements with similar properties. This "Periodic Table" is a consequence of the repeating pattern of outermost electrons and their permitted energies.

Lesson	*Middle School Standards*	*High School Standards*

Bonds between atoms are created when electrons are paired up by being transferred or shared. A substance composed of a single kind of atom is called an element. The atoms may be bonded together into molecules or crystalline solids. A compound is formed when two or more kinds of atoms bind together chemically.

15   NA

Structure of Atoms

Matter is made of minute particles called atoms, and atoms are composed of even smaller components. These components have measurable properties, such as mass and electrical charge. Each atom has a positively charged nucleus surrounded by negatively charged electrons. The electric force between the nucleus and electrons holds the atom together.

Structure and Properties of Matter

The physical properties of compounds reflect the nature of the interactions among its molecules. These interactions are determined by the structure of the molecule, including the constituent atoms and the distances and angles between them.

16   Properties and Changes of Properties of Matter

Substances react chemically in characteristic ways with other substances to form new substances (compounds) with different characteristic properties. In chemical reactions, the total mass is conserved. Substances often are placed in categories or groups if they react in similar ways; metals is an example of such a group.

Chemical Reactions

Chemical reactions occur all around us, for example in health care, cooking, cosmetics, and automobiles. Complex chemical reactions involving carbon-based molecules take place constantly in every cell in our bodies.

Lesson	*Middle School Standards*	*High School Standards*

17 **Structure and Function in Living Systems**

Living systems at all levels of organization demonstrate the complementary nature of structure and function. Important levels of organization for structure and function include cells, tissues, organs, organ systems, whole organisms, and ecosystems.

Structure and Properties of Matter

Carbon atoms can bond to one another in chains, rings, and branching networks to form a variety of structures, including synthetic polymers, oils, and the large molecules essential to life.

The Cell

Most cell functions involve chemical reactions. Food molecules taken into cells react to provide the chemical constituents needed to synthesize other molecules. Both breakdown and synthesis are made possible by a large set of protein catalysts, called enzymes. The breakdown of some of the food molecules enables the cell to store energy in specific chemicals that are used to carry out the many functions of the cell.

18 NA

The Cell

Cells store and use information to guide their functions. The genetic information stored in DNA is used to direct the synthesis of the thousands of proteins that each cell requires.

The Molecular Basis of Heredity

In all organisms, the instructions for specifying the characteristics of the organism are carried in DNA, a large polymer formed from subunits of four kinds (A, G, C, and T). The chemical and structural properties of DNA explain how the genetic information that underlies heredity is both encoded in genes (as a string of molecular "letters") and replicated (by a templating mechanism). Each DNA molecule in a cell forms a single chromosome.

19 **Structure and Function of Living Systems**

Cells carry on the many functions needed to sustain life. They grow and divide, thereby producing more cells.

The Cell

Cells have particular structures that underlie their functions. Every cell is surrounded by a membrane that

This requires that they take in nutrients, which they use to provide energy for the work that cells do and to make the materials that a cell or an organism needs.

separates it from the outside world. Inside the cell is a concentrated mixture of thousands of different molecules, which form a variety of specialized structures that carry out such cell functions as energy production, transport of molecules, waste disposal, synthesis of new molecules, and the storage of genetic material.

Specialized cells perform specialized functions in multicellular organisms. Groups of specialized cells cooperate to form a tissue, such as a muscle. Different tissues are in turn grouped together to form larger functional units, called organs. Each type of cell, tissue, and organ has a distinct structure and set of functions that serve the organism as a whole.

Plant cells contain chloroplasts, the site of photosynthesis. Plants and many microorganisms use solar energy to combine molecules of carbon dioxide and water into complex, energy-rich organic compounds and release oxygen into the environment. This process of photosynthesis provides a vital connection between the sun and the energy needs of living systems.

The human organism has systems for digestion, respiration, reproduction, circulation, excretion, movement, control and coordination, and protection from disease. These systems interact with one another.

Cells can differentiate, and complex multicellular organisms are formed as a highly organized arrangement of differentiated cells. In the development of these multicellular organisms, the progeny from a single cell form an embryo in which the cells multiply and differentiate to form the many specialized cells, tissues, and organs that comprise the final organism. This differentiation is regulated through the expression of different genes.

20   Reproduction and Heredity

Reproduction is a characteristic of all living systems; because no individual organism lives forever, reproduction is essential to the continuation of every species. Some organisms reproduce asexually. Other organisms reproduce sexually.

The Molecular Basis of Heredity

Most of the cells in a human contain two copies of each of 22 different chromosomes. In addition, there is a pair of chromosomes that determines sex: a female contains two X chromosomes, and a male contains one X and one Y chromosome. Transmission of genetic information to offspring occurs through egg and sperm cells that contain only one representative from each chromosome pair. An egg and a sperm unite to form a new individual. The fact that the human body is formed from cells that contain two copies of each chromo-some—and therefore two copies of each gene—explains many features of human heredity, such as how variations that are hidden in one generation can be expressed in the next.

In many species, including humans, fe-males produce eggs, and males produce sperm. Plants also reproduce sexually—the egg and sperm are produced in the flowers of flowering plants. An egg and sperm unite to begin development of a new individual. That new individual receives genetic information from its mother (via the egg) and its father (via the sperm). Sexually produced offspring never are identical to either of their parents.

Every organism requires a set of instruc-tions for specifying its traits. Heredity is the passage of these instructions from one generation to another.

Hereditary information is contained in genes, located in the chromosomes of each cell. Each gene carries a single unit of information. An inherited trait of an individual can be determined by one or by many genes, and a single gene can in-fluence more than one trait. A human cell contains many thousands of differ-ent genes.

The characteristics of an organism can be described in terms of a combination of traits. Some traits are inherited, and others result from interactions with the environment.

21   Diversity and Adaptations of Organisms

Millions of species of animals, plants, and microorganisms are alive today. Although different species might look dissimilar, the unity among organisms becomes apparent from an analysis of

Biological Evolution

Species evolve over time. Evolution is the consequence of the interactions of (1) the potential for a species to in-crease its numbers, (2) the genetic vari-ability of offspring due to mutation

Lesson	***Middle School Standards***	***High School Standards***

internal structures, the similarity of their chemical processes, and the evidence of common ancestry.

and recombination of genes, (3) a finite supply of the resources required for life, and (4) the ensuing selection by the environment of those offspring better able to survive and produce offspring.

Biological evolution accounts for the diversity of species developed through gradual processes over many generations. Species acquire many of their unique characteristics through biological adaptation, which involves the selection of naturally occurring variations in populations. Biological adaptations include changes in structures, behaviors, or physiology that enhance survival and reproductive success in a particular environment.

The great diversity of organisms is the result of more than 3.5 billion years of evolution that has filled every available niche with life forms.

Extinction of a species occurs when the environment changes and the adaptive characteristics of a species are insufficient to allow its survival. Fossils indicate that many organisms that lived long ago are extinct. Extinction of a species is common; most of the species that have lived on the earth no longer exist.

Natural selection and its evolutionary consequences provide a scientific explanation for the fossil record of ancient life forms, as well as for the striking molecular similarities observed among the diverse species of living organisms.

Regulation and Behavior

Changes in DNA (mutations) occur spontaneously at low rates. Some of these changes make no difference to the organism, whereas others can change cells and organisms. Only mutations in germ cells can create the variation that changes an organism's offspring.

All organisms must be able to obtain and use resources, grow, reproduce, and maintain stable internal conditions while living in a constantly changing external environment.

The Behavior of Organisms

Regulation of an organism's internal environment involves sensing the internal environment and changing physiological activities to keep conditions within the range required to survive.

Organisms have behavioral responses to internal changes and to external stimuli. Responses to external stimuli can result from interactions with the organism's own species and with others, as well as environmental changes; these responses can be either innate or learned. The broad patterns of behavior exhibited by animals have evolved to ensure reproductive success. Animals often live in unpredictable environments, and so their behavior must be flexible enough to deal with uncertainty and change. Plants also respond to stimuli.

Behavior is one kind of response an organism can make to an internal or environmental stimulus. A behavioral response requires coordination and communication at many levels, including cells, organ systems, and whole organisms. Behavioral response is a set of actions determined in part by heredity and in part by experience.

Like other aspects of an organism's biology, behaviors have evolved through natural selection. Behaviors often have an adaptive logic when viewed in terms of evolutionary principles.

An organism's behavior evolves through adaptation to its environment. How a species moves, obtains food, reproduces, and responds to danger are based in the species' evolutionary history.

22   Populations and Ecosystems

A population consists of all individuals of a species that occur together at a given place and time. All populations living together and the physical factors with which they interact compose an ecosystem.

The Interdependence of Organisms

The atoms and molecules on the earth cycle among the living and nonliving components of the biosphere.

Populations of organisms can be categorized by the function they serve in an ecosystem. Plants and some micro organisms are producers—they make their own food. All animals, including humans, are consumers, which obtain food by eating other organisms. Decomposers, primarily bacteria and fungi, are consumers that use waste materials and dead organisms for food. Food webs identify the relationships among producers, consumers, and decomposers in an ecosystem.

Energy flows through ecosystems in one direction, from photosynthetic organisms to herbivores to carnivores and decomposers.

Lesson	*Middle School Standards*	*High School Standards*

For ecosystems, the major source of energy is sunlight. Energy entering ecosystems as sunlight is transferred by producers into chemical energy through photosynthesis. That energy then passes from organism to organism in food webs.

The number of organisms an ecosystem can support depends on the resources available and abiotic factors, such as quantity of light and water, range of temperatures, and soil composition. Given adequate biotic and abiotic resources and no disease or predators, populations (including humans) increase at rapid rates. Lack of resources and other factors, such as predation and climate, limit the growth of populations in specific niches in the ecosystem.

Organisms both cooperate and compete in ecosystems. The interrelationships and interdependencies of these organisms may generate ecosystems that are stable for hundreds or thousands of years.

Living organisms have the capacity to produce populations of infinite size, but environments and resources are finite. This fundamental tension has profound effects on the interactions between organisms.

Human beings live within the world's ecosystems. Increasingly, humans modify ecosystems as a result of population growth, technology, and consumption. Human destruction of habitats through direct harvesting, pollution, atmospheric changes, and other factors is threatening current global stability, and if not addressed, ecosystems will be irreversibly affected.

Bibliography

Books

Davis, Raymond E., H. Clark Metcalfe, John E. Williams, and Joseph F. Castka. *Modern Chemistry.* Austin, Tex.: Holt, Rinehart, and Winston, 2002.

Feldkamp, Susan. *Modern Biology.* Austin, Tex.: Holt, Rinehart, and Winston, 2002.

Fix, John D. *Astronomy: Journey to the Cosmic Frontier.* New York: McGraw-Hill, 2001.

Fleming, Michael F. *Science Teacher's Instant Labs Kit.* Upper Saddle River, N.J.: Prentice Hall, Center for Applied Research in Education, 1992.

Hamilton, Debra. *Earth Trek—An Environmental Learning Manual for Educators.* Atlanta, Ga.: Earth Lab, the Educational Division of the Georgia Conservancy, 1991.

Hassard, Jack. *Science as Inquiry.* Parsippany, N.J.: Good Year Books, 2000.

Hsu, Tom. *Foundations of Physical Science with Earth and Space Science.* Peabody, Mass.: CPO Science, 2003.

Kenda, Margaret, and Phyllis Williams. *Science Wizardry for Kids.* New York: Barron's, 1992.

"Living and Working on the New Frontier." *NASA Information Summaries.* Huntsville, Ala.: National Aeronautics and Space Administration, Marshall Space Flight Center, Sept. 1991.

National Science Education Standards. Washington, D.C.: National Academy Press, 1996.

Project Learning Tree, Supplementary Activity Guide K–6 and 7–12. Washington, D.C.: American Forest Council, 1992.

Sousa, David A. *How the Brain Learns.* Thousand Oaks, Calif.: Corwin Press, 2001.

Sugarman, Carol. "Americans Go Overboard with Fat-Free Foods." *Atlanta Journal and Constitution,* May 24, 1994, p. B5.

Web Sites

The American Institute of Physics, www.aip.org/history/curie/periodic.htm. The work of Dmitry Mendeleev is explained at this site.

Chemistry.org, www.chemistry.org/portal/a/c/s/1/home.html. This is the Web site of the American Chemical Society, and it provides links to articles on various topics in chemistry.

The Geological Society of America, www.geosociety.org/educate/resources.htm. This Web site offers tutorials, lessons, and general information on all topics of earth science.

Imagine the Universe, http://imagine.gsfc.nasa.gov/index.html. NASA's Web site for anyone who wants to know more about the universe.

Nasaexplores, www.nasaexplores.com. This Web site is maintained by NASA, and it provides information for students of all ages.

The Physics Classroom, www.physicsclassroom.com/Class/newtlaws/newtltoc.html. This Web site presents tutorials on several basic principles in physics.

U.S. Geological Survey, www.usgs.gov. Maintained by the U.S. Geological Service, this Web site provides information on the geology of the earth.

WeatherEye, http://weathereye.kgan.com/expert/index.html. An excellent Web site to learn more about the science of meteorology.

Index